WEST AFRICAN KINGDOMS IN THE NINETEENTH CENTURY

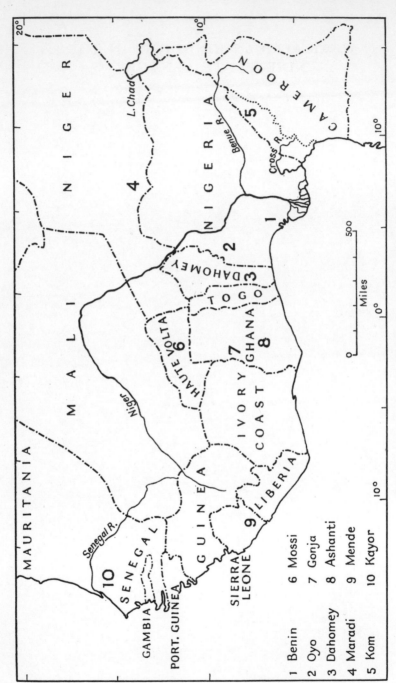

Sketch Map of West Africa showing Location of Peoples

1 Benin
2 Oyo
3 Dahomey
4 Maradi
5 Kom

6 Mossi
7 Gonja
8 Ashanti
9 Mende
10 Kayor

WEST AFRICAN KINGDOMS IN THE NINETEENTH CENTURY

Edited with an Introduction by
DARYLL FORDE
and
P. M. KABERRY

Published for the
INTERNATIONAL AFRICAN INSTITUTE
by the
OXFORD UNIVERSITY PRESS

Oxford University Press, Ely House, London W. 1

GLASGOW NEW YORK TORONTO MELBOURNE WELLINGTON
CAPE TOWN SALISBURY IBADAN NAIROBI LUSAKA ADDIS ABABA
BOMBAY CALCUTTA MADRAS KARACHI LAHORE DACCA
KUALA LUMPUR SINGAPORE HONG KONG TOKYO

First published 1967
Reprinted 1969

Printed in Great Britain

CONTENTS

LIST OF MAPS

LIST OF TABLES AND FIGURES

INTRODUCTION

Daryll Forde *and* Phyllis Kaberry

This collection of studies brings together in a single volume some of the results of the considerable body of recent research on the later development and organization of the larger states which played so great a part in the earlier economic, political, and cultural life of West Africa. We hope it will be useful to a wide range of readers.

Powerful kingdoms with complex political organization and elaborate state ritual had early developed in the wide region that lay between the Western Sahara and the Guinea Coast. Some were among the earliest societies of Tropical Africa to become known to the Mediterranean and Western World. They were also the first with which enduring external relations were established. From the tenth century onwards, Arabic-speaking merchants and Islamic proselytizers regularly crossed the Sahara in caravans to the courts and cities of Ghana, Mali, Songhai, and Kanem, and celebrated journeys were also made to North Africa and Mecca by some of the rulers of these states. Accounts of them in the writings of Arab travellers and geographers filtered through to Mediterranean Europe.

From the late fifteenth century, when the Portuguese established their first trading stations on the Gold Coast and in the Bight of Benin, fragmentary knowledge of other kingdoms lying in the forest and savannah hinterlands of the Guinea Coast began to flow directly to Christian Europe. Over the next centuries, as the slave trade built up to considerable dimensions, some accounts were published not only of the trade but of some of the kingdoms involved in it. We have such classics as the works of Pereira (1505–20), Dapper (1668), John Barbot (1732), Clapperton (1829), and R. and J. Lander (1832) relating to what was later to be Nigeria; of Bosman (1704), Snelgrave (1734), W. Smith (1744), Norris (1790), Dalzel (1793), and M'Leod (1820) for what is now Dahomey; of Bowdich (1819), Hutton (1821), Dupuis (1824), and Freeman (1843) for the Gold Coast; of Ogilby (1696), Astley (1745–47), and J. Matthew (1788) for Sierra Leone; and of Mollien (1820) for Senegal and the Gambia.

But it was not until the later nineteenth century, when the sea traffic with West Africa, which had reached considerable dimensions over more than three centuries, had been revolutionized by the suppression of the slave trade and the coming of the steamboat, that the increasing involvement of Europeans on the Coast with the political and economic ambitions of powerful centres in the interior, led to the series of explorations, embassies, punitive expeditions, and protectorates that culminated in the imposition of colonial governments. The establishment of colonial administrations created both the need and opportunity to investigate the character and organization of the many complex chiefdoms which were now incorporated in the various territories.

Whether once powerful chiefdoms had been already disrupted by internecine strife, as among the Yoruba, or were forced into submission like Dahomey and Ashanti; whether the indigenous political system continued to provide the basis for administration as in the Fulani emirates of Northern Nigeria, or was virtually ignored as in Benin and among the Mossi and Bambara, the efforts for pacification, orderly administration, and the development of peaceful trade all called for an understanding of the economies and institutions of these hitherto independent polities. Moreover, their exotic character and questions concerning the earlier history and significance of their own traditions aroused and sustained the curiosity and scholarly interest of some of the early European administrators. A vast mass of *ad hoc* documentation of varying detail, objectivity, and penetration also accumulated in the administrative files. Although the multitude of chiefdoms and the fewer large hegemonies in West Africa were not, of course, equally well served, two generations of scholar-administrators and a few independent ethnographers, in the earlier years of this century, laid the foundations for further studies in their detailed accounts and interpretations of the political organization, religious life, and history of some of the great kingdoms. Delafosse's *Haut-Sénégal-Niger* included a monumental conspectus of the ethnic diversities and the traditions of origin of the Mande-speaking peoples. Richmond Palmer and Urvoy, from their respective points of vantage, sought to do the same for the empire of Kanem-Bornu, as did C. K. Meek for the Jukun, and earlier both Johnson and Frobenius for the Yoruba. Unfortunately, the traditions of past glories and the quest of remote origins distracted some of the writers of this period from presenting and analysing both contemporary political and economic life and also the evidence of the immediately pre-colonial situation which was available to them from living elders. Rattray, in his studies of Ashanti, was exceptional in his concentration on the working of social institutions as he saw them, and he limited historical considerations to the immediate past for which his informants could provide direct evidence, although even here, as one of the studies in this book will show, his perspective was not adequate for the pre-colonial phase.

New concepts and field research methods which were being developed in social anthropology during the thirties had little immediate influence on the study of the larger West African chiefdoms. They had been developed mainly with reference to the interpretation of custom and understanding of social processes in small communities, in which political obligations and status differentiation were predominantly determined by relations of kinship and affinity. Interest in uncentralized segmentary societies was fostered both by theoretical interest in the processes whereby social structures were maintained in the absence of any institutionalized hierarchy of authority and by the practical problems posed for colonial governments in attempting to integrate such societies in their administration. The conceptual and field research problems involved in the study of complex centralized societies with marked economic and political differentiation were only beginning to be tackled. Only one comprehensive field study and analysis of a large West African chiefdom—Nadel's work on the Emirate of Bida in Northern Nigeria—appears to have been attempted.

But over the last twenty years detailed studies of the economy and of the political and religious aspects of institutions of West African kingdoms have multiplied. Focused initially on exploring in detail and in the field both the specific procedures and relations and the general processes and ideas involved in contemporary economic and political organization, they have been able, by the critical evaluation in the light of such knowledge of oral tradition, administrative records, and the earlier writings of travellers, traders, and of African scholars like Sarbah and Johnson, to reconstruct the workings of the independent pre-colonial polities, extending them, in some cases, over considerable periods of time. We have also been able to obtain evidence for some particular developments and to document the emergence of new institutions, as well as changes in the scale and mode of organization and in the economic and political circumstances and objectives of ruling groups. It is thus becoming possible not only to describe and analyse convincingly the economic and political conditions in some of the West African kingdoms on the eve of the colonial phase at the end of the nineteenth century but also to work out in some detail the course of earlier changes and developments and the factors which underlay them. Such a task is, of course, far from completed. For some peoples and chiefdoms it has scarcely begun. And it must be expected that some of the reassessments of the history of particular states will themselves undergo substantial revision as a result of the researches which are being undertaken by a new generation of scholars, notably those who are working intensively in the West African universities. The position is somewhat similar in East Africa, where we already have the first two volumes of a collective *History of East Africa*, to which anthropologists as well as historians have contributed, and a symposium by anthropologists, *East African Chiefs*, edited by Dr. A. I. Richards, to which this book is in some respects complementary.

The recovery and analysis of the working of political institutions in African societies before colonization involve a number of special difficulties and pitfalls. Some of these arise from the fact that the societies themselves have undergone substantial and often sudden and drastic cultural changes in their institutions, as a result of the establishment of the superordinate authority of colonial government. However acceptable and beneficial the actions of a colonial administration, they inevitably altered both the balance of political forces within a society and the means and range of political action. Thus, the political system that was open for detailed study during the colonial period was in greater or less degree something other than that which had existed before. Research, concerning the character and conditions of the earlier political system, which does not take fully into account the often considerable effects not only on current political relations but also on ideology and oral traditions concerning the past of changes in the situation under colonial government, will not succeed in recovering and presenting the former setting and the significance of earlier institutions and events, however well their mere occurrence may be documented.

In the meantime, however, it can already be fairly claimed that the pre-colonial political and economic past of West African kingdoms has emerged from the realm of myth and vague speculation. Through a combined operation of intensive field ethnography and documentary research, sound critical standards and techniques are now being established for further studies. Some of these have recently been discussed in *The Historian in Tropical Africa*, edited by Vansina, Mauny, and Thomas (1964).

The studies in this volume present some of the results of these researches. Like all such collections of work by different hands, the coverage and the particular approaches have depended on the availability of relevant research and the special interests of those who have been good enough to contribute. Accounts of some of the larger and more famous kingdoms, for example among the Mande of the Upper Niger or in the Futa Jallon highlands, could not be obtained. And where, as in the case of the Fulani-ruled kingdoms of Northern Nigeria, studies were already available in the detailed monographs of Nadel on Bida and of M. G. Smith on Zaria, duplication has been avoided. Although his own special researches have been among the Bariba chiefdoms to the north, M. Lombard kindly agreed to write on the political development of the kingdom of Dahomey in view of its prominence and distinctive character.

The scale and the cultural, economic, and political contexts of the kingdoms described in this volume are, as will be seen, very diverse. So, too, have been the range of field and documentary material available for their study. This, together with some differences in interests and conceptual background, has led to some inevitable limitation and specialization in the selection of the aspects presented by the different authors.

But to render the volume more valuable for comparative study by those who will use it as a source in attempting to elucidate the more general conditions and processes, as well as the operation of specific factors in the later growth of state organizations in West Africa, the contributors were asked when preparing their several essays to include as far as possible consideration of a number of topics and aspects which would contribute to this end. Thus, an outline of existing knowledge of the earlier historical development of each kingdom has been called for as a background to the main emphasis on the character of its organization in the nineteenth century and of changes during that period. The territorial structure of the state and its economic basis in the control and exploitation of resources, and their distribution through tribute and trade, provide a foundation for the analysis of politically significant social groups and categories, of the prerogatives of politically dominant elements, and of the modes of incorporation of subject peoples. The principles of succession and of appointment at the various levels in the hierarchy of offices, and the modes of competition for power and the balance of power among offices and between different parts of the system, are also central themes. These involve consideration of the ideology and ritual of kingship, the administrative machinery of the state, the operation of judicial institutions, and the organization and control of military forces. External relations of a kingdom have also, in some cases, played a dominant part in determining internal organization, and have called for special emphasis as a factor in its internal development and change. Our thanks are due to the authors for co-operating in following, as far as the character of their sources and special knowledge allowed, this general plan in their expositions.

As is well known, authors are often very much attached to particular styles of orthography. The contributors have varied in their concern for a close rendering of the phonetic values for words in African languages and in the conventions for expressing these. Some have kindly agreed to a simplification and, since this is not a linguistic study, we have not thought an elaborate and completely uniform orthography to be essential. Where, as in the case of Yoruba terms, some place names, as well as names of offices and persons, are spelled differently in various chapters, this should not give rise to obscurity or confusion and will we hope be excused, by purists, in a collection of studies by different authors.

THE KINGDOM OF BENIN

R. E. Bradbury

I. *The Historical and Territorial Background*

The Dynastic Myth

In March 1897 a British military expedition took possession of Benin City (*Edo*); in the following September Ovonramwen, the thirty-fifth *Oba* (king) of Benin, was deported to Calabar. Thus ended the independence of what had been one of the largest and longest lived of the West African forest states. It was not the end of the kingship, however, for when Ovonramwen died in 1914 his son Aiguobasimwin was made Oba. Conscious that his accession marked the beginning of a new era, Aiguobasimwin styled himself Eweka II after the first king of the dynasty. According to tradition, it was in the reign of the fifteenth Oba, Ozolua, that European visitors had first set foot in Benin City. As this event probably took place in 1485, it is unlikely that the dynasty was founded later than the early fourteenth century. The Edo believe that it was preceded by other dynasties. We are told that when the last of these came to an end the country fell into chaos, so the elders of Benin—today identified with the *Uzama* nobles (see p. 14)—dispatched messengers to the *Oghɛnɛ n'Uhɛ*, asking him to send them a prince. The *Oghɛnɛ* (*Oɔni*, to give him his Yoruba title) was the ruler of Ile Ife, the cosmic metropolis of the Yoruba people to the west and, for most of the states of the Bight of Benin, the cradle of divine kingship. He sent his son Oranmiyan, who, however, found Benin uncongenial, so after a short stay he departed for home, but not before he had impregnated the daughter of an Edo village chief. She bore a son, who in the course of time was enthroned under the name Eweka.

It is impossible to say, with assurance, what historical reality underlies this myth, but its symbolic meaning is plain. It states that the kingship is of alien provenance but that it came into being by the will of the Edo and was nurtured in Edo culture. The same assertions are expressed in other myths, and they are recurrent motifs in state ritual. At various points in the annual cycle of kingship rites, the Oba receives fictitious gifts from his 'father', the Ɔghɛnɛ. Before 1897 part of the remains of a dead king were sent 'back' to Ife by his son, who sought the Ɔghɛnɛ's formal approval of his own accession. These and other symbolic acts,

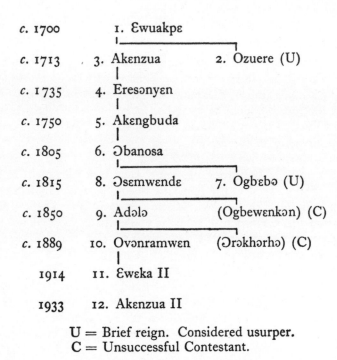

c. 1700	1. Ɛwuakpɛ	
c. 1713	3. Akɛnzua	2. Ozuere (U)
c. 1735	4. Eresɔnyɛn	
c. 1750	5. Akɛngbuda	
c. 1805	6. Ɔbanosa	
c. 1815	8. Ɔsɛmwɛndɛ	7. Ogbɛbɔ (U)
c. 1850	9. Adɔlɔ	(Ogbewɛnkɔn) (C)
c. 1889	10. Ovɔnramwɛn	(Ɔrɔkhɔrhɔ) (C)
1914	11. Ɛwɛka II	
1933	12. Akɛnzua II	

U = Brief reign. Considered usurper.
C = Unsuccessful Contestant.

Fig. 1. The Benin dynasty (from 1700)

and the myths with which they are associated, establish the roots of the royal line outside Edo society and link it up, through Ife, with the dynasties of other kingdoms. Thus, they make explicit the Oba's apartness and his right to rule. In many contexts 'Oba' and 'Edo' are opposed concepts. Yet in another sense the Oba *is* Edo, for while Oranmiyan was an alien, his son Eweka was Edo-

born and the latter's successors were bound to rule through Edo
institutions and according to Edo customs.

The dynastic myth links up the Benin kingship with the dynasties of most Yoruba states, especially with that of the great Oyo
empire, for Oyo, too, claims Oranmiyan as the founder of its royal
line. Thus, the traditions of the two great empires, which for
several centuries dominated the greater part of what is now south-
western Nigeria, converge in a single hero-figure. It seems certain
that the political innovations which gave rise to these states were
set in motion at Ife. Yet however similar the central political
institutions of Ife, Oyo, and Benin may have been at the outset,
they developed along very different lines. Though the political
systems of the Yoruba states differ considerably in detail (Lloyd,
1954 and 1962), they share many common basic features. The
Benin kingdom, however, is located among the Edo-speaking
peoples, whose social institutions are in many respects more akin
to those of the small-scale Ibo societies to the east. It has been
suggested elsewhere (Bradbury, 1964) that the characteristic
features of the Benin polity resulted from a lengthy process of
accommodation between the central notions of divine kingship,
that were current in this part of Africa, and the basic patterns of
Edo culture and society.

The Benin Kingdom

It is useful to distinguish what we may call the Benin kingdom
from the outlying territories which at various times accepted the
Oba's suzerainty. Roughly coterminous with the present-day
Benin Division of the Mid-West State of Nigeria, the Benin
kingdom was the area in which the Oba's writ ran most strongly
and consistently. It was not a single administrative unit, and its
boundaries cannot be precisely drawn. The great majority of its
inhabitants spoke Edo, the language of Benin City, with negligible
dialect variations, but there were Ibo settlements on the eastern
borders, Itsekiri and Ijaw lining the rivers in the south-west, and
Yoruba villages on the north-west whose relations with the Oba
were, in most respects, similar to those of the Edo themselves.
Generally speaking, the Benin kingdom may be defined as the area
within which the Oba was recognized as the sole human arbiter
of life and death. Within it no one could be put to death without
his consent, and any person accused of a capital offence had to

B

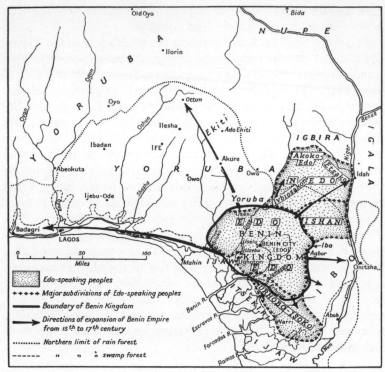

The Kingdom of Benin

be brought before his court. In accordance with this principle, he retained control over the administration of sasswood to suspected witches. Outside the Benin kingdom authority to inflict capital punishment, make human sacrifices or order the sasswood ordeal was delegated to, or retained by, local rulers.

The inhabitants of the Benin kingdom considered themselves to be the true *eviɛn-Ɔba*, 'slaves' of the Oba, that is free subjects of the throne. They wore the same body markings, and they regarded themselves as superior to all their neighbours. All male commoners in the Benin kingdom were the Oba's retainers in that they were nominal, if not initiated, members of the associations that administered his palace. Finally, throughout the Benin kingdom virtually every community or domestic ritual of a confirmatory or periodic nature made reference to the worshippers' allegiance to the Oba.

The Extent and Decline of the Benin Empire

In its heyday the boundaries of the Benin state stretched far beyond its solid core, taking little account of linguistic and cultural divides. The kingdom was bounded by Yoruba speakers on the west and north, Ibo on the east, Ishan and Northern Edo on the north-east, and Urhobo, Itsekiri, and Ijaw on the south. The Edo of the Benin kingdom, together with the Ishan, Northern Edo, Urhobo, and Isoko, make up the Edo-speaking peoples, and they share a basic cultural substratum (Bradbury, 1957: 13–17 and *passim*).

In the late fifteenth century Benin was a well-established state with a large army conducting long campaigns far afield. It was already approaching the peak of its power and prosperity. By the late sixteenth century its frontiers had reached out westwards along the coast to beyond Lagos, north-west through the country of the Ekiti Yoruba to Ottun, where there was a boundary with Oyo, and eastwards to the Niger. Thus, it embraced considerable populations of eastern Yoruba and western Ibo. The former largely retained their characteristically Yoruba political systems. Their titles, regalia, and ceremonial forms were influenced by Benin, but these were matters of style rather than structure. Within a limited framework of controls exercised by the Oba—tribute, assistance in war, facilities for Edo traders—they enjoyed internal autonomy. Many western Ibo groups developed into small central-ized states in which Benin-type institutions, copied with varying degrees of similitude, were superimposed on and accommodated to local social forms. Most of their chiefs (*obi*) accepted the Oba's suzerainty, but others, some of them founded by dissident groups from Benin itself, lay beyond his control.

While the Benin empire embraced non-Edo peoples, it is im-probable that firm control was ever established over the whole Edo-speaking area. To the immediate north-east of the Benin kingdom were the Ishan chiefdoms (Bradbury, 1957: 61–80), whose chiefs (*enigie, enije*) paid tribute to the Oba, provided contingents for his armies, and required his consent for their accession. To the west of Ishan the non-centralized Ivbiosakon (Bradbury, 1957: 84–99) had a similar allegiance, as did some of the nearer Urhobo chiefdoms and village groups to the south. But, to the north, the open rocky hill country of Etsako (ibid.,

100–9) and North-West Edo (Akoko-Edo) (ibid., 110–26) and, to the south, the swamp-encompassed lands occupied by the remoter Urhobo and Isoko (ibid., 127–64), were resistant to enduring Benin control.

The last three centuries of Benin's independence saw a gradual shrinking of the area from which its government could enforce delivery of tribute and military service and secure safe passage for Benin traders, though this decline was by no means uninterrupted. During the eighteenth century there were many campaigns aimed at maintaining control over the western Ibo area. In Osemwende's reign, in the early nineteenth century, control over the Ekiti Yoruba to the north was reconsolidated. Throughout the nineteenth century this latter area was the most important, though not the only, hinterland for Benin traders. Overseas goods, such as guns, powder, salt, and cloth, were obtained at the river 'beaches' on the south-west fringes of the kingdom from European merchants and Itsekiri middlemen, who, in return, bought Benin palm-oil, kernels, ivory, vegetable gums, and, in earlier times, slaves. The European goods were head-loaded to inland markets along well defined routes, the return traffic being in slaves, livestock, stone beads (from Ilorin), leather, and other commodities. This long distance trade was controlled by various trading associations, each operating in a different direction. The most important of these associations was called *Ekhɛngbo* (*ekhɛn*, traders; *ɛgbo*, forest). It monopolized the route from Benin to Akure, which was the main base for trade in the north-east Yoruba country. *Ekhɛngbo*, and similar associations operating towards the east and north-east, were controlled by title-holders and other prominent men from Benin City. The Oba of Benin is said to have been a member of all of them. It was in the interests of the traders to uphold the integrity of the Benin polity in order to ensure a state of security in which trade could flourish. Competition for power and prestige in the state itself provided a major incentive to engage in this trade. On the other hand, the interests of free trade were in potential conflict with the interests of the Oba, and the ruling policy had always been highly protectionist. No 'foreign' traders from the interior were permitted to operate in the Benin kingdom itself, and stringent controls were exercised over the waterside commerce with European and Itsekiri merchants. Heavy dues were demanded from visiting ships, the

Oba's monopolies in certain exports were strictly enforced, and general trading was allowed only when he and his chiefs had completed their business. Disagreements between the palace officials, who supervised this commerce, and the European and Itsekiri merchants often led to the latters' withdrawal or to the Oba's placing an embargo on all trade with them. State control aimed at maintaining the economic power of the ruling élite and, by limiting the distribution of firearms and powder, at preserving the integrity of the kingdom. These aims were largely achieved, but at the expense of economic vitality. It was no accident that the immediate cause of the expedition which led to Ovonramwen's deposition was the massacre of a British mission which sought to persuade him to facilitate free commerce.

In the period leading up to the expedition Benin fortunes were at a low ebb. Protected by its forest environment, the kingdom itself had remained secure from Fulani attacks and infiltrations such as had helped to break up the Oyo empire. Indeed, the Benin kingdom had apparently suffered no serious external attack since the legendary war with Idah in the sixteenth century. But in the second half of the nineteenth century the Nupe–Fulani swept down to the northern borders of Ishan and Ivbio-sakon, forcing most of the Northern Edo groups to pay regular tribute to the Emir of Bida. Meanwhile, the penetration of European commerce through Lagos on the west, and up the Niger on the east was slowly whittling away the Benin trading hinterland and loosening the Oba's hold over his subject populations. When the Ekiti states were beset by Fulani raiders from Ilorin and by the growing military forces of Ibadan, the Oba was able to afford them little protection. Benin warriors played some part in the Ekiti wars, but on a freelance basis; they took advantage of the confused situation to raid for slaves and loot. They sent gifts to the Oba, for they were dependent on the Benin route for their supplies. In return he occasionally dispatched reinforcements to help them, but his control over them was minimal. In the 1880s the official Benin army, under the *Ezɔmɔ*, was occupied subduing rebellious villages on the very north-west borders of the kingdom itself, no more than fifty miles from the capital. Some Ishan and Western Ibo chiefdoms continued to pay tribute, but payment was becoming more difficult to enforce and revolts more difficult to put down. By the 1890s the Oba and his chiefs were becoming increasingly apprehensive of the intentions of the British, who by this time were firmly established in the rivers to the south.

In these circumstances it is indeed remarkable that the Benin kingdom suffered no serious internal collapse. The capacity for survival shown by the Benin polity can be put down partly to the immense value attached to the kingship, which, over the centuries, had accumulated a great aura of mystery, fear, and respect. These attitudes were deliberately fostered by the Oba's retainers and priests and, though there is a hint of desperation in the apparently great increase in human sacrifice during this period, they were largely successful. But the strength of the state lay also in the structure of its central institutions and in the balance between competing power groups. The nature of these institutions and key role of the kingship form the main subject of this essay.

Territorial Administration

The population of Benin Division, which we equate with the Benin kingdom, was reckoned at about 292,000 in the 1952 census. Some 54,000 of these lived in the capital, Benin City, and the rest in several hundred compact villages, ranging in size from less than 20 to (in one case only) more than 6,000 souls. The great majority of villages had populations of less than 1,000; 400 or 500 may be taken as typical. Before 1897 Benin City probably had less than half its 1952 population. Even so, its urban, metropolitan character contrasted sharply with the small scale of village society.

The village was made up of a number of households containing simple, compound, and patrilineally extended families. Households were grouped into wards on a territorial basis, though a small ward might correspond to a descent group. Villages were not associated with kin groups, and all but the smallest of them contained members of many different clans. The kinship system had a marked agnatic bias, but the effective lineages (Bradbury, 1957: 30–31) were small, and neither at the village nor the state level was the balance of power conceived of in terms of lineage representation.

The narrow range of Benin lineages can be partly explained in terms of a high incidence of population movements between village and village, village and capital, and between the Benin kingdom and neighbouring areas. The primary factor, however, was the unusual pattern of land rights, which itself may have been related to population movements. Outside the capital population density was low, land was abundant, and rights in its exploitation were vested in the village community rather than in its component descent groups. Along with this lack of lineage control of land went primogenitary succession. Those offices that were hereditary passed, in principle, from father to eldest surviving son. Lloyd has shown that common interests in land and political offices were the basis of lineage solidarity among the northern Yoruba. The absence of such common interests in Benin had far-reaching implications for the political as well as the land-holding system.

In the village the predominance of community over kin-group interests was maintained through a three-tier age-grade organization (Bradbury, 1957: 32). The oldest man, subject to 'citizenship' qualifications, was in most villages the sole village head (*ɔdiɔnwere*). He and his fellow elders (*ediɔn*) made policy, controlled access to village resources, kept order, settled disputes, and mediated with the central authority. The elders directed the warrior and executive grade of adult men (*ighele*) and the grade of youths (*iroghae*) which performed 'public works'. Supernatural sanction for their authority came from their access to the spirits of past elders of the village (*ediɔn-ɛbho*) and from their collective superiority in magic.

In many villages, however, the *ɔdiɔnwere*'s authority was shared with and limited by that of a chief (*onogie*) whose office descended by primogenitary succession. Most *enigie* were descended from the immediately junior brothers of past kings, but some claimed lines going back beyond the incorporation of their chiefdoms into the state; and a few were descended from non-royal appointees of the Oba. The chiefdom might consist of one or several villages. In the central area round the capital and in the territory to the west of it there were few *enigie*, and here each village dealt directly with the central authority through its *ɔdiɔnwere*, though it might combine with neighbouring villages for certain purposes. To the north and east a much larger proportion of the population was included in chiefdoms. The more remote they were from Benin, the larger the chiefdoms tended to be and the greater their internal autonomy. The more distant *enigie* might control up to a dozen or more villages, some of which themselves had hereditary *enigie*. The more important *enigie* conferred titles on their 'palace' officials and on their agents in the subordinate villages. They had rights to game and tribute and they held courts for the settlement of disputes between their subjects. Having some of the attributes of kingship, they were the focus of rituals patterned on, though less elaborate than, those which took place at the Oba's palace.

The *onogie*'s authority was checked both from above and below. Each of his villages had its own council of elders headed by the *odionwere*, and he could do little against their combined will. If his rule was oppressive they could appeal to the Oba to restrain him. To the Oba the *onogie* had such obligations as to collect and dispatch tribute, to supply labour and military recruits, and to refrain from and prevent hostile acts against the king's subjects in other chiefdoms and villages. Some *enigie* held official positions in the state military organization. Unlike the Oba's Ishan, Yoruba, or Ibo vassals, the *enigie* of the Benin kingdom lacked the authority to put their subjects to death; all capital offences committed in their chiefdoms had to be referred to the Oba's court. Finally, they held their offices at the Oba's will. It was he who settled cases of disputed succession, and the *onogie*'s heir could not be installed until the Oba had given him permission to carry out his father's mortuary rites. Generally, the heir spent a period of instruction at the Oba's palace before he was escorted home and presented to his people by palace officials. In the last resort the Oba could depose him.

Twice yearly, every village in the Benin kingdom was required to send tribute to the Oba in the form of yams, palm-oil, and other foodstuffs.[1] The more remote vassal chiefs sent slaves and live-stock. Refusal to contribute, on the part of a village or chiefdom, was construed as revolt (*isɔtɛ*) and its headman or chief was designated 'the Oba's enemy' (*oghian-Ɔba*). Such revolts were put down by force. Apart from regular tribute, *ad hoc* levies were raised for particular purposes. Thus, if the Oba needed palm kernels for export (one of his monopolies) he could send out his palace officials to organize their collection.

For administrative purposes the Oba's domains were divided not into major provinces but into a large number of tribute units—single villages, village groups, and chiefdoms. Most of these 'fiefs' (as for convenience sake we may call them) served the Oba through the agency of one of his appointed counsellors of the Palace or Town orders, but other fief-holders included the hereditary *Uzama* nobles, the *Iyɔba* (Oba's mother), *Edaikɛn* (Oba's heir), non-titled palace retainers, and, it is said, some of the Oba's wives.

The fief-holders' main reward lay in their right to receive tribute, usually reckoned as half the amount passed on to the Oba. They could also demand labour services and received gifts from those who sought their aid and protection, but they had no direct control over land or resources. A fief-holder could arrange with the *onogie* or elders of his villages to settle his dependants or slaves there to farm for him, but this was not an exclusive right, for the village authorities could make similar arrangements with other residents of the capital. His chief functions were to see that tribute was paid and to conduct its carriers to the palace; to recruit labour for such works as the rebuilding of the Oba's palace; and to assemble men for service in the state armies. Fief-holders were required to live at Benin City. They used their own servants and kin to carry instructions to the *enigie* and *ediɔn-were*. From the point of view of his 'subjects' the fief-holder was their official sponsor through whom they could communicate requests, complaints, and disputes to the Oba. Benin villagers strongly maintain that their sponsors had no judicial authority over them, but, while they had no official courts, it is clear that they did often settle disputes without bringing them to the Oba's notice.

Though each of the higher-ranking counsellors controlled many fiefs, these were dispersed throughout the Oba's territories. If this arrangement had administrative drawbacks, it also had the advantage of preventing any one chief from building up too much personal power in a large consolidated area. Since most fiefs were in the hands of non-hereditary officials, they did not become permanently controlled by particular aristocratic lines. Nor were fiefs and titles indissolubly linked. When a man was awarded a title he expected to be given the fiefs that his predecessor had controlled, but the Oba had the right to redistribute them and, used with circumspection, this right could be a powerful political weapon.

It must be stressed that the fief-holders were not the sole channel of communication between the Oba and his subjects. Some *enigie* had the right of direct access to the king. In the more distant vassal chiefdoms the Oba stationed his own agents to watch over his interests and convey intelligence to him. Within the Benin kingdom his palace officials were constantly going out to the villages on a variety of secular and ritual missions.

II. *The Central Political Institutions*

The Capital

The Benin capital was encircled by a massive earth wall and ditch some six miles in circumference. Within the wall the town was divided into two unequal parts by a long, broad avenue running approximately north-west to south-east. This spatial division corresponded to a Palace/Town dichotomy of great political significance. Ogbe, the smaller area to the south-west, contained the Oba's palace (*Eguae-Ɔba*) and the houses of most of his Palace Chiefs (*Eghaɛbho n'Ogbe*). In Orenokhua, to the north-east, lived the Town Chiefs (*Eghaɛbho n'Ore*) and here, too, were located most of the wards of occupational specialists. There were forty or fifty of these wards, occupied by groups having special skills or duties which they performed, full or part time, primarily for the Oba. Each ward had its internal political organization, based on the grading of its male members, and headed by an *ɔdiɔnwere*, an hereditary chief, or an appointed leader.

On the western and southern sides of the town were a number of settlements that lay outside the main wall but within a second wall, standing a mile or so farther out. Some of these were inhabited by groups of ritual specialists and must be considered wards of the capital. Idunbhun-Ihogbe, for example, contained one section of the *Ihogbe*, priests of the past kings and of the living Oba's Head. In the same area were located the villages of six of the Seven *Uzama* (*Uzama n'Ihinrɔn*), hereditary nobles and 'kingmakers'. The seventh *Uzama* was the Oba's eldest son and heir, the *Edaikɛn*, whose court was at Uselu, just outside the second wall to the north-west. In fact, as we shall see, no *Edaikɛn* was installed during the nineteenth century. Uselu also housed the court of the Oba's mother, who ranked with the Town Chiefs rather than the *Uzama*.

The hereditary *Uzama* and the two groups of *Eghaɛbho*, whose titles were non-hereditary, constituted three great orders of chieftancy which, between them, were responsible for the continuity and government of the state. In order to understand the administrative system and the nature of political competition at Benin, it will be necessary to describe the manner of recruitment to these orders, their respective competences, and their relationship to each other and to the king.

The Uzama n'Ihinrɔn

Tradition identifies the *Uzama* with the 'elders' whose request resulted in Oranmiyan being sent from Ife to found a dynasty at Benin.[2] This is consistent with their role as 'kingmakers' (the *Edaikεn* being excluded from this role) and with their position as the highest-ranking order of chieftancy. As the elders of the state they take up the position of greatest honour at palace rituals, directly facing the Oba. In the ceremonial 'salutations', through which all the chiefs reaffirm their loyalty, the *Uzama* are the last to make obeisance and the first to receive the Oba's kola nuts and palm wine. *Oliha* alone does not kneel before the king, for it is he who speaks the words that inaugurate a new reign. When *Oliha* himself dies his heir is installed by the Oba in person, whereas all other state chiefs are inducted by the *Iyasε*, as senior Town Chief, on the Oba's instructions.

In the last centuries of independence the *Uzama*'s power, as a group, was not commensurate with their exalted rank. Some of them, especially *Ezɔmɔ* and *εro*, had important executive functions, but collectively they played a smaller part in the day-to-day direction of the state than did either of the *Eghaεbho* orders. They had few administrative duties, controlled relatively few fiefs, and attended policy-making and judicial councils at the palace only on the most critical occasions. Nevertheless, as guardians of custom and of the kingship, they retained considerable prestige and moral authority. An Oba could not be lawfully installed, nor could he properly worship his predecessors, without their participation; and new laws and major policy decisions required their formal consent. Ritual sanction for their authority lay in the cult of their collective predecessors, the *Ediɔn-Uzama*, whose worship, at a shrine in *Oliha*'s custody, was essential for the nation's well-being.

The authority of the *Uzama* was probably most effective in times of serious disagreement between the Town Chiefs and the Palace. Their ability to act as a 'third-force'—sometimes allying themselves with the Town group against the Palace, sometimes identifying themselves with the Oba's interests *vis-à-vis* his appointed counsellors—derived not only from their status as

The Palace Associations

Uzama (Hereditary nobles)	*Eghaebho n'Ore* (Town chiefs)	*Isebo*	*Iweguae*	*Ibiwe-Eruerie*	
1. Oliha*	n'Enɛ Eghaebho	1. Unwague	1. Esere	1. Inɛ	1. Osodin
2. Edohen*	1. Iyasɛ	2. Eribo	2. Obazelu	2. Obazuaye	2. Uso
3. Ezomɔ*	2. Esɔgban	3. Osague	3. Obaseki†	3. Obahiagbɔn	3. Ezuakɔ
4. Ɛro*	3. Eson	4. Ayobahan	4. Obadagbonyi	4. Obabhonyi†	4. Obazowa
5. Eholɔ n'Ere*	4. Osuma	5. Ɔlaye	5. Akenuwa	5. Obayuwana†	
6. Ɔlɔton*		6. Obaraduagbon			
7. Edaiken* (Ɔba's heir)	5. Esama	7. Esasɔyen			
	6. Ologbosɛ*	8. Ɔbamarhiaye†			
	7. Osula				
	8. Ighama (Ima)	*Eghaebho n'Ogbe* (Senior Palace Chiefs)			
	9. Ɔbarisiagbon				
	10. Ɔbasuyi				
	11. Ɔbaraye				
	12. Ɔbayagbona†	Many titles†	Many titles†	Many titles†	
	13. Aiweriogh-henɛ†				
		Ekhaenbhen (Junior Palace Chiefs)			
	Ibiwe Nekhua (Junior Town Chiefs)				
	1. Edogun*				
	2. Ɔza				
	3. Eso	Uko n'Iwebo	Uko n'Iweguae	Uko n'Urhoerie	
	4. Ezomurogho, etc.	Ɔdafɛn	Ɔdafɛn	Ɔdion	
		Ibierugha	Ibieruga	Eruerie n'Ibie	
			Emada		
		Grades of Untitled Officials (Simplified)			

* Titles hereditary by primogeniture.
† New titles created by Ovonramwen.

Fig. 2. The principal orders of chieftaincy in Ovonramwen's reign 'elders' but also from the considerable autonomy that they retained in their own settlements. They were not the Oba's equals; they could not sit in his presence nor put anyone to death without his consent. Yet in another sense they were his peers. Like the Oba, and unlike the *Eghaɛbho*, they were hereditary territorial rulers in their own right. Their territories consisted only of the villages or hamlets in which they lived with, in some cases, one or more villages farther afield; but in the internal affairs of these territories the Oba ought not to interfere. Their inhabitants were subjects of the *Uzama* rather than of the Oba. Freemen of Uzebu, for example, were *eviɛn-Ezɔmɔ* rather than *eviɛn-Ɔba*. *Ezɔmɔ* could make direct demands on their services and confer titles on them; the Oba could not. The *Uzama* themselves had some of the attributes of kingship. They had their own priests to bless their Heads, whereas the *Eghaɛbho*'s Heads were blessed by the Oba's priests, *Ihogbe*. They lived in 'palaces' which, in principle at least, were organized along the same lines as the Oba's palace, with associations of retainers bearing titles similar to those conferred by the Oba on his own courtiers. In the nineteenth century most of the *Uzama's* courts were more nominal than effective, but some of them, especially *Ezɔmɔ*, were able to keep up impressive establishments.

The *Uzama* had not always been set apart from the management of the state, if reliance can be placed on traditions of a prolonged struggle waged by the early kings to assert their supremacy over them. Up to the reign of the sixteenth Oba, Esigie, *Oliha* is portrayed as the Oba's main antagonist, but as time goes by this role passes to the *Iyasɛ*, the leader of the Town Chiefs. Ritual expression is still given to the ancient opposition between the Oba and *Uzama*, in the *irɔn* rite, which forms part of the annual Festival of the Oba's Father (*Ugie-Erha-Ɔba*). *Irɔn* takes the form of a pantomimic battle in which the *Uzama*, after challenging the Oba by showing him their archaic 'crowns', are defeated by loyal warriors. Then they accept the Oba's kola nuts and palm wine in token of their submission. This rite, and myths relating how various kings got the better of the *Uzama*, have a continuing social meaning in that they reassert the Oba's unchallengeable supremacy over those who are closest in rank to him. But it is likely that they refer, also, to an historical decline in the power of the *Uzama* correlated, the evidence suggests, with the rise of the

Eghaɛbho orders; and with a shift towards a doctrine of automatic primogenitary succession to the kingship. The successful assertion, by the kings of Benin, of the right to assign major administrative and judicial functions to counsellors appointed by themselves gave them considerable power *vis-à-vis* the *Uzama*. The rule of primogeniture, though ineffective in eliminating succession strife, made the *Uzama*'s role as kingmakers more ceremonial than political. They continued to receive the new king's installation fees and to inaugurate his reign, but they had no more effective voice in determining his identity than did the *Eghaɛbho*.

It is instructive to compare the nineteenth-century position of the *Uzama* with that of their analogues at Oyo (Morton-Williams, 1960: 362–7).[3] The *Oyɔ Misi* formed the central policy-making council, played a major administrative role in capital and state, and had a decisive voice in selecting the *Alafin* (king) from candidates put before them by the royal lineage. Moreover, their ultimate authority over the king was complete for, if his rule proved unsatisfactory, their leader, the *Bashɔrun*, could order him to commit suicide. At Benin no one could claim the right to bring a reign to an end.

Whereas the *Oyɔ Misi* titles were vested in powerful land-holding lineages, the *Uzama* titles descended by primogeniture through narrow lines of descent. Though it did not always prevent succession conflict, the rule of primogeniture at least set narrow limits on the range of possible aspirants, for, unless an *Uzama* died without sons, his brothers and the latters' descendants were automatically excluded from a direct interest in the title. Nor, since land was not lineage-held at Benin, were they dependent upon him, nor he upon them, for access to resources. Thus, two strong motives for lineage solidarity present among the Yoruba were absent from Benin. Wealthy *Uzama* could extend patronage to their kinsmen but, on the other hand, succession disputes were destructive of lineage unity. Many *Uzama* collaterals evaded the authority of their noble kinsmen by, for example, moving into the capital and seeking the Oba's preferment. Those *Uzama* who had many subjects seem to have recruited them mainly from slaves and clients rather than on a descent basis. A further difference between the two groups lay in the fact that, unlike the *Oyɔ Misi*, the *Uzama* did not have administrative and judicial authority over major sections of the capital.

Thus, the *Uzama* depended for their influence on personal wealth and following and, in this respect, their hereditary status gave them (with the *Ezɔmɔ* a conspicuous exception) no special advantages over the Oba's appointed counsellors. In Benin great wealth was attained through fief-holding, control of political patronage, long-distance trade, and participation in war and slave raiding. Wealth was invested mainly in buying slaves, who were set down in villages to farm for their masters. Except for the *Ezɔmɔ*, the *Uzama* controlled relatively few fiefs—the result, probably, of deliberate policy on the part of the kings. Since they exercised few administrative functions, they had little patronage to offer. Successful traders needed to move about freely, making new contacts and closely supervising their agents. In this respect the *Uzama* were hampered by the dignity of their quasi-kingly offices, which demanded that they remain in their palaces rather than wander about in search of wealth. Nor, except for the *Ezɔmɔ*, did they have any special role in the state's military organization.

The *Ezɔmɔ*'s position was unique. Though third in rank in its order, this was one of the great offices of state, and its holder most nearly approached kingly status. The wealth and prestige of successive *Ezɔmɔ*, remarked by many European visitors in the eighteenth and nineteenth centuries, was derived from their function as war captains, in which respect only the *Iyasɛ* equalled them. It was the *Ezɔmɔ* who took charge of most national campaigns, and their military activities enabled them to accumulate many slaves, subjects, and fiefs. However, this role had little to do with their *Uzama* status. They were directly responsible to the Oba, and there is no evidence that they regularly used their power in the interests of their order. The specific character of the *Ezɔmɔ*'s military functions meant that his relationship to the king was sharply defined and lacked the element of polar opposition which bedevilled the king's relations with the *Iyasɛ* or, in earlier times, the *Oliha*. The *Ezɔmɔ*'s military power could be an important factor in succession disputes, but he had no monopoly of physical force, for there was no standing army at his command; when warriors were needed they were recruited by the Oba through his fief-holders, most of whom were *Eghaɛbho*. In at least one nineteenth-century succession dispute the *Ezɔmɔ*'s support for one of the candidates appears to have been crucial, but he was not automatically in a position to dictate the succession. In the dispute which occurred when Adolo died, *Ezɔmɔ* Osarogiagbon seems not to have taken an overt stand.

The Palace Organization

The palace was the religious and administrative centre of the nation. The Oba's living quarters were incapsulated in a vast assemblage of council halls, shrines, storehouses, and workshops surrounded by a high compound wall. Immediately behind this wall, where it bounded the avenue separating Ogbe from Orenokhua, stood rows of huge walled quadrangles containing the altars of past kings. Beyond these was the main palace block, where the Oba lived and conducted his government; and, behind it, the *Eriɛ*, where his wives (*iloi*) lived in strict seclusion.

The main palace buildings comprised three major divisions— *Iwebo, Iwɛguae*, and *Ibiwe*. These were the names of three associations (*otu*) of freeborn retainers that administered the royal court and participated in the government. Access to the apartments of each *otu* was confined to its initiated members, except that a court in *Iwebo* served as a common forum for the chiefs of all three associations. The Oba could move .freely through the palace. In one of the courts in each division there was a dais on which he sat when he met privately with its chiefs to discuss palace affairs or public policy. Other courts lay outside the jurisdiction of any *otu*, and in these the Palace Chiefs joined with the Oba, the Town Chiefs, and, on occasions, the *Uzama*, in a general council of state assembled for decision-making and judicial purposes.

The three associations were characterized by their primary duties at court. First in rank were the *Iwebo*, who had charge of the Oba's state regalia, including his throne and his ceremonial wardrobe and accoutrements. *Unwaguɛ*, as head of *Iwebo*, was head of the palace organization. This was one of the key offices of state, conferring great prestige and patronage on its holder.

The *Iwɛguae* division contained the Oba's private apartments. Its chiefs were his household officers, and his cooks and domestics were chosen from its lower ranks. It also included his pages (*emada*, lit. 'swordbearers'), boys and young men who had been given to the Oba by their fathers and who were bound in absolute service to him until, well into manhood, he saw fit to give them wives and send them into the world as free men. They provided him with a small personal reserve of force and, as they moved about the palace on their errands, they used their eyes and ears to furnish him with intelligence about the intrigues of his courtiers. They also helped him to maintain direct contact with his subjects by arranging private audiences for people who wanted to see him, thus by-passing the official channels of communication through the fief-holders.

Also associated with *Iwɛguae* were the *Ewaisɛ*, the Oba's doctors and diviners, though in some contexts these were regarded as a separate *otu*. They lived in Orenokhua under their own chiefs, but had apartments in the palace, where they prepared and stored the medicines and magical paraphernalia used to protect the king and foster his vitality.

The *Ibiwe* were the keepers of the Oba's wives and children. Their chiefs were divided into two hierarchical series, *Ibiwe* and *Eruɛriɛ*. *Inɛ n'Ibiwe* was the senior chief, but *Osodin*, as head of *Eruɛriɛ*, had direct charge of the *Ɛriɛ*. He and his subordinates maintained discipline there, settled disputes between the wives, and reported to the Oba on their conduct and condition. The *Ibiwe* chiefs cared for them in their own homes when they were sick or pregnant and acted as guardians for the Oba's sons, who left the palace in early childhood. *Ibiwe*, as a whole, were responsible for provisioning the *Ɛriɛ*—a major task, for, including the servants of the Oba's wives, it housed several hundred women.

Apart from these retainer duties the palace associations performed important political functions, which may be summarized as follows:

(1) They were institutions for recruiting and training personnel for specific administrative, judicial, and ceremonial tasks and for the general exercise of royal authority.

(2) They were organized into an elaborate system of grades and hierarchies which served to channel competition for power.

(3) They were a powerful instrument of centralization and a force for stability in the state.

Every freeborn man in the Benin kingdom considered himself a member of one of the palace *otu*. In nearly every village there were a few men who had actually 'entered the palace', that is had been initiated into an association, but the majority had only a nominal affiliation inherited from their fathers. Nominal

c

membership gave no access to the *otu*'s apartments, no voice in its affairs or share in its revenue. Nor, so far as one can tell, did differential palace affiliations give rise to regularly opposed groups within the village community. What they did was to afford each individual a sense of personal identification with the central institutions of the state, and thus they helped to maintain popular support for a highly exploitative political system. In its relation to the capital, the village had the quality of a peasant culture. Except for the heirs to *enigie* and hereditary priests of community cults, the ultimate pinnacles of ambition lay outside the village. Relatively few managed to transpose themselves from the age-ascriptive hierarchy of the village to the achievement hierarchy of the state, yet virtually everyone had a kinsman or neighbour who had succeeded in doing so. When a man was made an elder (*ɔdiɔn*, *ɔdafɛn*) of his palace *otu* he automatically became an elder of his village and, to this extent, there was a measure of integration of village and palace hierarchies. Such men gained prestige and influence if they returned to their villages, for they had consorted with the great and might still be used to curry favour with them. The odd villager, even achieved a state title. By doing so he was lost to the village as a resident, but could use his influence at the centre on behalf of his kith and kin.

To 'enter the palace' was the first step towards a state title in either the Palace or (but see above, p. 14) the Town order. Apart from the heirs to some hereditary offices and subjects of the *Uzama*, any freeborn commoner (but no close agnates of the Oba)[4] could enter the palace, provided he could meet the expense of initiation. Many young men from all over the kingdom were initiated as *ibierugha* ('children' or 'servants' of the apartments). The candidate spent an initial period of seven days in the apartments of his *otu*, during which he paid fees to its chiefs, swore oaths of loyalty and secrecy, and received instructions in his duties. He was then liable to be called upon to perform the more menial tasks that fell to his *otu*, to act as a servant to its chiefs, and to accompany the Oba's emissaries on their missions. By paying additional fees, providing more feasts, and undergoing further rites of passage, the retainer could then seek promotion to the *ɔdiɔn* or *ɔdafɛn* grade and, subsequently, to the highest untitled grade of *ukɔ* (messenger, emissary). To the *ediɔn*, *edafɛn*, and *ikɔ* fell more responsible tasks inside and outside the palace.

With increasing responsibility went emancipation from menial tasks, more perquisites, and a greater voice in the association's affairs. Some, like the bead-workers of *Iwebo*, were craftsmen; others had organizational, ritual or ceremonial duties or undertook missions to the villages on the instructions of the Oba and the chiefs.

Once a man became *ukɔ* he was eligible to apply for a title. All non-hereditary titles were at the Oba's disposal when they fell vacant through the death or promotion of the previous holder. There was no constitutional means of preventing him awarding a title to whomsoever pleased him, simply by sending his messenger to inform the successful applicant. Nevertheless, the chiefs of the relevant order or association expected to be consulted, and any aspirant was well advised to seek their advocacy, for they exercised great influence with the Oba. Moreover, if they could not stop the Oba from awarding a title they could prevent its recipient from enjoying its privileges, for the latter had to pay fees to the king and both orders of *Eghaɛbho*, after which, at a public ceremony held in the Oba's presence, he was formally inducted by the *Iyasɛ*. Until this was done he could not begin to exercise the prerogatives of his office. Clearly the mechanism for awarding titles afforded much scope for the political arts of compromise and patronage.

In each *otu* there were two main grades of titles—*ekhaɛnbhɛn* and *eghaɛbho*. The latter had precedence over the former, and in each grade of each association all the titles were arranged in a single hierarchical series. In a normal career a retainer would take one or more of the lesser titles before achieving *eghaɛbho* rank, and the senior *eghaɛbho* titles—*Unwaguɛ, Ɛribo, Esere, Ɔbazelu, Inɛ, Ɔbazuaye, Osodin*—normally went to men who were already *eghaɛbho*. However, promotion was not automatic. The death of a senior chief did not mean that all those below him moved up one step. All titles were open to competition each time they fell vacant. Moreover, each time a man gave up one title for a more exalted one he had to pay increasingly higher fees and be installed afresh. On the other hand, a title was an investment, for it afforded its holder new opportunities for acquiring wealth.

A high proportion of initiates were sons of retainers and Town Chiefs, and this proportion was undoubtedly higher in the senior grades. This was partly because courtiers' sons were in a better position than most men to afford admission and promotion, but it was also because families resident around the palace maintained a continuing tradition of retainer service. Thus, wealth and family tradition combined to produce something in the nature of an hereditary aristocracy of retainers, through the generations of which administrative and political skills were passed down. Yet, at any one time, all ranks of the palace associations included a leavening of 'new men' who had risen from lowly origins. The strength of the palace organization as an instrument of centralization and stability lay, in part at least, in the way it thus combined a solid core of continuity with an open system of recruitment.

The sons of a senior palace official or Town Chief were distributed between the various *otu*. The manner of their distribution was not rigidly fixed, though the first son and one or more others always joined the father's association. What is significant is that brothers were assigned different palace affiliations. Particular associations did not become identified with particular descent groups, and the non-hereditary, competitive nature of palace titles was strongly maintained. The fact that a man entered his father's *otu* did not imply that he would necessarily remain in it, for it was possible to transfer from one *otu* to another in pursuit of advancement. Once a man became *ukɔ n'iwebo* or *ukɔ n'urhoɛriɛ* (*Ibiwe*) he was eligible for either a Palace or Town title. Initiates of *Iwɛguae* did not transfer to *Iwebo* or *Ibiwe* because, it is explained, they were too closely acquainted with the mysteries of the Oba's personal life, but they could take certain Town titles. Though most retainers probably remained in the same *otu* throughout their careers, many men held titles consecutively in different associations or orders.

Thus, while most retainers were drawn from a limited section of the population of Benin City, the mechanism of transfer and the non-hereditary status of palace offices ensured that neither the *otu* as groups, nor particular offices within them, were directly representative of descent group interests. The unity of an *otu* was based on the common interests of its members in preserving their prerogatives, but unity was not always easy to maintain in the face of the obligations of individuals to their kinsmen and fellow members of other groups, such as trading associations. Competition between the *otu* existed, but it was limited partly by the need for the palace to present a common front to the Town

Chiefs and *Uzama*, and also by a fairly strict segregation of administrative competences.

All three associations were concerned with palace revenues and stores. The *Iwebo* had charge of the Oba's reserves of cowrie shells, beads, cloth, and other trade goods. Tribute in yams, etc., was stored partly by the *Iweguae*, who catered for the Oba's personal household and for the feasts he gave his chiefs; and partly by the *Ibiwe*, who were responsible for the provisioning of the wives' quarters. Certain commodities, such as fish, palm wine, and wooden utensils, were supplied to the palace by particular village communities, and certain *ekhaɛnbhɛn* were responsible for seeing that they met their commitments. *Unwaguɛ* and *Ɛribo*, the two senior *Eghaɛbho* of *Iwebo*, had the important and lucrative task of supervising trade with European merchants at the river port of Ughoton, and some of the *ekhaɛnbhɛn* performed similar functions at the river beaches where the Itsekiri came to trade. Among the *Ibiwe* were a group of 'buyers' (*idenbhin*) who purchased goats, fowls, and other materials for sacrifice at palace rituals. *Ibiwe* were also ultimately responsible for the Oba's own livestock, but most of their missions were concerned with girls betrothed to the Oba, some of whom became his wives, while others were bestowed on men whom the Oba wished to favour. *Osodin* controlled the *igban* oath. This was a custom whereby any subject could declare his own wife or any other woman to be 'the Oba's wife'. He might do this out of anger at the woman's conduct, or as a means of bringing a personal dispute to the Oba's notice. Once the matter had been settled, *Osodin* was called upon to revoke the oath, a service for which he expected remuneration from those concerned.

Apart from these and other regular tasks, officials of all three *otu* were sent to the villages to organize levies, gather information, investigate complaints, represent the Oba at village rituals, and present *enigie* to their people. Assignment to these missions was keenly sought after, for they could be very rewarding. The emissaries not only received customary gifts from the recipients of palace favours but often lived for extended periods at the villagers' expense, and they are said to have been adept at extracting presents from men who wanted to make use of their influence, or fines from those whom they held to have broken taboos and regulations. They could also use their missions to establish trading contacts, negotiate marriages, and make arrangements for loaning out animals, or for settling their dependants in villages to farm for them.

The Palace Chiefs were also responsible for the special occupation groups in Benin City. Each 'guild' was affiliated to one of the palace associations, The craft guilds (such as the bronze-casters, smiths, carvers, leather-workers) were linked with *Iwebo*, the keepers of the royal regalia, as were most of the bands of musicians who performed at palace ceremonies. To the *Iweguae*, the keepers of the Oba's person, were allied various groups of ritual specialists, while the *Ibiwe*, who looked after his wives and children, also controlled his sheep- and cattle-keepers. The Palace Chiefs mediated between the Oba and the guilds and received fees from the successors to hereditary guild heads in validation of their titles. The Chiefs were able to draw on the services of the guilds, and they also, no doubt, received their share of the gifts that the Oba bestowed on specialists who pleased him.

Thus, there were many ways in which palace retainers could enrich themselves, and there was a constant flow of wealth from the lower ranks towards the chiefs who distributed tasks. However, the Palace Chiefs were not wholly dependent on these perquisites, for they, and many of the *ekhaɛnbhɛn*, were assigned fiefs from which they drew tribute and labour, and gifts for acting as sponsors and settling disputes. The number of fiefs held by a chief was broadly proportionate to his rank, and the senior *Eghaɛbho* each controlled many villages. They invested their wealth in trade and the purchase of slaves whom they set down in camps, or attached to existing villages, to farm for them under the surveillance of their own kinsmen.

Finally, the Palace Chiefs were not mere executives carrying out the Oba's instructions. They were his inner circle of advisers and had much influence over him, for he was largely dependent upon them for the exercise of his authority. This was especially the case in the early years of his reign, when the governmental and political experience of the palace staff who had served his father greatly exceeded his own. Together with the Town Chiefs, they formed a council of state which met frequently with the Oba himself to take decisions, try capital charges, and hear appealed disputes. Indeed, the only political sphere from which they were excluded was the military one.

The Town Chiefs

There were two main orders of chiefs associated with Orenok-hua, the *Eghaɛbho n'Ore* and the *Ibiwe Nekhua*. According to tradition, the former order was constituted by the twelfth Oba, Ewuare, who included in it two already existing titles, *Iyasɛ* and *Esɔgban*, and two others, *Esɔn* and *Osuma*, of his own creation. By the 1890s there were thirteen titles, of which eight had been added by eighteenth- and nineteenth-century kings.

Apart from *Ologbosɛ*, which was hereditary, all the titles were in the Oba's gift, and any of his freeborn subjects (except the heirs to certain hereditary offices, subjects of the *Uzama*, and the Oba's close agnates) could aspire to them. They were arranged in a single hierarchical sequence, the first four title-holders making up a senior grade. Variously known as *Eghaɛbho n'Ene* (the Four *Eghaɛbho*) or *Ikadal'Ene* (The Four Pillars), the latter were associated with the four days of the Edo week. On his own day each one performed, in his home, the rite of *zematɔn*, which corresponded to a similarly named rite that took place daily at the palace when, as the Edo say, 'the king who is like the day gives food to the day'. It was an act of purification and a renewal and release of the Oba's mystical power. That it had to be performed by the Four *Eghaɛbho* is one manifestation of a constant motif in Benin ritual, namely that the Oba and the Edo are in a relationship of mystical interdependence. In many contexts, this mutual dependence is expressed through acts of ritual communion between the Oba and his predecessors, on the one hand, and the people and their dead, on the other; but the notion underlying *zematɔn* is that the mystical power of the living king has its complement in the living community.

As we have suggested, the conceptual opposition of 'Oba' and 'Edo' was linked up with the alien origins of the royal clan. It also had continuing political connotations. The Oba/*Uzama* opposition, as we have seen (p. 15), was expressed in a mock battle. The potential hostility between the Oba and Town Chiefs was also played out in ritual. For example, when the Town Chiefs, swords in hand, danced homage to the king they were shadowed by his palace retainers, swords upraised as if to strike them down should they attack him, Unlike the *Uzama*, who were hereditary nobles, the Town Chiefs were commoners who, by their enterprise and the Oba's favour, had risen to positions of power. In many contexts it was they who were 'the Edo', in opposition to the Oba and the Palace, for they were held to embody the will and power of all the people. As the fingers are to the thumb, say the Edo, so are the Four *Eghaɛbho* to the Oba.

In one context, the Oba's authority, derived from his descent from Oranmiyan, was opposed to that of the *Uzama*, derived from their predecessor, the *ediɔn-Uzama*, originators of the state. In another, it was the *ediɔn-Edo*, the collective dead elders of the whole people, that stood opposed to the line of dead kings. Every descent group, village and association had its cult of the *ediɔn*, the past elders who laid down its customs and continued to uphold its values. Just as the *ɔdiɔnwere*, the oldest man, was the village head and priest of the dead *ediɔn* of the village, so the *Esɔgban* was *Ɔdiɔnwere-Edo*. In his official house, which directly faced the palace across the open space between Ogbe and Orenokhua, he kept a staff symbolizing the *ediɔn-Edo* whom, with his fellow *Eghaɛbho*, he served on behalf of the Oba and the people. Why, one may ask, was *Esɔgban* and not *Iyasɛ* the *Ɔdiɔnwere-Edo*? The Edo explanation is that the *Iyasɛ* was a war captain who was sent on long campaigns while *Esɔgban*, his deputy, remained behind to look after the town. Another explanation, perhaps, is that the *Iyasɛ* was seen as the chief protagonist of the people against the power of the Palace, a role hardly consistent with that of a priestly guardian of national peace and harmony.

A Benin writer has described the *Iyasɛ*, with some truth, as 'the prime minister and the leader of the opposition'. When the Oba wished to propose a new law, prosecute a war, or take important administrative action he was bound to seek the advice and approval of the *Uzama* and his Town and Palace Chiefs. After meeting separately to formulate their views, the three orders assembled with the Oba in a full council of state. The sole right to argue with or censure the Oba in public was held to lie with Town Chiefs and, more especially, with the *Iyasɛ*. When one of them died, the Oba sent his men to claim his lower jaw, 'the jaw he had used to dispute with the Oba'. This act symbolized the ultimate supremacy of the king over the Edo.

Except in this last symbolic act, it was difficult for the Oba to impose his will on the Town Chiefs. They controlled many fiefs, and he was dependent on them for tribute, labour, and troops. Many of them had great personal followings, since the people saw them as their main protection against the demands of palace officials. Apart from *Iyasε*, they included two other senior war chiefs, *Ologbosε* and *Imaran*, on whom the king regularly depended for the prosecution of his campaigns against rebel vassals. Since no state chiefs could be installed without their acquiescence, the Town Chiefs could render the Oba's appointments ineffective. Finally, the king himself often needed their support lest he became too dependent on his Palace Chiefs.

The best interests of the common people lay in the maintenance of a balance of power between the Town Chiefs and the Palace. Even in the present century, political factions have tended to gather round the Oba and the *Iyasε*, and popular support has swung from one side to the other. In tradition, the *Iyasε* is regularly portrayed as the focus of opposition to the Oba's power. However, we must beware of over-simplifying. We cannot assume that the interests of the Oba and the Palace Chiefs always coincided, or that the orders themselves always presented unanimous fronts towards each other or towards the Oba. Kin and other loyalties cut across obligations to fellow chiefs. Moreover, it was in the Oba's interests, as in his subjects', to keep a balance between different power groups and to advance his own interests by dividing theirs.

We have already seen that any man who had reached *ukɔ* rank in the palace was qualified for a Town Chief title. An alternative avenue of advancement lay through the *Ekaiwe* association, composed mainly of descendants of the Oba's daughters. From *Ekaiwe* the Oba appointed men to titles in the *Ibiwe Nekhua* order, which had mainly military and ceremonial functions. These titles were regarded as a step towards Town Chief rank. Since it was customary for the Oba to marry his daughters to the Town Chiefs, many of the latters' children became *Ekaiwe* and *Ibiwe Nekhua*. Thus there was a degree of descent continuity within the Town order. However, since *Ekaiwe* status was not the only qualification for Town titles, the Oba was able to inject men of his own choosing into the order. Frequently he filled these titles from the palace ranks, but others were given to men who had made their way in life independently, acquiring wealth through trade, farming, or the pursuit of crafts or war. It was in the Oba's interests to bring such men into positions of authority and to bind them in oath and obligation to him. By allying himself with them he could strengthen his position *vis-à-vis* the palace establishment. Moreover, since there was always a danger that the Town Chiefs would grow too powerful and come into conflict with the king, it was useful to introduce among them men who were as yet little involved in political intrigue. It is worth noting that the *Iyasε* title was often given to men who, though Edo-born, had made their fortunes by trading or slave raiding on the fringes, or beyond the bounds, of the Benin state.

The Oba

It should already be clear that the Oba of Benin was neither a mere ritual figurehead nor a constitutional monarch, but a political king, actively engaged in competition for power. His main political weapon lay in his ability to manipulate the system of Palace and Town offices. By making appointments to vacant titles, creating new ones, transferring individuals from one order to another, introducing new men of wealth and influence into positions of power, and redistributing administrative competences, the kings tried to maintain a balance between competing groups and individuals.

The distribution of authority was such as to prevent any one group from obtaining too much power in a particular administrative sphere. While the Oba depended on his fief-holders for the administration of his territories and the collection of revenue, these were not drawn from a single order, and the holdings of any one of them were fragmented. Moreover, the fact that a village or chiefdom 'belonged to' a chief did not prevent the palace staff entering it on specific royal assignments. The same principle of overlapping authority operated in other contexts. In Benin City the Town Chiefs were associated with and lived in Orenokhua, but they had no *ex-officio* authority in the ward-guilds that made up Orenokhua; the guilds served the Oba through the Palace Chiefs. Nor was there any concentration of military offices in one order. There were two alternative commands, one led by *Ezɔmɔ* (*Uzama*) assisted by *Ologbose;* the other by *Iyasε* with *Edogun* (*Ibiwe Nekhua*) as his second-in-command. Their warriors were recruited by the fief-holders on the Oba's instructions. To take a last example, while *Unwaguε* and *Εribo* were in charge of overseas trade, the Oba appointed their assistants from all three palace *otu*.

Though the Oba had considerable room for manœuvre in exercising his prerogatives, he was not free to act entirely according to the expediency of the moment. He had to operate within the framework of conventions sanctioned by tradition and sanctified by ritual. To a certain extent he could rearrange the hierarchical orders, but the uppermost titles in each series remain fixed. Their holders had indispensable ritual functions, and any attempt to displace them met with general opposition. Nor, once he had appointed a man to a title, could he lawfully remove him, except by ordering him to commit suicide, if a treasonable charge was made out against him. Moreover, though in principle the Oba was free to reallocate duties and privileges, if he did so too often, or too arbitrarily, he risked consolidating the chiefs against him. To prevent this he had to play them off against each other, and this could be done only by a judicious devolution of power. His interests lay in fostering competition for his favours, both within and between chiefly orders and palace associations, and competition for titles was worth while only so long as the relationship between rank, prerogatives, and privileges remained fairly constant. When a man applied for a title he did so in the expectation that he would succeed to the fiefs and perquisites that his predecessor had enjoyed. If these expectations had not been regularly fulfilled competition would have broken down.

All monarchies have to face the problem of the succession, and their success in solving it has an important bearing on their continuity and integrity. The succession at Benin had a complicated history, but by the nineteenth century the principle of primogeniture was firmly established. According to tradition, it had been introduced in Ewuakpe's reign, in the early eighteenth century, with the purpose of avoiding succession conflict (Egharevba, 1960: 40). This aim was not achieved, for two of the last three successions before 1897 involved civil war, and in the third it was avoided only because one candidate had secured overwhelming support. In theory there should have been no dispute, for it was the Oba's right to make his heir apparent by installing him as *Edaikɛn* of Uselu. In fact, none of the nineteenth-century kings did this, because, it is said, they were afraid that their heirs, once officially recognized, would begin to accumulate too much power. The result was that, in each case, factions formed round two of the Oba's oldest sons. The rewards of success lay in the patronage that the new Oba could dispense, and in the influence that his backers hoped to exert through him. In the last resort force was the decisive factor, but each faction was concerned to validate its candidate's right to succeed. The dispute was conducted in terms of the relative age and legitimacy of the rival brothers, the arguments employed being too complicated to detail here. What is significant is that the factions that emerged seem to have cross-cut rather than followed cleavages between the main power groups described above. Competition for the kingship was not, as in Fulani Bida (Nadel, 1942) or Zaria (Smith, 1960), between dynastic segments, but between two brothers. The royal clan had no corporate existence as a power segment and no say in the choice of a successor. The rival candidates had to assemble support piecemeal from each of the main chiefly orders and from influential men outside them. When the Oba died it was the senior Palace Chief, Unwaguɛ, who formally named his successor, in a public gathering of chiefs—the convention being maintained that the late king had disclosed the identity of the legitimate heir to him. But he did so in response to the Iyasɛ's inquiry, and it was the latter who installed the heir as Edaikɛn, after he had paid fees to the Town and Palace orders. Before he could be enthroned he had to pay further fees to the Uzama, and it was they who inaugurated his reign. Only then could he enter his palace, which, in the meantime, remained in Unwaguɛ's custody. Thus, if civil war was to be avoided one of the candidates had to secure overwhelming backing in all three orders.

The new Oba had no right to dismiss the chiefs appointed by his father, and since at the beginning of his reign they were more experienced in the direction of state affairs than he was, he was highly dependent on them, especially the Palace Chiefs. At the same time he had to satisfy his personal supporters, many of whom, up to the time of his enthronement, had lacked official positions. It was customary for a new king to create two new titles in the Town order and in each palace association, so he could give immediate rewards to his closest and most ambitious henchmen. It was difficult, however, for him to place these new titles anywhere but at the bottom of the various hierarchical series. In the early years of Ovonramwen's reign there was a bitter contest between 'those who came with the Oba' (*iguɔmɔre*) and the old palace guard. Between 1889 and 1897, as a result of this struggle, and through dissension within the palace *otu*, a number of chiefs were murdered and others put to death or ordered to commit suicide by the Oba. Ovonramwen was able to use the vacancies caused by these killings and by natural deaths to introduce and promote his favourites into positions of power. Traditions suggest that this may have been the normal pattern of events in the early part of a reign and that, as time went by, the Oba was in a position gradually to increase his personal power.

The kings of Benin seem to have had more security of tenure than many of their African counterparts. It is true that two kings of the eighteenth and nineteenth centuries were removed by force, shortly after they had occupied the palace, and replaced by their brothers, but once the Oba had survived the initial succession crisis it became progressively difficult to remove him. It is conceivable that some kings may have been dispatched by secret regicide, but there was no instance of constitutional dethronement after the introduction of primogenitary succession. The explanation lies partly in the mode of succession itself, in the doctrine that succession can be validated only by the proper performance, by the senior son, of his father's funeral rites. The dogma was that kings were chosen in 'heaven' not by men. This did not prevent violent conflicts for the throne, but it did ensure that the ideological issue in such contests lay in the age and legitimacy of the rival aspirants, not in their personal qualities. As the Oba was not, in theory, chosen on the basis of his fitness to rule—whatever happened in practice—he could not, in theory, be removed if his conduct did not live up to expectations. But the explanation lies, too, in the balance of right and power between the main orders of chieftancy. We have seen that no single order could, by itself, determine the identity of the legitimate heir. Nor could any of them claim undisputed right to bring his reign to an end. While the *Uzama* 'owned' the kingship, the Town Chiefs represented the people's will, and the Palace Chiefs were both the king's servants and the custodians of his person. Nor was there, in Benin, any institution corresponding to the *Ogboni* of Oyo (Morton-Williams, 1960: 364-6) which could co-ordinate public opinion and bind the chiefs to common action. The Oba may have feared that he would be secretly disposed of, yet his best chance of survival lay not in accepting the role of a passive constitutional monarch, but in using his power to maintain competition and dissension between his chiefs.

In emphasizing the more obviously political aspects of the Benin kingship, as we have done in this essay, we inevitably distort that institution. For the Oba was, of course, no ordinary political leader. In succeeding his father he gained access to powerful instruments of political control and manœuvre. But by that same act of succession he ceased to be a mere man. Once installed, dogma had it, the king needed neither food nor sleep, nor would he ever die. In short, he was a divine king, the living vehicle for those mystical forces by which his predecessors, from the inception of the dynasty, had ensured the vitality and continuity of the nation. His principal sacred functions were: first, to maintain the bonds of ritual communion between himself and his predecessors, on the one hand, and his people and their dead, on the other; and, secondly, to foster his own magical powers and to deploy them for the good of his people. The sanctity of his authority lay in the indispensability of these functions, which only a legitimately enthroned king could perform.

In an essay of this length it has been impossible to do more than hint, from time to time, at the extent to which the political and mystical aspects of kingship interpenetrated. The key problem of the Benin polity—the relationship between political kingship and divine kingship—is left unresolved. Here we can only suggest some of the lines along which it might be approached. Firstly, we would need to consider how, in both organizational and ideological terms, divine kingship performed its general unifying functions; to show, for example, how the worship of past kings was interwoven, in contrapuntal fashion, with the worship of various categories of the dead, at all levels of the social system; and to consider the links between ideas and practices relating to the person of the living Oba, and the general Edo dogma of personality and its expression in ritual. We would have to explore the role of the kingship in Edo notions about the interaction of the natural with the social world; and to show how local cults of nature deities were incorporated, by organizational and mythological techniques, into a state pantheon in which the Oba, as 'king of the dry land', was identified with *Olokun*, 'king of the waters'.

More specifically, it would be necessary to demonstrate how

mutual ritual obligations, sanctioned by the general world-view, served to counter disruptive tendencies in the pursuit of conflicting political interests. Every political role, we would find, implied ritual roles. The distribution of rights, duties, and privileges among the complex hierarchies of officialdom received constant expression in an endless series of palace rituals. The continuity of the state and the sanctity of its institutions were reiterated in ritual by linking each significant office and institution with the king who had created it or shown it special favour, and by giving it a part to play in the rites addressed to him. The loyalty of the chiefs to the king was constantly reaffirmed. One may mention here the Festival of the Beads, in which the regalia of the king and his chiefs, symbols of their authority, were brought together and re-dedicated, by human sacrifice, to the common purpose. At *Igue*, the central rite of divine kingship, the royal priests blessed not only the king's Head but those of his *Eghaɛbho* too.

Finally, it would be necessary to consider how the whole ideational complex centred on the king's divinity interacted with individual and group interests in the day-to-day political life of the kingdom. This would be the most difficult of our tasks. For it would be necessary to balance those factors which contributed to the strength of the Oba's position against those factors which placed restraint on his freedom of action. On the one hand, we should have to try to assess the force of the universal belief in his supernatural powers, a belief sustained and fostered by the king himself, by the multitudinous ritual functionaries who were directly beholden to him, and by the chiefs themselves, whose authority, in the eyes of the people, derived from him. Attitudes towards the kingship were a complex of affection and awe, pride, and fear, but the overriding notion, I believe, was one of fearfulness. He was the giver of life but also the giver of death. 'Death, Great One', 'Child of the Sky whom we pray not to fall and cover us, Child of the Earth whom we implore not to swallow us up'—these are the kinds of epithets most frequently used of him. One of the most important meanings of the human sacrifice, for which Benin became notorious, lay in its capacity to demonstrate the sole right of the Oba to take human life. He was addressed as *Omo* 'Child' to distinguish him from all other men, who, in relation to him, were *eviɛn*, 'slaves'. On the other hand, we would have to take account of the fact that the Oba was unable to fulfil his ritual and mystical functions without the active participation, in their sanctified roles, of the representatives of the people. Refusal, on the part of the chiefs, to perform their ritual obligations was one of the most powerful weapons that they could use against monarchical tyranny, for, as we have suggested, the sanctity of the king's authority lay in acceptance of his ability to control those mysterious forces on which the vitality of human society depended.[5]

NOTES

1. The yam was the basis of the subsistence economy, and its cultivation was mainly men's work, each man with a yam farm being expected to contribute to the village tribute. Subsidiary crops, such as corn, groundnuts, peppers, melons, and beans, were planted and tended by women. Kola and coconut trees were individually owned, but oil palms belonged to the village collectively, any member being free to use them at will, except where they were growing on current farms. See Bradbury, 1957: 23–26, for a brief account of the economy.

2. Strictly speaking, this applies only to the first five titles, *Oliha*, *Edohen*, *Ezɔmɔ*, *Ero*, and *Ehɔlɔ n'Ere*. The first *Ɔlɔtɔn* was a follower of Oranmiyan, and the *Edaikɛn* was added to the order by Oba Ewuare.

3. These comparisons were made before I had read the study on Oyo by Morton-Williams which appears in this volume.

4. It was a feature of the Benin political system that the Oba's close male patrikin were excluded from political office at the centre and from membership of the palace organization. In theory, the Oba's oldest legitimate son succeeded him, the next two or three sons being appointed *enigie* of villages outside the capital, where they were supposed to remain, taking no part in the central direction of state affairs. Younger sons were supposed to reside, after childhood, in a ward of the capital set aside for them under the supervision of a non-royal headman. Though membership of the royal clan conferred a measure of prestige, it afforded little material benefit. The lack of lineage-held land, the exclusion of royals from office, and the rule of primogenitary succession to the kingship meant that neither a single royal lineage nor a series of lineage segments existed as corporate power-seeking groups. The king's daughters and sisters, who were married to senior chiefs, often enjoyed his favour and became rich and powerful. Their descendants were powerfully represented in the *Ibiwe Nekhua* and *Eghaɛbho n'Ore* orders (see p. 14).

5. The data used in this essay were gathered during field researches

supported by the Royal Anthropological Institute (Horniman Studentship) and the International African Institute (Research Fellowship), and during the period 1956–61 when I was attached to the Benin Historical Research Scheme (Director, Dr. K. O. Dike), University of Ibadan. To all these bodies and to their relevant financial sponsors, my grateful thanks are due.

REFERENCES

Bradbury, R. E. 1957 *The Benin Kingdom and the Edo-speaking Peoples of South-Western Nigeria.* Ethnographic Survey of Africa, Western Africa, Pt. XIII. London, International African Institute.

1964 'The Historical Uses of Comparative Ethnography with special reference to Benin and the Yoruba', in *The Historian in Tropical Africa*, Eds. J. Vansina, R. Mauny, L. V. Thomas. O.U.P. for International African Institute.

1959 'Chronological Problems in the Study of Benin History', *Journal of the Historical Society of Nigeria*, Vol. I, 4, 263–87.

Egharevba, Jacob 1960 *A Short History of Benin*, 3rd ed. Ibadan University Press.

Lloyd, P. C. 1954 'The Traditional Political System of the Yoruba', *South-western Journal of Anthropology*, Vol. 10, 4, 366–84.

1962 *Yoruba Land Law.* O.U.P. for Nigerian Institute of Social and Economic Research.

Morton-Williams, P. 1960 'The Yoruba Ogboni Cult in Oyo', *Africa*, Vol. XXX, 4, 362–74.

Nadel, S. F. 1942 *A Black Byzantium.* O.U.P. for International African Institute.

Smith, M. G. 1960 *Government in Zazzau.* O.U.P. for International African Institute.

THE YORUBA KINGDOM OF OYO

Peter Morton-Williams

I. *The Earlier Empire*

The nineteenth century was a period of turmoil, disaster, and shaky reconstruction for the kingdom of Oyo. Having enjoyed for perhaps three centuries, or even longer, a dominant and unchallenged position among the Yoruba-speaking peoples, the Ɔyɔ Yoruba had in the late eighteenth century, under King Abiɔdun, extended their empire to the south-west to secure access to the Atlantic along a trade route of more than two hundred miles. The administration of new territory was conducted by officials of the palace of Oyo, and was thus in the hands of the king, or Alafin, whose powers were in consequence so greatly increased that the earlier constitutional balance of power in Oyo itself was destroyed. The Ɔyɔ Yoruba failed to evolve a new and adequate pattern of authority. Internal political rivalries opened their territory to Fulani invaders (the last thrust southwards of Usman dan Fodio's *jihad*), who drove them far to the south. They regrouped themselves on the borders of the forest lands, where, in spite of many determined efforts of the Fulani to conquer them and of attacks from the various forest Yoruba states, they built a new capital, the present town of Oyo. There the Alafin Atiba in *c.* 1838 established a system of government which he intended to be very similar to that of the former kingdom.

The ideas and institutions of government in Oyo in the middle of the nineteenth century had been formed, then, in an earlier period; and a review of the rise of the kingdom, concentrating on the pattern of territorial relations developed in its heyday, will make its structure in the nineteenth century more intelligible. Although a considerable amount of further research is now being undertaken, at the moment only tentative conclusions can be drawn from research into the Yoruba past.

Ɔyɔ, and its archiac variant Eyɔ or Eyeo, is the name of a town, the capital of a kingdom also called Ɔyɔ, of the inhabitants of the kingdom, and of their dialect. There are legends of several localities of the capital, the present town of Oyo (New Oyo) being the seventh or eighth to bear that name. The first three are said to have been north of the Niger; subsequent capitals (from perhaps the late fourteenth century) were still in the extreme north of the wide region occupied by Yoruba-speaking peoples. There is other evidence to support the view that the ruling dynasty of Oyo, if not the rest of the populace, had moved into the area from farther north.

Old Oyo and its Empire

Oyo asserted its power over its Yoruba neighbours, extending its conquests southwards down to the edges of the forest and indeed penetrating it to some extent. This expansion was achieved through the use of cavalry. Legends attribute the building of this empire to their earliest kings, who may have reigned at the beginning of the fifteenth century. The territory of the early empire, which was some ten thousand square miles in extent, was not incorporated into a centrally administered unitary state, but consisted of a large number of internally autonomous kingdoms whose rulers were said to derive their crowns from Oyo and were the vassals of the Alafin. It was this area that Johnson, in his invaluable *History of the Yorubas* (1921: 16), called the 'Metropolitan Provinces' or 'Yoruba Proper', and it formed—if we except its eastern and south-western extremities, far from Oyo—a region remarkably uniform in culture and dialect. The large and strong vassal state of Owu, almost due south of Oyo and just within the forest (and excluded by Johnson from Yoruba Proper), guarded the southern frontiers of the metropolitan provinces against the Ifɛ, Ijɛbu, and Ɛgba Yoruba, and, forty miles north-east of Owu, the smaller kingdom of Ɛdɛ faced the Ijɛsha, who might otherwise have raided the open savannas of the Ɔyɔ from their wooded hills across the river Oshun.

Oyo began to participate in the coastal trade in slaves with Europeans in the middle of the seventeenth century, using the port of Ouidah in the Gun (Popo) kingdom of Allada. There is a break in the forest belt here, and the terrain between Oyo and Ouidah is grassland, for the most part flat or gently undulating and, although there is a steep broken escarpment half-way along the old route, the Oyo cavalry could ensure the safety of the caravans all the way to Allada.

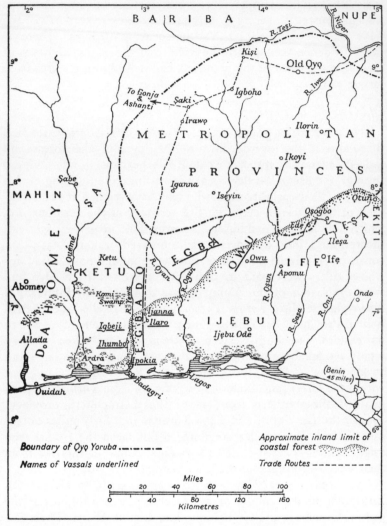

The Kingdom of Old Ọyọ and its Neighbours *c.* 1800

The eighteenth century saw the emergence of Dahomey to the west as a military power. In 1724 it conquered Allada, and Ouidah then became the port for Dahomey, while Oyo took to ports farther east. Oyo recognized the emergence of Dahomey as a threat, and the Oyo cavalry were sent on a series of devastating raids until, in 1747, Dahomey agreed to pay tribute to the Alafin. Nevertheless, the kings of Dahomey succeeded for a time in pursuit of a policy of crushing ports that were in competition with Ouidah, especially to the east (for these were fed with slaves from the same sources), until ordered by the Alafin to leave the last of them free. Dahomey's eastward expansion was halted, leaving Oyo with access to the beaches of Offra, or Little Ardra (now the site of Porto Novo), in the rich little kingdom of Ardra, whose rulers eagerly bought the alliance and protection of the Alafin. A little later Oyo used Badagri as well.

In the eighteenth century Oyo reached the height of her strength, and in the second half was one of the most powerful and wealthy kingdoms in Africa. It has not yet proved possible to make full historical reconstructions of the territorial relations between Oyo and independent neighbouring states at this period. Oyo had certainly for long secured the nearby frontiers of the nuclear kingdom against the large and powerful Nupe kingdom occupying the lands on the north bank of the Niger, little more than fifty miles to the north-west. Nothing can be confidently asserted about the relations between Oyo and her inland neighbours in the eighteenth century, although Johnson (1921: 197) claims that parts of Nupe and Bariba were tributary to Oyo. South of Nupe (and the Niger), Oyo had thrust deeply through the Igbomina Yoruba eastwards into the savannas of northern Ekiti and the Yagba, Gbɛdde, and Kabba Yoruba had probably suffered raids, if not the imposition of regular tribute. A frontier had been established, it seems, for at least a century with the Benin empire at Otun in northern Ekiti, though Benin can have exercised little effective military control. Farther to the south-east was the frontier with the Ijɛsha at the Oshun river; and southwards again Ifɛ and Ijɛbu were left unmolested in their forest territories by the Oyo and discouraged from breaking the peaceful relations by the military reputation of the Owu, who also guaranteed free access to Apomu in Ifɛ territory, where there was a large market for slaves and for goods imported through Lagos and Ijɛbu. Between Owu

and the Ɛgbado trade corridor were the Ɛgba Yoruba, who had
been subjugated by the Ɔyɔ perhaps only in the eighteenth
century; and farther south were the Awori and Lagos. Lagos and
the coastline as far west as the right bank of the Yewa estuary
had earlier been held by Benin (Lander, 1832: 47–52), and there
is some slight evidence to support the view that Oyo may have
destroyed the last vestiges of Benin power in the area before
establishing the trade route through Ɛgbado; by the end of the
century Oyo had no contact with Benin on the coast. In the west,
but north of Dahomey, were the Mahin people, who seem for a
time to have been subject to Oyo (Labarthe, 1803: 105), though
they were overrun later by Dahomey.

Sadly little is known about the rule of Oyo over the 'metropolitan provinces'. The region was divided up into a number of
areas of jurisdiction or ɛkun—four according to Johnson (1921: 68);
three, according to Bowen (1858: xv); and six, according to
Ajaye (1964: 4), but neither their boundaries nor their relationships to Oyo are adequately known. Possibly their main function
had been for the raising of armies in support of an army from the
capital to fight local wars. Each consisted of a dozen or more
vassal kingdoms, whose rulers were required to go in person once
a year to the Alafin at the Bɛrɛ festival (an archiac ceremony which
involved presenting the Alafin with thatching grass—bɛrɛ—for the
palace). Some of them had access to the Alafin only through lesser
overlords, royal or other incumbents of high offices in Old Oyo.

More is known of the newer territories in the south-west,
through which the trade route passed to the coast. It was one of
the major achievements of the Alafin Abiɔdun towards the end of
the eighteenth century, that, in the face of the expansion of
Dahomey, he had reorganized the 200-mile-long trade route to
the sea by moving the southern part of it farther eastwards.
He colonized an area separated from Dahomey by the rivers
Oueme and Yewa and lying well within his own dominions, and
he established members of the Ɔyɔ royal dynasty—his own sons,
according to current traditions—as vassal rulers of the small towns
that were the staging posts on the new road. Among the Ɛgba,
across the Ogun river to the east of the route, he posted state
officials of the *ilari* order (see p. 63) as overlords (Biobaku,
1957: 8); at Ijanna in the Ɛgbado area he stationed an officer of
high rank and a large number of other officials to administer the

highway and toll stations (Clapperton, 1829: 4 ff., 39; Lander R. & J., 1832: 30, 68).

The extension of the power of Oyo along this trade route ensured not merely its protection and the Alafin's supplies of various commodities and valuables. It increased his revenues both directly, through his own commerce, which was mainly in the hands of royal wives and eunuchs, and through the revenues derived from the frequent toll gates (Lander, 1832: 68), and also indirectly through the tribute and accession fees paid him by the vassal rulers of the territories along the route, who had, of course, themselves been enriched by the commerce of the markets in their respective territories. When Abiɔdun died, c. 1810,[1] he left Oyo an extremely prosperous kingdom with an empire which had been brought under a remarkable degree of centralized administration. In assuring Oyo safe access to its port he had set up an executive system to administer the route itself and to control the external relations of the petty kingdoms along it. The officials were all recruited from the staff of the palace in Old Oyo, many of them slaves and eunuchs and responsible through the administrative hierarchy to him alone. From this imperial expansion the Councillors of State, the Ɔyɔ Mesi, did not gain territorially, for they were not made patrons of subordinate rulers; but they profited greatly from the share of booty and tribute and from the flow of wealth into Oyo.

The Fall of Old Oyo

In increasing the power and authority of Oyo over its dependencies, Abiɔdun also strengthened the kingship. During the middle years of the eighteenth century there had been a long struggle for decisive control of the policies of the Oyo kingdom between a rapid succession of feeble kings and the Ɔyɔ Mesi, powerful hereditary office-holders, the most senior of whom was Gaa, the Bashɔrun of Ɔyɔ. His wealth and following enabled him to dominate the Ɔyɔ Mesi and to exercise arbitrarily the prerogative of the Ɔyɔ Mesi to demand the suicide of a king before the latter could gain firm enough control over his retinue and vassals and enough popular support to resist the demand.[2] The struggle was conclusively settled, though for his lifetime only, by Abiɔdun, who slew Gaa and the men of his lineage. Thereafter he dominated the Council and directed the policies of the kingdom. This was a situation which members of the most prominent, non-royal lineages of Oyo could have viewed only with misgivings.

Although the Yoruba could not conceive of government without kingship (they can hardly do so nowadays), they believed that kings in general had a tendency to exploit their immense powers to the disadvantage of their subjects. The powers of the Alafin, however, were limited in practice not only by the ceremonial and ritual restrictions hedging his activities but by opposing to them those of certain strong corporations. The Ɔyɔ Mesi was the most important of these. Second to it in its capacity to sanction the king's rule was the Ogboni cult of the Earth, a priestly corporation whose members mediated relations between him and the Ɔyɔ Mesi. A succession of strong kings would have menaced the capacity of these corporations to exercise their powers and check those of the king, and it seems to have been the practice, not only in Oyo but in other Yoruba kingdoms too, to choose as the successor of a strong king (however much his subjects might have gloried in his achievements) a man whose disposition was judged to be more amenable to pressure from his various bodies of councillors.

Considerations of this sort must have influenced the Ɔyɔ Mesi in their selection of Abiɔdun's patrikinsman, Awole Arogangan, to succeed him. The consequences were dire. He quickly forfeited the military power of Oyo by a series of political blunders during his short reign (1810/11–1816/17?). The first and capital mistake breached his northern and western frontiers. The office of *Kakamfo*, commander-in-chief of the Ɔyɔ armies, had fallen vacant at the beginning of his reign. Awole was deceived into giving the office to an ambitious kinsman, Afɔnja, thus breaking the accepted rule that it should not go to a royal (Johnson, 1921: 189). Afɔnja, who coveted the throne, insisted on stationing himself not on a frontier, as was proper, but in Ilorin, 35 miles SSW. of Oyo itself. There he increased his personal following into a body large enough to threaten the king, partly by coercing neighbouring villages to move into his town and recruiting their men into his army, but principally, and fatally both for himself and the Oyo, by attracting Hausa and Fulani from the north: among the Fulani who joined him was a priest named Alimi, to whom Usman dan Fodio had given a missionary's *tuta* (standard), and who was resolved to carry the *jihad* into Yoruba.

The Alafin also became locked in a struggle for power with the Ɔyɔ Mesi, creating a situation in which the ancient vassal kingdoms of the central metropolitan provinces near Oyo allied themselves to the King's opponents. Misjudging his position again, the Alafin sent the Oyo army and Afɔnja on an expedition he had seen was bound to fail. He had hoped that Afɔnja, defeated, would follow convention and commit suicide; instead the army mutinied and the king's own contingent was massacred. The Bashɔrun now demanded the king's suicide, and Awole, after dramatically cursing Oyo, took poison and died (Johnson, 1921: 190 ff.; Crowther, 1852: iv).

The interplay between four factors dominated the politics of the next twenty years, ending in the evacuation of Old Oyo and the substantial depopulation of the surrounding area. These were: (1) the Fulani penetration; (2) an ambitious rival to the king; (3) the mistrust of the Ɔyɔ Mesi; and (4) fears of the rulers of the chiefdoms in the metropolitan provinces that their support of the Alafin would result only in their greater subordination to Oyo. The most important results of the interplay of these factors were, first, that the Alafin could never command at the same time the thorough-going allegiance of the Oyo town army under the Bashɔrun and of the provincial armies, which were led by the Onikoyi, the premier provincial king; and, second, that Ilorin was often aided in battle by disgruntled provincial rulers.

Awole's successor failed to subdue Afɔnja, whose plans to conquer Oyo and seize the throne ended only when he attempted too late to reassert his command over his indisciplined and rapacious troops. He died fighting outside the doors of his burning house, and control of Ilorin passed to the Fulani. The attempts of successive kings of Oyo to drive them out failed, and instead the Fulani army entered Oyo and compelled the then Alafin to pay tribute.

The prolonged warfare between Oyo and Ilorin led to immense changes in the areas far south of the battlefields, the results both of a vast flooding southwards of people from the devastated north and also of the termination of the Alafin's power to influence the Yoruba-speaking peoples of the forest zone—the Ifɛ, Ijɛbu, and Ɛgba. Many thousands from the north went to settle in a suburb of the oldest Yoruba town, Ifɛ, considered sacrosanct until it was sacked later, in the middle of the century. Others went to the Egbado town of Inubi, blind to the menace of Dahomey, which took it in 1841. Owu had fallen in the 1820s, her soldiers, skilled in hand-to-hand fighting, no match for the Ijɛbu and Ifɛ, now efficiently equipped with firearms.

A large body of Oyo settled near the razed site of Owu, founding the town of Ibadan, soon to become the largest and most powerful Yoruba town, and others grouped themselves near by, at Ijaye. Both towns were organized on a war footing and ruled by redoubtable warriors, Oluyɔle in Ibadan, Kurunmi in Ijaye. Several Oyo adventurers camped on northern edges of the forest, where they were tolerably secure from attack by the Ilorin cavalry and able to raid for slaves on their own account. Among them was the warlike Ɔja, from a chiefly family of Oyo, who settled at a spot known as Agɔ Ɔja, Camp Oja. He was joined by another adventurer from Oyo named Gbenla, and soon afterwards by Atiba, a son of Alafin Abiɔdun.

Atiba had determined to become Alafin. He had his father's ability, and was also more cunning and ruthless than Afɔnja in pursuit of his ambition. He correctly saw that Old Oyo had become untenable as a capital town. He bought the alliance of Oluyɔle of Ibadan with the promise that, after becoming Alafin, he would install him as Bashɔrun, a title that had been held by some of Oluyɔle's ancestors, though it had been transferred to another lineage by an Alafin many generations before; and then he secured the alliance of Kurunmi, who had fought in Afɔnja's army, with the promise of the title Kakamfo. According to current traditions, Atiba then instigated the deaths of Ɔja and of his lineal successor and assumed the chiefship of Agɔ Ɔja.

Alafin Oluewu was now, in the middle 1830s, on the throne in Oyo. At his accession he had paid homage to the Fulani ruler of Ilorin, but rebelled when called upon to declare for Islam. He assembled a huge army from Oyo, Ibadan, Ijaye, and the metropolitan province, got the aid of Bariba allies, and routed the Fulani in the first engagement; but delayed three months before risking an assault on Ilorin. This was long enough for the leaders of the Yoruba forces to conclude that Oluewu and his Bariba allies would make intolerable masters and to resolve to betray him. In the battle for Ilorin, Oluewu was slain, largely, it is said, through the treachery of Atiba, who, with his supporters, retreated without firing a shot; the Bariba were routed and Ilorin was safe.

Atiba Creates New Oyo

Atiba, judging his time had come to seize the rule of Oyo, bought the body of Oluewu from the Emir of Ilorin, since without it he could not properly be installed Alafin (see p. 53). Yet the Ɔyɔ Mesi offered the throne to another royal son, and only after he had declined it in favour of Atiba, did they, too, consent to his being made Alafin (Johnson, 1921: 279).

The Ɔyɔ Mesi and most of the court officials were in refuge in towns near Oyo: they reached an understanding with Atiba that he would join them and lead them back to Oyo (just as his ancestor Alafin Abɛpa had done two centuries earlier, ending an earlier period of exile in Igboho). They found themselves, how-ever, no match for Atiba, who suborned their thirty-four royal and other emissaries, detaining them in Agɔ Ɔja, and making them install him Alafin there with proper ritual *c.* 1838. He next decreed that Agɔ Ɔja was now Oyo, interred the corpse of Oluewu in a new royal mausoleum, summoned the remnant of Oluewu's court, filled those offices of state that were vacant, and dismissed and replaced any office holders who failed to join him at once. The royal leader of the emissaries who had installed him was rewarded with the title of Ɔnashokun (ranking as the king's official father); while that of Bashɔrun went to Oluyɔle, Chief of Ibadan (and Atiba's uterine nephew), and that of Kakamfo to Kurunmi, Chief of Ijaye, as Atiba had promised they should. Gbenla, his ally at Agɔ Ɔja, was given the title of Laguna, one of the Ɔyɔ Mesi, with the promise of succeeding Oluyɔle as Bashɔ-run; and the head of Ɔja's house was made Ashipa (Head of the Hunters' Association and Leader of the Vanguard), now to rank as one, the most junior, of the Ɔyɔ Mesi.

The pattern of political relations between New Oyo and its neighbours that was to last for the twenty years or so of Atiba's reign formed quickly. The political situation was still hazardous. Although the New Oyo was 70 miles south of Ilorin, there was still danger from the Fulani, who continued to raid deep into Yoruba territory; but a large army attempting to take Oshogbo, 45 miles east of Oyo, was defeated by a combined Ibadan–Oshogbo force in about 1841.[3] After this exemplary defeat, vitally important to the Oyo, the Fulani confined their attacks to settlements close to their southern frontier with Oyo; but constantly intrigued with and allied themselves to other Yoruba-speaking groups (especially Ilesha and Ekiti) at war with Ibadan, which was thus engaged on more than one front. In the south, not far from Oyo, Oluyɔle and Kurunmi both ruled towns that were much larger than Oyo and organized on a war footing. Atiba had to keep both of them effectively loyal to him, ready to defend Oyo as well as their own towns against other Yoruba enemies, against the Fulani, and also against Dahomey. There was the further problem of the rivalry of Oluyɔle and Kurunmi.

To safeguard the frontiers of the remaining Oyo provinces and to keep the rivals apart as far as possible, Atiba arranged with them a division of Yoruba territory for protection and tribute. Ibadan under Oluyɔle was to guard the territory from the south-east to the north, and thus to confront Ilorin; while Ijaye under Kurunmi was to defend those to the south-west and west, confronting Dahomey. Both were free to launch offensives beyond their territories, gaining what had been exclusively the Alafin's pre-rogative. Finally, the Alafin was no more to go to war in person, but was to confine himself to religious, civil, and diplomatic affairs (Johnson, 1921: 282). A few towns in the north-west, including Igboho and Kishi, places of refuge for royals and other state officials from Old Oyo, were also permitted to be vassals directly of the Alafin. Unable either to aggrandize himself by conquests or to attract to the new capital more than a small proportion of the scattered population of the former one, Atiba had to content himself with enlarging his town through compelling the inhabitants of the smaller nearby villages to settle in it.

Such power as the king had to influence political developments outside Oyo itself stemmed from the rivalry of Ibadan and Ijaye, which gave him some scope for diplomatic manœuvre; yet his policy, if fostering rivalry, had to prevent hostilities between them, lest one should destroy the other and then, as Afɔnja had attempted from Ilorin, seize the throne. Oluyɔle in the mid-forties did attempt just this, but the king managed to put an end to his siege of Ijaye and to restore the *status quo*. For the rest of Atiba's life, that is, until 1859, while Ibadan and Ijaye were almost continuously engaged in wars or raids beyond the frontiers of the kingdom, within them there was, on the whole, peace.

Oyo in the middle of the nineteenth century, on a different site from the Oyo of the beginning of the century, was no longer

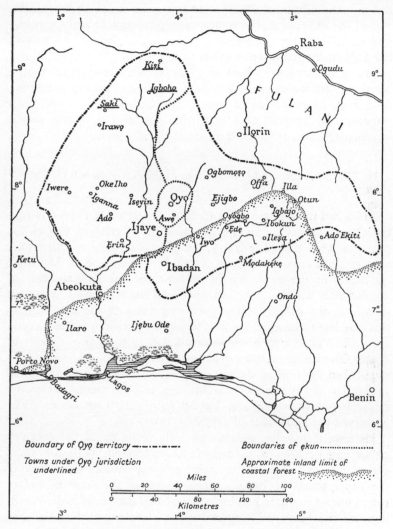

Territory held by the Oyo Yoruba at the death of Atiba

the metropolis of a large empire commanding extensive trade routes and receiving the tribute of many vassals. Nevertheless, through the efforts of Atiba, who had done much to hasten the end of the old capital, the structure of government and organization of his new Oyo duplicated as far as possible the pattern of the ancient kingdom. In relation to the needs of the smaller new capital and kingdom, whose inhabitants were converting to the Muslim faith, the structure was both over-elaborate and anachronistic, with its multitude of state officials whose offices had been important in imperial Oyo and with powerful sanctions vested in reinstituted cults of the traditional Yoruba gods.

II. The Structure and Constitution of Mid-Nineteenth Century Oyo

Atiba had most scope and success in his attempt to reconstruct the Oyo of Abiɔdun, in the organization of religion and of the palace, least in that of territory and of military affairs. During his sojourn in Ilorin, he had presumably behaved as a Muslim.[4] As Alafin of the new Oyo he reinstituted the annual cycle of ancient rites for the principal gods and built temples or set up shrines in the palace for the gods important to the kingship, in this way legitimizing and guaranteeing his position. It has already been said that one of his first deeds was to bury the remains of Alafin Oluewu in a new royal mausoleum; in doing so, he reestablished the cult of the ancestral kings. Probably a substantial proportion of his subjects was Muslim, and he was by no means intolerant of their religion, but in recreating Oyo he carefully preserved the ritual side of kingship.

He also, it appears, restored as fully as he could the complex palace organization of Abiɔdun's day; though, with his small capital city and reduced territory, and the greater autonomy of the other towns of his kingdom, many of the host of palace functionaries can have had little more to do than reflect the splendour of the king and emphasize the remoteness of the sacred kingship from the ordinary citizen.

Territorial Organization

On the territorial side, Atiba could not bring back the empire or even reproduce the old pattern of administration in what remained of the metropolitan provinces or towns where he was the acknowledged titular sovereign (see map). These towns needed military protection, and for that purpose were divided into two *εkun*, one including such large towns as Iwo, Oshogbo, and Ogbomosho, east and north of Oyo (with populations estimated by contemporaries at 50,000 or more) under the Bashɔrun of Ibadan, and the other including Ado, Erin, Iseyin, Igana, and Irawo, west and north-west of Oyo (ancient kingdoms but with rather smaller populations) under the Kakamfo of Ijaye. The nature of the relationships of these towns with their respective military overlords is not known at present, except that Ibadan stationed political agents (*ajεlε*), to whom travellers had to report before presenting themselves to the local ruler, in the towns of Oshogbo, Ejigbo, Ibukun, Abajo, Illa, Gbatedo, and presumably others (May, 1860: 212–30), and collected tribute from them, and also tolls on the Ilorin road. Both Ibadan (population *c.*100,000) and Ijaye (population *c.* 80,000) claimed exclusive and paramount military and political interests in their respective *εkun*, but how far their authority was regarded as legitimate on the grounds that their rulers were the Alafin's officers of state is an open question. Some of the towns, indeed, such as Iseyin and Ogbomosho, still referred to the Alafin for the confirmation of their rulers in office. A number of the rulers had the title and insignia of *ɔba* (king) and governed a number of subordinate villages ruled by *balε* (land fathers) as well as their own towns (Lloyd, 1960: 230–2).

Commerce was carried on mainly by women, as far as the circumstances of war permitted, both within and beyond the area protected by Ibadan and Ijaye; but it is not yet known whether Ibadan or Ijaye asserted the right to collect tolls beyond their own walls or what income they derived from the towns in their respective *εkun*. The whole area had in any case become impoverished. When Old Oyo was deserted its role as a commercial centre was taken over, not by Ibadan, Ijaye, or Atiba's Oyo, but by Ilorin.[5] It is true that some trade still flowed intermittently through these towns, but the Ijεbu and Εgba frequently closed the roads from the sea. Atiba could not even restrict all payments from vassals to himself: some palace officials were given the patronage of villages as benefices; Atiba's son and official heir was given others; and among the State Councillors one, the Ashipa, already held several villages seized by his ancestor, another—

Atiba's ally Gbenla—was rewarded with the patronage of nearby Awe, and a third gained that of the town of Shaki because of its traditional links to his office. Before his accession Atiba had made a fortune from slave raiding and used it to attract a following; afterwards he had to supplement his income from tribute and fees and feed a large palace staff by setting a multitude of slaves to work on his farms.

The organization of the new capital was dominated by a division into two sectors: the royal sector—inhabited by members of the royal lineage, their wives, slaves, eunuchs, and other retainers, and the families of some of Atiba's former companions in arms—and the rest of the town, where the free Ɔyɔ lived with their own slaves. Both areas were subdivided into wards (*adugbo*), the royal wards headed by titled royals, and the others by some members of the Council of State. The largest wards were further subdivided into areas under the authority of the holder of the highest titled office living there, or else of a member of the pre-eminent lineage there, who would then be titled *magaji*. The smallest territorial units were the large walled structures (*agbole*) or 'compounds' housing an agnatic group, its wives, and dependants. The heads of some large compounds, too, ranked as *magaji*. There were, besides the royal sector, two areas belonging to the Alafin, one being the royal mausoleum (*bara*), just within the walls of the eastern edge, and one known as Koso, where the Alafin's temple for his deified ancestor Shango, the Thunder God, and the *agbole* of some of Shango's priests, were.[6] During Atiba's reign this simple pattern of residence became modified by the inclusion of the inhabitants of the villages forced to settle in New Oyo: they were placed in separate localities attached to the existing wards, including the royal ones, and their heads (*balɛ*—'land fathers') ranked as *magaji*.

Social Categories

Four clearly differentiated social categories, forming status groups, as they may be called following M. G. Smith's usage (1960: 37), existed in Oyo. They were royals (*ɔmɔba*), free people of Oyo (*ara Ɔyɔ*), eunuchs (*iwɛfa*), and slaves (*ɛru*). There were in addition, two other statuses so distinct and their occupants so separated from ordinary life that they, too, might be regarded as separate status groups: the one, the women called king's wives (*ayaba*), and the other, the category of palace officials called in Yoruba *ilari* (lit. 'scar heads'). Various orders of rank were recruited from members of all these social categories.

Ranking was characteristic of all levels and forms of Yoruba social organization. In all corporate groups the most general organizing principle was that of seniority, i.e. ranking by order of admittance into the group (cf. Bascom, 1942 and 1951). For instance, in the *agbole* (compound) members of the agnatic group owning it were ranked by age; wives, in relation to them and to one another, were ranked according to the time of their marriage, that is, from the time they began to reside in it. In the field of kinship relations generally, all kin regarded one another as ranking in the order of seniority by birth; thus, kinsmen of the same generation called one another 'senior sibling' or 'junior sibling', irrespective of sex or of lineal or collateral relationship. In cult associations seniority was reckoned from the time of admission to a particular grade. In society at large the junior person had to show respect for the senior by obeisance (increasingly profound the greater the difference in seniority or rank, though influenced, too, by relative wealth) and use of the honorific plural pronoun. The highest ranks were restricted to state and cult offices. With such emphasis on rank differences, and the privilege and right to command service accorded to high rank, competition to achieve it was intense. Wealth was essential for attracting the following usually needed to contest succession to high rank and to maintain or increase the following once in office. The Yoruba themselves emphasized this, but they also recognized that part of an office holder's ostensible wealth was committed to a process of centralized redistribution among his following. The process included making indefinite loans and taking one of the borrower's children in pawn (*iwɔfa*); the child's labour was supposed to stand in lieu of interest, but, when it was a matter of keeping a following, the office holder usually maintained the pawn and educated him like his own children (Aderemi, 1956: 17). Polygyny as a means of securing many children was also important for advancement, not so much because wealth could be increased through the labour of children while young, but rather because a wide network of affinal alliances could be set up through them.

There were in Oyo as constituted by Atiba and surviving to the present day, several orders of rank, each order being usually

E

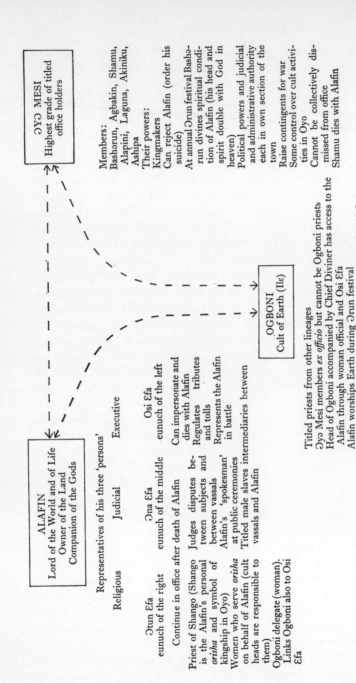

Fig. 3. Government in Atiba's Oyo

recruited from a single social category. The relations between these rank orders were conditioned in the first place by the structural opposition between the king and the Ɔyɔ Mesi (Council of State), which entailed a cleavage between the royal sector of the town, on the one hand, and the sector controlled by the Ɔyɔ Mesi, on the other.

The King and the Council of State

Something has already been said about the struggle for power between successive kings and the Ɔyɔ Mesi in the eighteenth century, with the Ogboni cult of the Earth occupying a mediating position in the political arena (see p. 42). Ideologically, there was no political arena. The king nominally held absolute power, the Ɔyɔ Mesi were his advisers,[7] and the Ogboni added to his ritual powers. Moreover, the Ogboni priests played an important part in a series of rites during his installation which embodied in him the power of his ancestors. When a king died they were summoned to the palace, and after the corpse had been washed they were given its head and cleaned the flesh from the skull. A palace official removed the heart and put it in the charge of the Ɔtun Ɛfa, the titled eunuch responsible for the Shango cult (see p. 62). During his installation the succeeding Alafin was taken by the Ɔtun Ɛfa to sacrifice to Shango and was given a dish containing the heart of his predecessor which he had to eat. Later he was taken to the Ogboni shrine, where the senior priest, the Oluwo, handed him the skull of his predecessor, which had been filled with a corn gruel for him to drink. This rite was said to open his ears to distinguish truth from falsehood, gave his words compelling power, and assigned to him alone the authority to execute criminals and his enemies at home, and to make war on enemies abroad (Morton-Williams, 1960: 371; Johnson, 1921: 42–46). He was praised with titles that attributed omnipotence to him: he was called *Alayeluwa*, 'Owner of the World and of Life' ('World' here connoting all social activity); *Onilɛ*, 'Owner of the land' (*Ilɛ*, besides Earth, means also territory, and territory is equated to the people owning it: 'The town and its territory, they are the same thing'); and *Ekeji Orisha*, 'Companion of the Gods' (referring to his status as sacred king and religious head of the Ɔyɔ Yoruba).

The structural opposition, central to Ɔyɔ politics, lay in a division of roles. On the one side, the Alafin was head of the administrative and executive arms of government, entrusted with the implementation of external policy by diplomacy or war, the management of markets and trade, the investigation and punishment of crime, and the celebration of the principal annual rites in the state cults of the Yoruba gods and ancestors. Having to implement policy in all its aspects, he was in a strong position when arguing what it should be. On the other side, the Ɔyɔ Mesi, on the orders of Alafin, raised the citizen army of Oyo, and the Bashɔrun commanded it. The cults were in the hands of free Oyo, and their titled priests ranked among the subordinate officials of members of the Ɔyɔ Mesi, who were themselves civil lords of the non-royal wards, and who severally had some judicial control in them, adjudicating disputes between the component lineages, and generally in matters where arbitration rather than punishment was the aim. Finally, the Ɔyɔ Mesi could dissuade the Alafin from embarking upon rash adventures because they held his life in their hands. Collectively, with the Bashɔrun as their spokesman, they could pronounce his rejection, whereupon he would have to commit suicide.[8] No Alafin has committed suicide since the death of Alafin Maku, c. 1820; but traditions of earlier suicides can be interpreted as indicating that, whatever the formal pretext, the main reasons for rejecting an Alafin were his insisting on an unpopular war, being defeated in battle after taking the field in person, or failure to prevent excesses of his Arɛmɔ (Eldest Son) or of his high-ranking slaves, and especially for failure in the execution of policy agreed with the Ɔyɔ Mesi. After the death of an Alafin they decided upon his successor.

While the Ɔyɔ Mesi held the ultimate power of life and death over the king he had no such power over them, for he could not dismiss them collectively from office. There were circumstances in which he could dismiss an individual member, who would then be expected to kill himself to remove the disgrace from his own lineage. He had also the right to alter the succession to the office of Bashɔrun; that is to say, he could vest the office in another lineage; and this right, according to Johnson, had been exercised four times. It is uncertain whether Atiba was also following precedent in altering succession to other offices in the Ɔyɔ Mesi, though it is likely that there were precedents for a change he made in the Council's composition (see below). Successors to members of the Ɔyɔ Mesi were elected by their respective lineages and, if the election was shown by his Ifa oracle to augur well, confirmed by the Alafin.

The Ɔyɔ Mesi met together twice daily and, after private discussion, went to the palace to pay homage to the Alafin and offer counsel. Its members had, besides their corporate relationship to the king, individual relations with him. There were seven Ɔyɔ Mesi, each with a title, and they constituted a rank order which, in Atiba's day, was as follows: The Bashɔrun, Agbakin, Shamu, Alapini, Laguna, Akiniku, and Ashipa. The Bashɔrun's role was much the most important. He was not only the commander of the citizen army of Oyo, he was also principal kingmaker and diviner of the king's spiritual condition. The Bashɔrun in Old Oyo had been the richest man in the kingdom, and Oluyɔle in Ibadan was the most powerful. His title was a contraction of *Iba-ashe-Ɔrun*, 'the lord who performs the *ɔrun*', which is related to his role of going once a year to the palace and presiding over the secret *ɔrun* rite to divine whether the king was on good terms with his own *ɔrun*, his spirit double, who was with God in the heavens. The divination might be made to show that the relationship between the king and his spirit double presaged misfortune, in which case further divination might reveal that the offering of sacrifice was needed to restore a favourable relationship; but it could show that the king's spiritual condition was so bad that he should no longer reign. The oracle was worked by casting, or letting fall, the pieces of a split kola nut, and could only give the answers 'yes/no' or 'favourable/unfavourable' or 'silence' to questions, which, although he did not himself throw the kola, were put to it by the Bashɔrun; hence the operation of the oracle could readily supply the Bashɔrun with a pretext for urging upon the Ɔyɔ Mesi the rejection of the king. The precedent that, in the absence of the Bashɔrun, the eunuch holding the state title of Ɔtun Ɛfa should officiate in his place, was followed while Oluyɔle in Ibadan was Bashɔrun during the first part of Atiba's reign; not until Atiba's friend Gbenla succeeded to the title after Oluyɔle's death in 1847 was the *ɔrun* performed in New Oyo by the Bashɔrun.

Next in rank to the Bashɔrun was the Agbakin, custodian of the temple of Ɔranyan, the legendary founder of the Alafin's dynasty. Ɔranyan had to be invoked with a human sacrifice as a pre-condition of success in war; hence, through the Agbakin's role, the Ɔyɔ Mesi had some control over the sending out of a military expedition.

The Shamu, the King's Friend, was second in importance only to the Ogboni in trying to restrain other members of Ɔyɔ Mesi from calling for the death of the Alafin. His title meant *Sha k'o mu!'*, 'Pick your choice!', and he had the privilege of first choice of gifts or booty the king distributed to the Ɔyɔ Mesi. His friendship also caused him to follow the king out of life. If the Ɔyɔ Mesi decided that the Alafin should be told to 'go to sleep' the Shamu would abide by the decision, go with them to the Alafin, and then afterwards, says the present Shamu, announce that the time had come for his own act of love (*olofε*) and he would take poison. His suicide was to be regarded as the exercise of love by a freeman, unlike the compulsory suicide required of certain palace officials.

The Alapini controlled the hierarchy of priests of the powerful, masked, Egungun cult in Oyo, which dealt with witchcraft and sorcery and brought the gods and ancestors embodied in masks visibly into the world at its festivals. At the beginning of their annual festival they could arrange for the disappearance of reputed witches, sorcerers, and people who had shown themselves contemptuous of persons of higher rank (Morton-Williams, 1956: 90–103). The Alapini had custody of the mask Jεnju, ostensibly the property of the Alafin, which was worn by a slave of the Arεmɔ (Eldest Son) who publicly executed convicted witches and sorcerers. He was also patron of the Ɔkεrε (ruler) of the town of Shaki, the centre of the cult (cf. Johnson, 1921: 72,160), and was the only free Oyo, apart from the Bashɔrun, to be appointed patron of a subject ruler.

The Laguna was described by Johnson as 'the state ambassador in critical times' (1921: 72). His traditional role seems to have been primarily a religious one as head of the cult of Orisha Oko, god of the fertility of the farm land and of the increase of game in the bush. He had charge of the first-fruits rite at the yam harvest, and until he had invoked Orisha Oko and sent a dish prepared with new yams to the Alafin, no one was permitted to taste new yams.[9]

The Akiniku's public role was to praise the Alafin when he appeared in the palace forecourt at the principal annual festivals.

Last in order of rank was the Ashipa, Ɔja's descendant (see
p. 44), head of the largest ward in Oyo and lord of extensive
territories outside it which had belonged to villages which Ɔja
had compelled to move into his settlement. He had charge of the
cult of Ogun, the Yoruba god of the use of iron and of hunters
and warriors. As such he was titular head of the guild of huntsmen,
and hence of the vanguard in offensive war, which was recruited
from it.[10]

Affinal alliances between members of the Ɔyɔ Mesi and the
Alafin were set up through the convention, said to have been
carried over from Old Oyo by Atiba, that each of them after his
induction into office should send a daughter to be married to the
Alafin.

Ranking below the Ɔyɔ Mesi were two orders of rank, one
military (Ɛshɔ), the other civil (magaji). Each of the Ɔyɔ Mesi
was responsible for nominating ten Ɛshɔ to the Alafin, who would
confirm them in office. Their duties were to raise troops for war,
to lead them, and to organize their supporting groups of non-
combatants and their supplies of food. Some of the Ɛshɔ were
invested with the rank of Balogun (War-Father), head of a main
division of the army. When necessary, the Alafin would appoint
a head of the ɛshɔ, the Arɛ Ɔna Kakamfo, to be commander of
military activities in some part of the kingdom under heavy threat
of attack or at the base for a campaign of conquest, Kakamfo
were not allowed to return to the capital, but lived in a frontier
town. The office seems to have been introduced at the time of
Oyo's military penetration southwards and south-westwards
towards the coast, perhaps at the beginning of the eighteenth
century. Afɔnja of Ilorin was only the sixth Kakamfo to be
appointed, though six more gained the office during the long period
of warfare in the nineteenth century (Johnson, 1921: 25).

Magaji, as heads of subdivisions of wards, or of large compounds, were responsible to their respective ward heads for the
good order of their charge and had to accompany disputants in
matters they could not arbitrate successfully themselves to their
ward heads. While in the sector of Oyo ruled by the Ɔyɔ Mesi,
the magaji were free Ɔyɔ, in the royal sector they could be members of the royal lineage, free Ɔyɔ settled in the sector as craftsmen
or as ritual specialists, or titled slaves and eunuchs.

Cults of the Gods

The gods were worshipped through a number of cults, which were independent of one another. Each cult was organized round a hierarchy of titled priests, whose offices had political aspects of varying importance (Morton-Williams, 1964: 243–61). It was a dogma of the kingship in Oyo, as in other Yoruba kingdoms, that the king 'owned' all the cults, i.e. that he was titular head of them all, with the implication that it was the duty of the priest-hoods to serve the gods for the satisfaction of his needs and to the public good. Each of the priesthoods was required to communi-cate, through its appointed agent at court (see below), with the Alafin before performing any rites affecting the public interest, and also to perform whatever rites he might order on the advice of his diviners. The need for ritual action of some sort might, of course, have been suggested in the first place by the Ɔyɔ Mesi. In spite of the dogmatic assertion of the Alafin's position, he did not in fact have untrammelled ritual, any more than secular, power. The Bashɔrun was priest of the Alafin's *ɔrun*, the priest of Ɔranyan was himself a member of the Ɔyɔ Mesi, and the Alapini, Laguna, and Ashipa had charge of important cults. In the affairs of all those cults, the Alafin's requirements were directly sanction-ed by the Ɔyɔ Mesi; his powers were further limited because the high priests of nearly all cults resided in wards of which the Ɔyɔ Mesi were lords and whom they were obliged to keep informed of their activities.

It was, indeed, in the field of ritual that the structural relations between the Alafin and the Ɔyɔ Mesi were most complex. For instance, in the cult of Shango, God of Thunder, that represented in its imagery the epitome of the absolute power of kingship (see Johnson, 1921:34–36, 149–52; Wescott and Morton-Williams, 1962: 27–33; Verger, 1957: ch. xii), the priest who exercised the most power was not the *Magba*, the hereditary high priest who resided in the precincts of the temple of Shango in the Alafin's sector of New Oyo, but the *Ɔdɛjin* (head of the set of possession-priests) who lived and served Shango within his own temple sited in the Bashɔrun's ward. Whenever fines were paid in expiation of an offence against Shango, the Magba and Ɔdɛjin divided them. half for the Alafin, half for the Bashɔrun. Initiated possession priests in the Alafin's sector did not serve the Ɔdɛjin; their

activities centred on the Alafin's shrine at Koso, outside New
Oyo.[11]

From the political point of view, however, there is no doubt
that the Ogboni cult of the Earth was of prime importance in
moderating the relationship between Alafin and Ɔyɔ Mesi,
since it could impose ritual sanctions on both. The fully initiated
members of this powerful and dreaded association were recruited
partly by hereditary right, partly by invitation from the Ogboni
priests from free Ɔyɔ lineages on a basis of age, presumed wisdom,
and some prominence in secular or religious life. As far as the
general public was concerned, the known function in government
of this cult was to punish the shedding of human blood, which,
however slight the wound, was a sin as well as a crime and resulted
in an inquiry by the judicial official of the cult, the Apena, who exacted heavy payments in expiation from all parties to the affray, as well
as referring the principal offenders to the Alafin for punishment.
The cult was believed, too, to perform vitally important rites
for the king and the community in the secrecy of its lodge in the
palace forecourt, rites that gave its members such magical powers
that any trespass on their activities or privileges was revealed
to them and condignly punished. But, politically speaking, those
of its activities that were most important to keep secret were its
deliberations on government policy.

All members of the Ɔyɔ Mesi were *ex officio* admitted to the
senior grade of the cult, but were debarred from the highest
ritual offices, which were vested in certain lineages (though
successors had to be acceptable to the Ogboni and the king, and
the choice confirmed by the Ifa oracle). The Alafin, too, was
represented in the cult by a woman who heard all that was said
and reported to him, but could not herself take part in the discussions. Thus, while they attended the plenary meetings that were
held at sixteen-day intervals, the Ɔyɔ Mesi did so in circumstances
that placed them to some extent under the discipline of sanctions
vested in a priesthood from which they were excluded and which
bound all Ogboni members to accept decisions taken at the meetings, even though the decisions might not have been unanimously
reached. The Ɔyɔ Mesi's knowledge that their opinions would
reach the king provided them with a channel for warning him as
well as perhaps causing them to moderate their opinions. It is
also of significance that the Ogboni leaders were shielded from

undue pressure from the Ɔyɔ Mesi because the holders of the highest titles (and the head of the women's section) resided in the royal sector of Oyo and so were not subordinate chiefs of any of the Ɔyɔ Mesi.

Finally, the Ogboni lodge was the scene of the Alafin's secret rite for Ilɛ (Earth and her spirits), which took place during the Bashɔrun's celebration of Ɔrun (Sky and spirits in the sky). The Alafin, with the woman who represented him there, and the Third Eunuch (Osi Ɛfa—Eunuch of the Left), joined the Ogboni high priest (Oluwo—Lord of the Mysteries) to divine whether Earth would sustain his rule during the coming year and if sacrifices were required in propitiation, or whether unconditional misfortune would befall him and the land. The Earth's verdict, it is said, would be compared with that obtained by the Bashɔrun when he divined in the central rite of the Alafin's Ɔrun. If both presaged disaster, the Ɔyɔ Mesi had grounds for demanding the suicide of the Alafin.

It would, however, be unwise to conclude that the Alafin's reign was necessarily liable to abrupt termination because of the forebodings of oracles, which in some degree might have been juggled by their operators. Special care was probably taken in appealing to the Ifa oracle before the king made decisions during the next months; but if disasters did come about, or the antagonism between Alafin and the Ɔyɔ Mesi increased, or the townspeople grew disaffected, then in judging the time had come to call for the Alafin to 'sleep', a retrospective view of the oracles would strengthen the resolve of the Ɔyɔ Mesi and give them the concurrence of the Ogboni.

If oracles were not of overriding importance in determining whether the Ogboni and Ɔyɔ Mesi should decide whether the king should or should not continue to rule, they were immensely important in the field of executive and administrative action that the Alafin controlled; and the principal Ifa diviner, the Ɔnalemɔlɛ, lived in his sector of the town and was in constant communication with him. The Alafin needed to know the intention of the gods (orisha); to have oracular sanctions for appointments of officials of all ranks, from a new Bashɔrun to a titled priest or a slave-envoy (ilari); to be told what must be done to secure a favourable omen for enterprises of every kind; and to have interpreted any events that were extraordinary and consequently portentous (Morton-Williams, 1964: 254 ff.).

Royals and Palace Officials

In the royal sector of Oyo the highest ranking men were five members of the royal lineage. Three were his 'official fathers', heads of the three principal branches of the royal lineage, two of the branches being debarred from putting forward successors to the throne. Of the three 'fathers', we need notice only the Ɔna-shokun, head of the line within which succession was confined. He was himself head of a large ward in the royal sector; and one of his principal duties was to bury deceased Arɛmɔ within his compound (Campbell, 1861: 50). In Old Oyo and, it seems, after Atiba's death, they submitted to the Ɔyɔ Mesi the names of eligible candidates for succession to the throne. The fourth royal bore the title of Magaji Iyaji in the nineteenth century; today, he is known as the Baba Iyaji, ranking, with the Ɔyɔ Mesi, above the *magaji*. He was the official 'Elder Brother' of the Alafin, and his role was to ward off insults directed at his 'Younger Brother', that is, assume responsibility for his failings (Johnson, 1921: 68 f.). On the other hand, he was the only man in the kingdom priveleged to rebuke the king. At the present day he joins the 'King's Father' in naming possible successors; but formerly, and perhaps at Atiba's death, the Magaji Iyaji died with the Alafin.

But the most powerful of the royalty, next to the Alafin, was the Arɛmɔ—the Eldest Son—who shared many of the king's powers and privileges, holding a large court, sharing market dues with him, and being lord of many towns and villages. Unlike the king, he was not secluded or confined to his palace. Although he was the official heir apparent, it had become the custom about two centuries before Atiba's succession that he should die with the king, to ensure his support rather than his rivalry. Atiba ended this custom, persuading the Ɔyɔ Mesi that he should be succeeded by the Arɛmɔ. Constitutionally the change was important in strengthening the Alafin and Arɛmɔ *vis-à-vis* the Ɔyɔ Mesi.

Other royals held offices of very minor importance, ranking with the *magaji*. Most of these offices, as far as has been ascertained, were confined to the section of the royal lineage headed by the Ɔnashokun,.and they were given to heads of branches that in course of time had become excluded from the succession; though one, the Atingisi, was the representative of Atiba's uterine kin (*iyekan*—one mother). Another of them, the Agunpopo, Compounder of Medicine for the pregnant wives of the Alafin, formerly vested in the royal lineage, was made over to one of Atiba's non-royal friends, who became *magaji* of a large ward in Oyo.

The principal function of the royal titles seems to have been that of binding the various branches of the royal lineage to the Alafin and preventing them from intriguing with the Ɔyɔ Mesi in the hope of a transfer of the line of succession.

The Alafin's eunuchs (*iwɛfa*) were the highest grade of palace officials, and three of them he appointed to very high rank indeed to represent and personify his three administrative roles, judicial, religious, and executive.

The Alafin might sit in judgement himself; but ordinarily he would be personated by the Ɔna Ɛfa, 'Eunuch of the Middle', or Principal Eunuch, who served too as his 'spokesman' (in the manner of the Ashanti Okyeame). The Ɔna Ɛfa was aided, just as the other leading eunuchs were, and deputized for, by a group of lesser eunuchs assigned to him. Judicial processes in Oyo may be here conveniently summarized. Homicide was the affair of the Alafin in the capital and was investigated and judged by the Ɔna Ɛfa. Bloodshed, because it polluted the Earth, was in the first instance the concern of the Ogboni association. *Lèse-majesté* was a matter for the Ɔna Ɛfa and was punished by decapitation, fines, or flogging, according to the gravity of the offence and the rank of the offender. Adultery with a royal wife, a special form of this crime, was punished by decapitation or by emasculation and incorporation in the palace eunuchs; this was so whether the adultery had been with a wife of the Alafin or of a vassal king. Territorial disputes between vassals were also referred to the Ɔna Ɛfa. Land disputes over farm boundaries or dwelling sites were investigated by compound heads, who might refer them to ward heads, and at this level the judicial process aimed at reconciliation and mutual accommodation. But intractable disputes were taken to the Ɔna Ɛfa. Suicide was an abominable crime, and the corpse would be taken by a high-ranking palace slave, the Ariwo, who, with his following, would impound the property of the suicide.

The Second Eunuch, the Ɔtun Ɛfa (Eunuch of the Right), represented the king's religious person. He was initiated into the priesthood of Shango, and played an important part in the ritual

of installation of a new Alafin. He had charge of the hamlet of
Koso, where the Alafin's Shango temple was, he was responsible
for ensuring that rites prescribed by the king's diviner were performed, and he supervised the elaborate arrangements for the
annual cycle of religious festivals.

The Third Eunuch, the Osi Ɛfa (Eunuch of the Left), represented the king in his executive and military roles. A group of
his subordinate eunuchs, the Arɛ-Ɔja (Market envoys), collected
the dues to be paid by retailers in the King's Market (Ɔja Akɛsan)
in Oyo. Others collected tolls on the trade routes and received
tribute for the Alafin, and in general executed fiscal and trade
policies. The Osi Ɛfa might receive the Ɔyɔ Mesi as the Alafin;
if the king were ill he could personate him at the great public
ceremonies, dressed in full regalia; and at Old Oyo he had sometimes personated him in battle. He had access to the king at all
times, saw him retire at night, and was the first to visit him in the
morning. Being so close to the king and exercising such important
prerogatives, he, unlike the other principal eunuchs, was required
to die with him.

Other high-ranking palace officials included slaves with specialized duties, among them the Ɔna Tɛtu, and his subordinates,
the king's executioners, who beheaded criminals in public,
beneath a palm tree outside the palace; the Ariwo who dealt with
suicide; and Ɔna Onsheawo and his subordinates, whose ritual
duties included preparing the body of the Alafin for burial. The
Olokun-Ɛshin (Master of the Horse), besides his duty of maintaining the royal stable and providing mounts for the Alafin,
Arɛmɔ, and their principal attendants, bore the body of the king
to the *bara* (mausoleum) and then ended his own life.

There was a numerous grade of titled slaves, the *ilari* (scar
heads), who performed many administrative services. They were
selected by the Osi Ɛfa from the palace slaves and distinguished
war captives, and the choice submitted to the Ifa oracle to divine
whether each one would serve the king well. In the rite admitting
them to the grade (Johnson, 1921: 60–63) they received eight
hundred small incisions on their breasts and shoulders, and two
larger ones on their heads, into which 'medicines' were rubbed
that were believed to change their characters so that they would
display characteristics suitable to the specialized roles required
of them; and they were then given new names. The choice of a

particular *ilari* for a diplomatic assignment, or to make demands on a vassal, would show the Alafin's feelings concerning the occasion. Instances may be found in Johnson (1921: 211, 468, 514, 531, 591, 627). The envoy's initiative was thus restricted to a degree that gave the Alafin assurance that his intentions would be communicated.

The *ilari* had an important role in the administration of dependent territory. The towns and villages in the Alafin's territories were linked to Oyo by making their rulers clients of the Alafin or other patrons at the capital. The relationship was expressed in the idiom of father and son. The 'fathers' and their 'sons' communicated through agents called *baba kekere* (Little Fathers). Whether the patron was the Alafin, the Aremo, the Bashorun, or the Alapini, the *baba kekere* was always an *ilari* delegated by the Alafin to the entourage of the patron, living in the patron's compound, but ultimately responsible to the king for his conduct.

The two senior *ilari* supervised, respectively, the Alafin's slaves concerned with matters outside and within the palace. The most senior, Arɛ Apeka ('They will call the king's name everywhere'), was titled *olori ɛru*, 'Head of the Slaves', and led the *arɛ* and other slaves in their twice daily act of greeting and submission to the Alafin. In public ceremonies he danced in front of the king carrying an iron rod. He was responsible for the conduct of the *ilari* outside the palace, and was himself *magaji* of a large compound. The second in rank, Arɛ Kudefu, received all visitors to the palace and supervised the work of all *ilari* working within the palace, such as Arɛ Tujani, in charge of all food, and Arɛ Mapemipa ('Don't call me to kill') in charge of the king's arsenal, of the discharge of guns on state occasions, and also of the slaughter of all animals sacrificed in the palace.

In his choice of wives the Alafin had to conform to the Yoruba rule prohibiting marriage between kin. Women had various roles of great importance in the palace. They were called in general *ayaba* (king's wives), but they were of various ranks and grades. Highest in rank were those of the grade Iya Afin, 'Mothers of the Palace'; next were *ayaba* proper, with whom the king enjoyed conjugal relations, then the order of female *ilari*, who were slave officials, and lowest in the rank the ordinary slave women. Of all the people who lived in the palace the Iya Afin (who were also known as *ayaba ijoye*, 'titled king's wives') were closest in rank to the king. Their numbers seem to have varied over the past century, but there were probably about twenty-four of them in Atiba's palace. No man was ever alone with the king and, whatever other men might be there, at least one *ayaba* would always be in attendance, and she would rank senior to the man received in audience and command his deference. All palace officials had official mothers. The three chief eunuchs had for theirs three of the Iya Afin. The *ilari* were individually matched by a female *ilari* as 'mother' and were collectively under the authority of the Iya-oke Ile Ɔsanyin, who was aided by two deputies. The king himself had an official 'mother' (his own mother had to die at his accession) who ranked higher than any of the Ɔyɔ Mesi and was present when they had audience with the Alafin; she was present even if the Bashɔrun wished to consult the Alafin by himself, and however private the matter might be. The Arɛmɔ had two 'mothers', the Iya Adodo, his own mother, or official step-mother if she were dead, and the Iya Ɔlɔrun Kunmɛfun, who attended and escorted him whenever he visited the king's palace. Most of the Iya Afin were priestesses, who were in charge of shrines in the palace, and were 'mothers' of cult organizations in the town, having *iya kekere* ('little mothers'), generally women *ilari*, to assist them. Of most importance in the king's political relations were the Iya Naso, 'mother' of the cult of Shango; the Iya Nkolara, 'mother' of the Ogboni cult and of the Ɔnalemɔlɛ, the Principal Diviner, who also had charge of the room where the rite of *ɔrun* was performed; and the Ɛni Ɔja (Person of the Market), who supervised the King's Market with the aid of three titled eunuchs from the Osi Ɛfa's group of subordinates, and was the 'mother' of the Osi Ɛfa himself.

Atiba died in March 1859, leaving to his son Adelu, who succeeded him, a town of about 40,000–60,000 inhabitants. The constitution bequeathed by Atiba consisted, in summary, of distinct fields of government, the political and the administrative. The internal administration of Oyo was on two levels—at ward level it was controlled by members of the Ɔyɔ Mesi or titled members of the royal sector as ward heads (the division into the two sectors being of political rather than administrative significance), and at the level of the kingdom as a unit it was administered by officials of the king. Politics within Oyo lay in the relations between the Alafin, Ɔyɔ Mesi, and Ogboni, but they were overshadowed by the paramount need for the Alafin to maintain the precariously peaceful relations between the ambitious rulers of Ibadan and Ijaye, who were masters of the large territory that had been saved from Fulani conquest. Adelu allowed hostilities to break out between Ibadan and Ijaye, and these resulted in the destruction of Ijaye, followed by the victory of Ibadan over Ijaye's allies the Ɛgba Yoruba, who had aimed to gain the territory formerly dominated by Ijaye. The result was both the military ascendency of Ibadan over all the Yoruba lands north of the forest and also the extension of the territories directly attached to Oyo, through its sharing the Ijaye dependencies with Ibadan. Atiba's constitution later survived the superimposition of the British Protectorate (and its selection of Ibadan as the seat of government in western Nigeria), though the judicial roles of the Ɔna Ɛfa— Head Eunuch—and the Ogboni were progressively taken over by newly introduced courts of law. It ended only in the 1950s after Alafin Al Haj Adeniran had denied the sanctions of the traditional cults, and he and the majority of the Ɔyɔ Mesi had quarrelled and had joined opposing national political parties. The intervention of the victorious party resulted in the Alafin being exiled and deposed and the Ɔyɔ Mesi reconstituted.[12]

NOTES

1. Dr. I. A. Akinjogbin puts the death of Abiɔdun as early as April 1789. In an interesting unpublished thesis on Dahomey in the eighteenth century, he quotes a letter from a French Officer, Gourg, at Ouidah, to the Ministre de Marine, 8 June 1789: '. . . le Roy des Alliots est mort . . . en Avril dernier' and continues 'I have taken into consideration all the events of this period, and have concluded that the "Roy des Alliots" could be no other than . . . Abiodun' (Akinjogbin, 1963: 257). There is no corroboration of the report, and putting Abiɔdun's death so early brings many grave difficulties into the chronology of the next three kings, conflicting with the traditions current in both Oyo and Ilorin of Yoruba relations with the Fulani. Assuming that the report does reflect some event in Oyo, among the possibilities is Abiɔdun's celebration of the *bɛbɛ*, or *iku* (death) festival. It is a lengthy rite of thanksgiving, including lavish sacrifices at the graves of the ancestral kings and has been performed by only a few Alafin, whose reigns were regarded as exceptionally successful (Johnson, 1921: 163 f.).

2. This analysis is based on the assumption that the traditions recorded by Johnson (1921: 178–185) are broadly true.

3. Samuel Crowther notes in his journal entry, 27 September 1841, that he was informed that the Fulani had been defeated at Oshogbo 'about three years ago' (Schön and Crowther, 1842: 318). Allowing for Yoruba time reckoning, the battle was probably fought in the dry season of 1839–40.

4. The present Emir of Ilorin says Atiba was brought as a captive from Oyo and adopted as a son by its Fulani ruler, Abdulsalami. Johnson (1921: 265) writes, 'He was all Fulani in his manners' (before he became Alafin).

5. Cf. T. J. Bowen (1858: x f.): 'Ilorin ... were defeated by the people of Ibadan since which time they have acted chiefly on the defensive ...

'Ilọriŋ is one of the great marts of Central Africa, and is much frequented by people from beyond the Niger, and even by Moors and Arabs. The principal exports are fine cotton cloths of Nufe manufacture, and slaves or prisoners captured in petty wars with neighbouring tribes. The imports consist of Arabian and common horses, salt, trona or crude carbonate of soda from the Great Desert, kola or goorah nuts, guns, swords, and European goods. Much of this traffic is carried on across the Desert, although Ilorin is not two-hundred and fifty miles by the road from the Bight of Benin.'

6. The *bara* and Koso of Old Oyo had been several miles to the north and east, respectively, of the town.

7. In 1963 an elder of the Bashọrun's lineage gave me an etymology of Ɔyọ Mesi. It is said to derive from Ɔyọ mɔ esi, 'Ɔyọ knows the reply', implying how to answer to the king's needs. This etymology, though said to be ancient, is not widely known (Morton-Williams, 1960: 364), and the Council is more often known as the Omesi or Ɔyɔ Misi, evidently through the influence of vowel harmony, which is potent in Yoruba.

8. The procedure in intimating to the Alafin that his suicide was demanded seems to have varied, sometimes taking the form of hints that he had disgraced himself beyond redemption; sometimes of silently presenting him with an empty closed calabash (for his head), or one containing parrots' eggs (a procedure used in other Yoruba kingdoms, a parrot's egg being the customary vessel for a suicide's poison); and sometimes of a formal speech of rejection.

9. The present incumbent of the title considers that Johnson's reference was to the exploits of his ancestor, the Laguna of Atiba's day, a notable warrior whose 'ambassadorial' activities were restricted to telling the heads of neighbouring villages that they had the choice of moving into the new Oyo with their people or fighting.

10. It is said that the title had been vested in Ɔja's lineage in Old Oyo, but it had not ranked among the Ɔyɔ Mesi there, where

F

the seventh member had held the title Ɔnamɔdeke, Head of the Young Men (ɔmɔde), organized there in an age-grade association, which carried out public works in the city.

11. In earlier times the Alafin had used possession priests at Koso, many of whom were his slaves, to add ritual sanctions to military coercion in controlling his distant vassals. Alafin Atiba is said to have sent 'priests of Shango', in company with a eunuch representing himself, on two occasions to impose an armistice in the Yoruba wars (Johnson, 1921: 301, 368 ff.), a sanction that was recognized by the Ijɛbu and Ɛgba, and later by the armies of Ibadan and Ijaye.

12. This chapter is based on field and documentary research. Fieldwork in Oyo Division, Western Nigeria, occupied about nineteen months during the period 1955–58 and was supplemented by a fortnight's visit to Oyo in 1963. Fieldwork in Egbado Division, for about twenty-seven months in 1950–54, provided material for the study of the trade route from Old Oyo to the Atlantic. The documentary material available for the study of relations between Old Oyo and Dahomey, of the fall of Old Oyo, and especially of the Oyo Yoruba in the mid-nineteenth century is much richer than my text references (scanty and rather arbitrary because of restrictions on space) may suggest. It is nevertheless admitted that the account of Atiba's Oyo rests very much on inferences from statements of informants, and it is the more tentative because I went to Oyo only after Alafin Al Haj Adeniran had been banished; and I left before his successor, the reigning Alafin Gbadegesin, had fully established his court.

REFERENCES

Aderẹmi, Sir Adesoji (The Ọni of Ifẹ)	1956	'Iwọfa', *Odù*, No. 3. Ibadan.
Ajayi, J. F. A. & Smith, R. S.	1964	*Yoruba Warfare in the Nineteenth Century*. London.
Akinjogbin, I. A.	1963	*Dahomey and its Neighbours, 1708–1818*. Unpublished Ph.D. thesis, University of London.
Bascom, W. R.	1942	'The Principle of Seniority in the Social Structure of the Yoruba', *Amer. Anthropologist*, Vol. 44, pp. 37–46.
	1951	'Social Status, Wealth, and Individual Differences among the Yoruba', *Amer. Anthropologist*, Vol. 53, pp. 490–506.
Biobaku, S. O.	1957	*The Ẹgba and their Neighbours 1842–1872*. Oxford.

Bowen, T. J.   1858   'Grammar and Dictionary of the Yoruba
                             Language' (*Smithsonian Contributions to
                             Knowledge*, x, 4). Washington.

Campbell, R.   1861   *A Pilgrimage to my Motherland*. New
                             York and Philadelphia.

Clapperton, H.   1829   *Journal of a Second Expedition into the
                             Interior of Africa* ... London and Phila-
                             delphia. (Page refs. to London printing.)

Crowther, S. A.   1852   *A Grammar of the Yoruba Language*.
                             London.

Johnson, S.   1921   *The History of the Yorubas*. Lagos.
(Johnson, O., Ed.)

Labarthe, P.   1803   *Voyage à la Côte de Guinée* ... Paris.

Lander, R. L. and   1832   *Journal of an Expedition to Determine
  Lander, J.   the Course and Termination of the Niger*.
                             London.

Lloyd, P. C.   1960   'Sacred   Kingship   and   Government
                             among the Yoruba', *Africa*, Vol. XXX,
                             pp. 221–37.

May, D. J.   1860   'Journey in the Yoruba and Núpe
                             Countries in 1858', *J. Roy. Geog. Soc.*,
                             Vol. XXX, pp. 212–33.

Morton-Williams,P.M.1960   'The Yoruba Ogboni Cult in Ọyọ',
                             Africa, Vol. XXX, pp. 362–74.

                      1964   'An Outline of the Cosmology and Cult
                             Organization of the Ọyọ Yoruba', *Africa*,
                             Vol. XXXIV, pp. 243–61.

Schön, J. F. &   1842   *Journals of the Rev. J. F. Schön and Mr.
  Crowther, S.A.   Crowther, who, with the sanction of H.M.'s
                             Government, accompanied the expedition
                             up the Niger*.

Smith, M.G.   1960   *Government in Zazzau*. London.

Verger, P.   1957   'Notes sur les cultes des oriṣa et vodun...'
                             Mém. de l'Inst. Français d'Afrique Noire,
                             No. 51, Dakar.

Wescott, J. & Morton- 1962   'The Symbolism and Ritual Context of
  Williams, P.M.   the Yoruba *laba Shango*', *J. Roy. Anthro-
                             pol. Inst.*, Vol, 92, pp. 23–37.

THE KINGDOM OF DAHOMEY

J. LOMBARD

In earlier times 'Danhomé' was the name given to the fabulous kingdom of Abomey; and it is by this name that the modern republic is known. Some of the first European travellers visited the country and left eye-witness accounts of the splendour and organization of the royal court. An employee of the African Company, Bullfinch Lambe, visited the Dahomey capital in 1724. Henceforth innumerable missions—English for the most part—arrived at the capital of the Abomey kings. Norris (in 1772 and 1773), Forbes, Richard Burton, and Dr. Répin (all in the nineteenth century) were a few of the travellers who left detailed accounts of their journeys.

On the eve of European penetration the Dahomey kingdom stretched from the important coastal ports of Whydah and Cotonou to the eighth parallel, excluding Savé and Savalou. Savalou formed a small allied kingdom. East to west, it extended from Ketu, on the present Nigerian border, to the district around Atakpame in modern Togo. Towns like Allada (the capital of the former kingdom of Ardra), Zagnanado, Parahoue (or Aplahoué), and Dassa-Zoumé came under the suzerainty of the Dahomean kings. Even the Porto Novo kingdom was at one time threatened by Dahomean forces at the time of the treaty agreeing to a French protectorate. The Dahomey kingdom thus stretched almost two hundred miles from north to south, and one hundred miles from east to west. Its population has been estimated roughly at two hundred thousand.

The founding of the Abomey kingdom dates from about the beginning of the seventeenth century. According to the consensus of local traditions, it was established by Adja invaders, members of the royal family of Tado, an important town now in modern Togo, which formerly dominated certain Ewe groups. Tado was nominally a tributary state of the Oyo–Yoruba empire in the sixteenth and seventeenth centuries. It is not improbable that Yoruba elements had contributed to the development of this

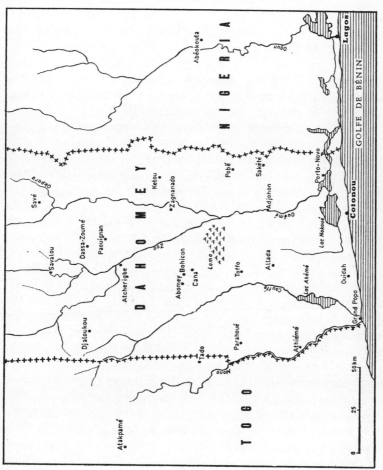

The Kingdom of Dahomey

kingdom (Bertho, 1949), After a dynastic quarrel a group of Adja nobles fled to the east and established themselves near Allada. A further family dispute ensued, and three brothers competed for their father's throne. The eldest succeeded, and the other two left the country, one to found the kingdom of Porto Novo, and the other to establish what was to become in the north the kingdom of Abomey. There the Adja immigrants intermarried with people of Yoruba provenance, the Gedevi, thus originating the Fon ethnic group. The Adja conquest was not achieved without friction and a number of conflicts between the invaders and the indigenous chiefs, but by the seventeenth century the new kingdom was established under Wegbadja, considered by Dahomeans as the true founder of the dynasty. Nine kings succeeded him until the French occupation in 1892. In the course of two and half centuries they sought to extend the boundaries of the kingdom and especially, until the nineteenth century, to escape from the tutelage exercised by the kings of Oyo, who regarded the kings of Abomey as their vassals and exacted an annual tribute in goods, money, and slaves as a symbol of allegiance. In the early part of the nineteenth century the collapse of the Oyo empire (see Chapter II, p. 41) gave Abomey the opportunity to free itself completely from the Yoruba yoke and even to carry war into territories formerly subject to Oyo. The history of Abomey was thus dominated by a series of wars designed to 'make Dahomey always greater' (the motto of their kings), and to acquire the largest number of captives to sell to European slave traders.

In the history of the Abomey dynasty two names have stood out in the memory of Dahomeans by virtue of the renown and the conquests of the kings who bore them. The first, Agadja, who reigned from 1708 till 1732, is considered the country's greatest warrior king. Despite a recent sacking of the capital by an Oyo invading army, Agadja was still master of the Abomey plateau and was determined to establish a direct route to the coast in order to reap the gains of a considerably augmented European trade in the Bight of Benin. His way was barred by the kingdoms of Allada and Whydah. With an invading army he defeated the former in 1724, and in 1729 a second attack brought the Whydah kingdom to heel. By the early eighteenth century Dahomey had conquered an important strip of coastal territory and was able to monopolize the slave trade there. This association with European traders made the kingdom's fortune and enabled the Dahomean army to become one of the most feared in West Africa.

Agadja's successors all extended the boundaries of the kingdom. In 1818 Gezo, the king who was to become the most revered in Dahomean history, came to the throne. He early proved himself a consummate politician and a skilful warrior and also established a close control over the whole kingdom by organizing a highly specialized administration. He managed to wrest independence from his Oyo suzerains, who were by now weakened by the Fulani invasions. He continued his predecessors' military expeditions against the Yoruba chiefdoms and kingdoms to the north and east of his kingdom. During his long reign the arts and crafts flourished at the royal court, which reached an unprecedented splendour. By 1858, the year of Gezo's death, the kingdom had reached its apogee. The abolition of the slave trade soon dealt a serious blow to the country's economy. Palm-oil, however, was found to be a new source of wealth, and Glele, the next king, continued his father's policy. He extended the eastern frontier beyond Ketu, formerly a Yoruba kingdom which had suffered an attack from the Dahomey army. But Glele's army was, in turn, routed before the ramparts of the great Nigerian town of Abeokuta. In 1892, three years after the accession of Behanzin, the last Abomey king, the French conquest brought about the collapse and disintegration of the monarchy (Dunglas, 1957, *passim*).

The Dahomey People—Social Categories

Despite the fact that the Abomey kingdom was established by conquest by foreign invaders, the population of the country exhibited a high degree of homogeneity. The Fon, inhabitants of the Abomey plateau, were the descendants of the conquering Adja and indigenous Yoruba. Small colonies of Fon were subsequently installed in all the conquered districts, particularly in the coastal towns, where they took full advantage of the lucrative European trade. By intermarriage with local inhabitants the Fon achieved a demographic revolution: over the years they successfully assimilated most ethnic groups in the region. Apart from the Yoruba, they all belonged to the same stock. But despite the high degree of ethnic homogeneity, Dahomean society was highly stratified. The four major categories were: royals—descendants of Abomey kings; officials or 'caboceers'; free commoners or *anato*; and slaves.

The servile class was recruited from war captives for the most part, their large numbers being due to the aggressive policies of the kings. They were foreign in origin since it was a rule that no free-born Dahomean could be enslaved. And they were all, in theory, the personal property of the king. Large-scale slavery was probably instituted under Agadja when Abomey first obtained a monopoly of the trade in this region. Slaves were differentiated according to their roles. One category was destined for the royal sacrifices at the 'annual customs' which the king carried out in honour of his ancestors; another worked the royal plantations, under Abomey overseers, and provided contingents for the Whydah slavers; a third, the domestic slaves, was in a more favoured position. They were presented by the king to notables and successful warriors as rewards for their services. In theory, the master had no power of life and death over such a slave. A slave worked in the house or fields and usually became accepted as a member of his master's family; after the second generation he became an unalienable Dahomean citizen. Apart from the stigma attached to his origin, the lot of a slave's descendant hardly differed from that of a free-born Dahomean.

The next rank in society was held by the *anato* or free-born commoners: they were mostly farmers and artisans descended from indigenous families. They formed the backbone of the army, and many of them held minor official posts.

The great officials of the Dahomean central organization ranked next in the social hierarchy. These 'caboceers' or *gbonugan* included the king's ministers (all *anato* in theory), provincial and village chiefs, military commanders, and high-ranking priests.

At the top of the Dahomean hierarchy stood the royal family—all those descendants of kings, past and present. They were ranked according to their genealogical proximity to the reigning king and enjoyed many privileges barred to the ordinary Dahomean. On the other hand—and this is typical of despotic monarchies—princes were not permitted to hold important political or administrative offices. This policy minimized their opportunities for rebellion against the king. Endogamous marriages, although forbidden the commoners, were of frequent occurrence among royals. Princesses were permitted wide sexual liberty. Most royals

lived as parasites within the walls of the palace; all of them were
to some extent the responsibility of the king (Herskovits, Vol. 2,
Chapter 23). The exclusion of royals from official functions demon-
strated the king's determination to retain political power in his
own hands. His policy towards the assimilation of conquered
groups was indicative of the centralizing policy of the Abomey
government.

The Incorporation of Conquered Groups

The Fon kingdom of Abomey did not remain confined to the
original plateau. It incorporated several subject provinces populated by people of varying relationships to their conquerors.
These relations seem to have been major criteria in determining
the policy of the central government towards them. If the conquered territory was inhabited by people dynastically or ethnically
related to the Fon, however distantly, assimilation was the rule.
This was true of the region between the capital and the coast,
especially the kingdoms of Whydah and Allada. Allada was a
'brother-kingdom'; its king had earlier been considered senior to
the Abomey monarch. After the conquest the defeated king
retained his important religious role; temporal functions were
stripped from him, however, and exercised by a provincial chief
who was appointed from the capital and resided at Allada. He was
the viceroy and to all intents and purposes wielded absolute
power in the district. In Whydah administrative control was
even more closely exercised. The defeated king was forced to
flee his capital and was later killed. His family went into voluntary
exile, and the Whydah kingdom came under the control of the
all-powerful *Yovogan*, provincial chief and minister at Abomey,
who was appointed by the king. In both these important trading
centres colonies of Fon were established. They intermarried with
the local inhabitants, thus greatly facilitating the assimilatory
policies of the Abomey kings.

In those regions where the people were of Yoruba origin—
mainly in the north—the incorporation of new provinces was not
followed by colonization on the part of the invaders. Provincial
chiefs were allowed restricted powers. Nevertheless, a practice
typical of Dahomean administration was followed: indigenous
village chiefs were permitted to remain in office, but they were
'doubled' by Dahomey officials, who supervised their political

activities. In all his conquered provinces the king practised a dual method of incorporation—or assimilation—religious as well as political. All village chiefs were placed under a provincial chief or governor who was appointed from the capital. Besides this, all local cults of any significance found in conquered areas were transferred to the care of a priest at the capital and incorporated into the state pantheon under the great cult of the mythical ancestor of the Dahomean kings, the leopard Agasu. The dominion of the Abomey monarchy was thus doubly assured.

Territorial Organization

The country was divided into provinces; and provinces were divided into villages, each with its own territory. If the province was of considerable extent it might be subdivided into districts. At the end of the nineteenth century Dahomey consisted of seven provinces. They included Abomey, the central province controlled most directly by the king; Whydah, administered by the Yovogan; and Allada, under the Akplogan, assisted by five district chiefs. These three provinces were the most important and came under the constant supervision of the king. The other four were of less importance, due to their distance from the capital or their economic insignificance, but were also administered by representatives of the king. Zagnanado bordering the Yoruba chiefdoms on the east, was mainly a military zone. The boundaries of the other provinces were ill-defined. Mahi, the northern province, was situated south of Savi and Savalou; Atakpame was to the west, now in Togo; the Adja region around Athieme in the south-west retained a high degree of automony.

The political influence and economic resources of a provincial chief or *togan* depended on the province he governed. The Yovogan was the richest and most powerful. He controlled Whydah trade and had judicial functions, but he was under constant supervision from the capital and could be dismissed by the king on the slightest pretext. Thus, provincial governors were royal agents: they were responsible for public order, collecting taxes, providing military quotas, maintaining national highways, and settling all land disputes. Conquered chiefs came under the judicial and political control of the provincial governor. The death penalty, however, remained a royal prerogative.

The smallest territorial unit in the kingdom was the village.

All its inhabitants, whether free or servile, came under the authority of the village head or *tohosu*. The *tohosu*'s office was hereditary, although his successor was obliged to accompany the provincial chief to the capital and be confirmed in office by the king. The village chief was assisted in his functions by a deputy or *tonukwe*, and the *donkpegan*, who was in charge of a body of young men who carried out communal work: weeding the chief's fields, or maintaining paths. Large villages were divided into wards; and ward-heads (*hagan*), with the *tonukwe* and *donkpegan*, formed the village council. The power of the village chief was far from being absolute; both the central government and local lineage heads could intervene if his decisions warranted it. If the chief overstepped the bounds of his authority lineage heads could take over in the interests of their members. Individual villagers had the right of appeal to the capital. The king exercised direct control at village level through his royal messengers; occasionally officials from the capital were appointed for longer periods.

The village chief advised rather than judged, arbitrated rather than laid down the law. His major role was settling land disputes and lineage affairs, particularly divorce. Witnesses were essential before decisions could be reached. During epidemics sacrifices were made at cult shrines which were chosen by the village chief and villagers in concert. In inter-village disputes—after a communal hunt or over the division of a palm grove—a royal councillor was asked to deliver judgement, with the further possibility of an appeal to the king. On the whole, the judicial role of the village chief was an important one, in spite of the limitation on the sanctions he was permitted to wield.

The King and the Central Organization

At the top of the Dahomey hierarchy, dominating all social categories and wielding absolute authority over all officials, stood the king. There could have been few African monarchs whose authority was so great, and whose powers were so wide. All state polities, in theory, possess a system of checks and balances: powers are shared with a body of officials residing at the capital who succeed in influencing royal decisions; or territorial chiefs enjoy a degree of political autonomy. In both centralized and decentralized states most kings were limited by some kind of control from subjects or royals. In Abomey, however, we are confronted by a form of absolute monarchy which reached its highest development in the nineteenth century. Absolutism must not be confused with tyranny, however. The king's powers were in fact limited by age-old traditions, established by his predecessors and bolstered by the great respect accorded the royal ancestors which precluded their violation.

One of the first rules which assured the concentration of political power in the hands of the king was the exclusion of members of the royal family from political or administrative office. Succession rules also contributed towards the stability and continuity of the monarchy. The kingship was hereditary within the royal lineage, and theoretically primogenitive. In practice, the king was free to choose as heir apparent the son who showed the greatest ability. This system of succession gave strength to the kingship and assured continuity under kings who were fully instructed in the art of government by their fathers, according to traditionally sanctioned methods. Above all, the dangers inherent in competition were reduced to the minimum: the number of eligible candidates was diminished by excluding collateral branches of the royal lineage and sons not expressly designated by their father to succeed him.

Tradition required that the king-elect should be nominated by the two principal ministers, the *Migan* and the *Meu*. In fact, these two officials were obliged to stand by the dead king's choice in this matter. The essential conditions for eligibility were as follows: to be the son of the king, preferably the eldest—the mother's status was irrelevant, she might even be of foreign or servile origin; to possess a name which did not exclude its bearer from the kingship—in the history of Abomey the rightful heir was once supplanted by his brother and his name remained cursed ever since; to be the son of a king who had died in office and been buried in the palace—in spite of these elaborate precautions there was one case of successful usurpation, but the descendants of this king were excluded from the throne; and, finally, to be *persona grata* with the royal ancestors—the king's diviners acted as go-betweens in this matter.

When the heir apparent (*vidaho*) had been chosen he was presented by the king to his councillors. He was taught the secret traditions concerning the origins of the dynasty and given a palace, with wives, slaves, and farmland attached. The *vidaho* did not exercise any political function during his father's life-time, apart from accompanying the king on his official tours of the country. On the king's death the heir apparent was installed as quickly as possible. The interregnum was always marked by several days of wild anarchy: royal wives killed each other so that they might accompany their husband to the grave; ordinary subjects were at liberty to indulge in all kinds of delict—theft and major crimes—without the slightest intervention of the law. Only the accession of the new king put an end to this chronic disorder—adequate proof of the state's need for a head.

Royal Absolutism

In judicial, military, and political spheres the king had absolute power. He was supreme judge, with power of life and death over his subjects. Neither his judgements nor his punishments—often exceedingly severe—were ever questioned. Punishments provided him with a means of coercion, not only of the victim but also of the public at large. Thus, floggings and executions were given the greatest publicity, in this way increasing their exemplary character. The same publicity was evinced when loyal subjects and successful warriors were rewarded at the annual ceremonies. The people were given models for conduct; and the king's prestige was augmented whether he was being severe or generous.

All administrative officers were appointed by the king; ministers, provincial and village chiefs, and military officers. He also con-firmed the election of priests of the national cults and even lineage heads in the Abomey province. His right to dismiss them at will sprang logically from his monopoly of all appointments. A perma-nent system of espionage was organized from the capital. Certain chiefs were supervised by royal agents, and in this way the king was kept informed of political decisions taken in every corner of his kingdom and was assured of the loyalty of his territorial officials. The slightest dispute or administrative problem was reported to the capital; after the king had been informed the matter was usually settled by his ministers.

The same policy was pursued in the religious field. In many African societies an equilibrium is established between secular chiefs and priest chiefs. In Dahomey, however, national cults were closely supervised by the king. The priests of these cults—which were of great importance and influence in the country—

were his loyal subordinates. Royal agents supervised their activities constantly. The king was also high-priest in a state religion. With the political elaboration of the kingdom the cults associated with the royal dynasty quickly assumed primacy over others. Unlike the chiefs of some West African societies, the king was never enstooled by an indigenous 'chief of the earth', a representative of the original inhabitants, but by the priest of the royal ancestor cult. Besides this, no religious ritual, however domestic or private in nature, could be performed before the annual celebration in honour of the royal ancestors. It is clear that the king stood in no danger of rivalry from affluent subjects, whether noble or commoner. The whole gamut of religious and political elements of society were subordinate to his might.

The king of Dahomey was also supreme commander of the army, which he often accompanied in its campaigns. If in general he left the direction of military operations to the officers responsible for them, it was he nevertheless who appointed them to the different posts of command. This army, as we shall see, was composed in the nineteenth century of a large contingent of female soldiers, the Amazons. This device was an example of the king's skill in foiling in advance any military plot. He placed in his army female companies who usually acted as his bodyguard, who were devoted to him, and charged in time of peace with his protection even within the palace.

The king's methods of reinforcing his authority and increasing his prestige were very subtle. At his court were innumerable families of craftsmen whose products the king monopolized: woodcarvers, smiths, weavers, tailors, copper-workers, jewellers, etc. Artistic themes served to increase the glory of the king. Drawings and bas-reliefs symbolized the 'strong-names' of the monarch and evoked the great events of his reign. Carved stools and richly ornamented figures were all designed to add to the power and wealth of the Abomey kings and the prestige of the dynasty. History was another royal monopoly. Traditions associated with the state, the kings, the royal clans, and the great lineages were confided to certain royal relatives only and a few of the king's wives. In some Western Sudanic states the king's authority was diminished by the influence of a caste-like group of minstrels, 'griots', who had acquired a monopoly of state traditions. The Dahomean monarchs, however, confided the secret traditions of their kingdom to a few people in their own entourage. The exploits of the great kings were translated into song and transmitted from generation to generation within the bosom of the royal family.

Religion was one sphere which escaped their complete control—especially divination, an art widely practised in Dahomey. Diviners, *bokonon*, interpreted the wishes of the royal ancestors when the king consulted them before appointments to posts in the administration were made.

Officials of the Court

The centralization of political activity at the capital required a highly specialized administration. Obviously the king was not able to cope with the minutiae of government himself. Most government business was dealt with by ministers and officials with well-defined functions, although they were not permitted to make final decisions on major questions without the royal consent. According to Forbes, who visited the capital in the middle of the nineteenth century, the royal retinue consisted of 296 nobles. In effect, however, most power was concentrated in the hands of six high-ranking ministers whose functions were considerably varied.

The first minister, the Migan (see p. 78), was the king's chief councillor. He had authority over all Dahomeans who were not members of the royal family. His original role had been that of royal executioner; he retained the official title, but the function was limited to the beheading of the first sacrificial victim at the 'annual customs'. His assistants decapitated the rest. He was always seated on the king's right; in theory, he acted as regent during the interregnum which followed the king's death. He and the Meu alone knew the exact spot inside the palace walls where the king was buried. The Migan and the Meu presided at the accession of the new king, who was usually chosen by his predecessor. The Migan had the important role of supervising the affairs of the province of Allada; the resident provincial chief was responsible to him.

The first minister of the 'left', so-called because he was always seated on the king's left, was the Meu, the second-ranking officer in the kingdom. He wielded authority over members of the royal family; and was given the task of executing royals who had intrigued or rebelled against the king. A prince, convicted of any crime, was 'given to the Meu', who 'lost' him, according to native parlance. The execution of a royal must be kept secret; and it must be done so that no royal blood flowed. The Meu also acted as the king's spokesman in public, since the head of the state was not permitted to speak directly to his subjects. The royal speeches at the 'annual customs' were repeated by the Meu. The provisioning of the palace was the Meu's responsibility; he also organized ceremonies concerning royals, such as baptisms, marriages, and funerals.

The third councillor—second on the king's right—was the *Adjaho*, overseer and administrator of the palace. The Adjaho was also chief of police; in this role he was known as the *legede*. He received reports from the king's spies on political developments in the country. He received visitors to Abomey and announced them into the king's presence. He was responsible for those royal retainers who resided outside the palace walls. The *Tokpo* was the second councillor on the left, and administered the royal plantations and agricultural affairs in general. He was consulted in land disputes and controlled the large markets. In time of war he guarded the palace.

The office of *Yovogan* belonged to one of the most powerful provincial chiefs, as we have seen, and was created after the conquest of Whydah. As governor of Whydah the Yovogan was responsible for all commercial dealings with Europeans. He was a councillor of the left, and as such came under the orders of the Meu. The *Akplogan*, councillor and governor of the province of Allada, was charged with the maintenance of the tombs of former kings of Allada, cradle of the Abomey dynasty.

It is almost impossible to discover whether other officials also held the rank of councillor or minister; we need merely note here the titles and functions of the more important officials at Abomey. The *Sogan* was head of the royal cavalry, never a large contingent due to the difficulty of acclimatizing horses in the forest zone. The *Binazon*, the royal treasurer, supervised the palace stores, where the king's trade goods and gold were kept. Under the Binazon was a host of minor officials who fulfilled multiple functions as stoolkeepers, butlers, organizers of royal ceremonies, etc.

All these councillors and officials were appointed by the king exclusively from commoner families. It was not until the eve of

European occupation that members of the royal lineage were given honorary positions in the administration.

Apart from exercising personal control over the state administration, the Dahomey monarch also ruled an elaborate court, itself organized like a little state. It consisted predominantly of women: relatives, wives, and servants. The palace was the nerve-centre of the kingdom; its very name—Homé or Danhomé —was given to the country as a whole. It covered an area of more than fifteen acres and was enclosed by twelve-foot-high walls. Successive kings built their own palaces beside that of their predecessor, whose huts, altars, and tombs they were obliged to maintain. In this fashion each king made his contribution to 'making Dahomey always greater', since the palace symbolized the kingdom, which should extend its frontiers during each reign. Several thousand people inhabited the palace—all women, apart from a few eunuchs, who exercised police functions within the palace and guarded the gates. There were two official courts where the king gave audiences, plus innumerable apartments for his private use. The palace, as the living symbol of the kingdom, was organized along similar lines. Senior women had the same functions and the same titles as 'outside' ministers: the prime minister's female counterpart was the *Miganon*; the Meu's was the *Meunon*, etc. Of the three or four thousand women inhabiting the palace, only a small proportion were actually wives of the king. Some were royal kinswomen, but the majority were servants or members of the royal bodyguard. The *kpodjito* or 'queen mothers' inhabited a special section of the palace; they represented mothers of past kings. They had large retinues of young girls and servants to help them in their functions, which were mainly honorary and ritual. There were also a number of older women (*tasinon*), members of the royal family, who saw to the upkeep of the royal tombs and offered the required prayers and sacrifices. They participated in royal ceremonies and enjoyed important privileges.

The king's wives were the *ahosi*. These were legitimate wives, as distinct from simple concubines chosen from the servant or slave class, who could not rank as royal wives. Among the *ahosi* was a small group who enjoyed the absolute confidence of the king. They acted as his personal servants and supervised all aspects of his private life. These were the *kposi* or 'leopard wives'; one of them was usually mother of the heir apparent. Other *ahosi* were

G

subordinate to them and were forbidden access to the king at ordinary times. Many of these were maintained at the palace only until they were given away in marriage to councillors or other notables whom he wished to favour. The king also took wives from this group. Finally, there were innumerable women who saw to the upkeep and provisioning of the vast palace, collecting supplies of water, food, wood, etc. One section was responsible for providing the royal table with game. Toughened by their endurances in the forest, they were chosen by the king to be his personal bodyguard. This may have been the origin of the Amazon corps (the name was given to the Dahomean female soldiers by European travellers), who occupied special apartments in the palace and saw to the protection of the king's person.

It is clear from the foregoing that the royal palace—with its own army, priesthood, and advisory council—was a reflection of the Dahomey kingdom itself.

Ritual and Ideology of the Kingdom

From our description of the royal prerogatives and the organization of the kingdom, it will not be difficult to appreciate the important role played by ideology and religious cults centred on the person of the king. *Dada*—the king—was an absolute ruler with sacred attributes. He was the symbol of the whole kingdom and the incarnation of the royal dynasty—all those past kings who continued to exercise a protective role over the land. His subjects prostrated themselves and smothered their heads in dust when they greeted him. At official ceremonies the area around the king's throne was delimited by bamboo poles which no ordinary subject was allowed to cross. When he drank in public everybody looked the other way. Only the king was allowed to wear ornate sandals. Only the king could be followed by a woman carrying an umbrella, richly embroidered with symbolic designs to protect him from the sun. He never appeared in public without his 'stick', a carved baton, slightly curved. The king's cloth was thrown over one shoulder; all lesser men were obliged to wear theirs tied around the waist, at least in the royal presence.

Of the great national cults, two dominated all others: one was associated with the Agasu leopard, mythical founder of the Abomey dynasty, the other with the royal ancestors. These cults occasioned splendid annual ceremonies of great significance and also played an important role during the accession rites of the king. In the early days of the kingdom the king-elect journeyed to Allada, where he was tattooed by the high priest of the cult, receiving five tiny marks on each temple and three on his forehead —symbols of a leopard's claws. Subsequent kings, however, refused to make the journey to Allada, which had become something of a trial, and a deputy replaced them on this ritual pilgrimage. On his enstoolment the new king was consecrated by the Agasu priest with holy water which had been brought from Allada. After a brief period of seclusion, which he spent meditating on his newly acquired responsibilities in a special recess of the palace which housed the ancestral stools, the king was presented to his people. His royal name was then publicly announced: it always consisted of the first syllables of an allegorical sentence.

The king was not considered properly enstooled until he had paid due homage to the late king, his father. This involved the execution of the 'grand customs', ceremonies which have been so well described by visitors to the Abomey court, such as Burton and Forbes. These ceremonies were held each year and lasted for three months, although the 'annual customs' (*anunugbome* in Fon) were of diminished splendour compared to the 'grand customs' held after the death of a king. The proceedings were primarily associated with the royal dynasty, but the kingdom as a whole was also involved. The implications were political and economic as well as religious. Loyal subjects from distant corners of the kingdom were united at the capital at this time. Territorial officers were rewarded or reprimanded according to their desserts. The king's court of appeal was in session. New laws were passed extending the royal prerogatives or further centralizing the administration of the country. Sacrifices offered to the ancestors infused the kingdom with a new spiritual force.

One of the major functions of the 'annual customs' was economic. The exchange of goods was intensified: lineages sent tribute to the king through their village chief or the provincial governor. In the days before the first ceremonies gifts poured into the palace and, in the ensuing months, were redistributed among the soldiers, officials, priests, dancers, and subjects. The extent of the king's wealth and his illimitable generosity increased his prestige and occasioned his subjects' gratitude. During the ceremonies Dahomeans were given the opportunity to admire the work of the royal

craftsmen—cloths, carvings, jewellery, etc. It all exalted the power
of the monarchy and consolidated the feelings of attachment
between ruler and ruled. The king did not display only the material
wealth of the court. During the three months of ceremony the
traditions of the kingdom and the royal dynasty were inculcated
into his subjects on innumerable occasions by the guardians of
Dahomean history—the court minstrels and royal wives.

The 'annual customs' were a convenient means of assuring
the king's absolute ascendancy in the country. He inspected his
officials, received reports, appointed and dismissed chiefs,
announced new laws to his assembled subjects, heard complaints,
judged important cases, gave orders, brought his soldiers' attention to the next campaign, and instilled into the people the history
of their country.

Two kinds of 'annual customs' alternated annually. Both
were organized in five stages: the preparatory stage, during which
the people assembled at the capital and attended the initial
sacrifices made over the kings' tombs—the famous 'platform
ceremony' (*ato*) when slaves were thrown down to the executioners
to have their throats slit before travelling beyond the grave to
serve past kings—the parade of men who marched and manœuvred
for the king; military exercises and demonstrations by the Amazons, who feigned attack on an enemy town; and, finally, the
parade of the king's wealth through the town. At the end of the
'annual customs' preparations were put under way for the next
military expedition.

The Military Organization and External Relations

Social cohesion and a feeling of unity in Dahomey were reinforced by a universally held hatred of an ancient enemy—the
Yoruba. The wars that resulted also benefited the royal treasury
through the acquisition of large numbers of captives who were
sold at the coast in exchange for arms and a variety of European
goods. By the end of the nineteenth century the Dahomean
standing army constituted a considerable force, due to its numbers
and its armaments. Forbes, the English traveller, estimated in
1845 that the army consisted of twelve thousand soldiers, five
thousand of whom were women.

The first kings had led their own armies to war. In the nineteenth century they were content to follow in the wake of the

main body with their retinues, spurring on their officers from the rear. Firearms were first introduced towards the end of the seventeenth century; in the eighteenth century the army even possessed a few cannon. Rapidly a gun became the indispensable part of a Dahomean soldier's equipment, replacing the bow and arrow entirely except for one or two companies. In the second half of the nineteenth century there were two armies: a standing army of male and female warriors, and a reserve army of all adult men and women capable of bearing arms. They were mobilized by the king in time of war. The regular army consisted of fourteen regiments of about eight hundred men strong, and three brigades of Amazons amounting altogether to three thousand. Two officers, ranked as councillors, commanded the army. The *Gau*, the commander-in-chief, led the right wing. During the campaign he shared the prerogatives of the king. The *Kposu*, second-in-command, led the left wing. In peace-time the Gau came under the Migan, on the king's right; the Kposu came under the Meu, on the king's left.

Regular soldiers wore blue-and-white tunics and were organized into regiments and companies, under the command of an officer, each with its own drums and standard. Veterans wore indigo tunics and were called *atchi*. Among the others, the more numerous were the fusiliers, who fought with bayonets, and the blunderbussmen, or *agbaraya*. The Ashanti company was the *élite corps*, formed of the king's hunters. Lastly, there were companies of archers, armed with poisoned arrows, a cavalry company, and a few artillerymen.

The Amazons were organized into two separate corps: a permanent army and a reserve. The reserve company guarded the capital, and especially the palace, in war-time. In the nineteenth century the Amazons were highly organized. They wore uniforms similar to the men's: sleeveless tunics, with blue-and-white stripes, reached to the knees; baggy breeches were held in at the waist by a cartridge belt. Members of the king's bodyguard wore a band of white ribbon about the forehead, embroidered with a blue crocodile. Amazons lived at the palace and belonged to the king, who recruited them from free Dahomeans and captives. They were celibate and were forbidden to marry until they reached middle age, when they still needed the king's consent. In peace-time they saw to their own needs by manufacturing pots or carving calabashes; both crafts were their exclusive monopoly.

During the campaign the Amazon army was organized into three groups: the Fanti company—royal bodyguard—constituted the main body, and the left and right wings came under female officers who corresponded to the Gau and Kposu of the male army. Individual companies were distinguished by the arms they carried: bayonets, muskets (each musketeer was accompanied by a carrier), and bows and arrows (borne by the youngest recruits). The *élite corps*, the Fanti company, consisted of the famed elephant huntresses, the boldest and toughest of the Amazons.

In spite of the efficiency and the size of the standing army, the wars of the nineteenth century necessitated the mobilization of a large proportion of the civilian population. A census system was instituted to achieve the recruitment of these men. Before each annual expedition lineage heads throughout the country were required to inform their village chiefs of the number of males aged over thirteen years in their group. Each man was represented by a pebble, and a short time before mobilization the village chiefs sent bags of pebbles to the capital embroidered with the symbol associated with their village. Pebbles corresponding to the number of arms-bearing men were counted at the palace and carefully distributed among the divisions of the regular army. Each village head was expected to send at least one-half of the available warriors.

When the army was assembled the campaign began. But first the ancestors had been consulted about the opportuneness of the expedition. The king announced that 'his palace needed thatch', making an allusion to the skulls of enemies, which were traditionally placed on the roofs of certain porches. The army left the capital, taking on departure a direction opposite to that of their destination. They were guided by scouts who knew the country and who had often been sent previously as 'traders' to acquaint themselves with the situation and possibilities of defence. When nearing the place of attack the army advanced by night. During the day any enemy farmers who had ventured into the forest were captured. The main assault was launched at dawn when the population was asleep: the object was to collect captives, but those killed in battle were beheaded, the king giving a reward for every head brought back. However, this form of razzia was not always employed. When the Dahomean army was fighting a powerful and well-entrenched enemy it was necessary to lay siege to a town or village, sometimes with serious losses.

Thus, by its aggressive military policies and by its unlimited need for slaves, the kingdom of Dahomey had with its neighbours only relations of war; scarcely any alliances with foreign kingdoms endured. The only possibility of escape for neighbouring populations was flight into the lagoons or the mountainous districts, refuge areas where the Dahomean army could not penetrate easily. By the end of the nineteenth century, at the time of European intervention, Dahomean expansion did not seem to have reached definitive limits.

Judicial Institutions

The king, as we have seen, was supreme judge, with power of life and death over his subjects. There was, however, a well-organized hierarchy of courts. Village chiefs dealt only with civil disputes. Criminal cases were adjudicated by the provincial governor or the king's councillors. At village level there was a court of first instance only; sanctions were limited to fines and short periods of imprisonment. Village chiefs supervised trials by ordeal.

The provincial chief had wider powers. He could inflict the bastinado or impose lengthy periods of imprisonment. In all cases, however, the death penalty was the king's prerogative. Capital crimes included recidivist housebreaking, arson, rape, and adultery with a royal wife—in the latter case the woman was also executed. If the convicted man was also head of an extended family his compound was destroyed and his people sold as slaves. Punishments were always executed in public, usually in the main market-place in Abomey.

Trade and the Economic Resources of the State

The king possessed a number of economic monopolies. He had certain traditional sources of income, which included: a capitation tax, instituted by the first king—it was paid in just before the 'annual customs'; an inheritance tax, aimed particularly at government officials; a palm-oil tax; tolls paid to local collectors installed on the major trading routes (the king did not receive duties on goods and slaves); market dues; special reductions made by all the Europeans on goods sold to the king; elephant tusks and part of game caught by hunters; the labour of royal slaves and the income from their sale; import duties paid on certain goods.

These taxes and dues formed a considerable part of government revenue; most of them originated in commercial transactions. The king monopolized the trade in slaves, who were sold at the coast—mainly at Whydah—by royal traders. Besides this, goods leaving European warehouses were taxed by royal officials stationed at the gates of their factories—a kind of royal tithe being exacted on each transaction. Trade was facilitated by the wide use of cowries, and occasionally iron bars and gold dust.

The slave trade proved profitable until about 1830, when the embarkation of slaves from the Slave Coast became more and more difficult due to the strict watch kept on coastal ports by British warships determined to stop the traffic. It was then that the Abomey kings began selling oil products which were in great demand in Europe. Inevitably the oil trade was much less lucrative. In return for slaves or oil the Dahomean trader received armaments (guns and cannon), cloth, alcohol, and precious metals. Royal control of the trade was strict, but the general prosperity which resulted allowed the development of a wealthy commercial class—descendants of those officials and royal traders who worked for the king on commission and also managed to trade on their own account.

Trade also boosted the development of a network of communications in the southern part of the kingdom. Messages between the capital and Whydah were incessant. The direct route between the two towns could be covered in three days by relays of royal messengers. In other regions communications were less efficient. Local markets served as centres of exchange for two or three villages only. Provincial capitals were linked with the capital by fairly well-kept paths.

The Abomey kingdom in the nineteenth century constituted an almost perfect example of absolute monarchy. Even in such African kingdoms as Buganda or Zululand there was nothing approaching the concentration of powers in the hands of the sovereign. In West Africa the Ashanti king ruled over a confederation of provinces, which enjoyed a certain amount of autonomy. The Mossi king presided over a more or less decentralized empire. In both states groups of nobles, related in some way to the king, enjoyed wide prerogatives as provincial chiefs. In Dahomey this was not so: the policy of centralization permitted neither any significant degree of regional autonomy nor the participation of members of the royal family in the government of the kingdom. The people had no more influence at the seat of power than the nobles. Commoner ministers were in no sense representatives of the people. On the contrary, they remained loyal retainers of the king, who had absolute control of their careers and their lives. In Dahomey the kingdom was concentrated in the person of the king and his ancestors.

REFERENCES

Barbot, John	1732	*A Description of the Coasts of North and South Guinea, and of Ethiopia Inferior . . .* , London.
Bertho, J.	1949	'La parenté des Yoruba aux peuplades de Dahomey et Togo', *Africa*, Vol. XIX, No. 2.
Bosman, W.	1705	*A New and Accurate Description of the Coast of Guinea . . .*, London.
Burton, R.	1893	*A Mission to Gelele, King of Dahome*. 2 vols. London.
Dalzel, Archibald	1793	*The History of the Dahomey*. London.
Duncan, John	1847	*Travels in Western Africa, in 1845 and 1846*. 2 vols. London.
Dunglas, E.	1957–58	'Contribution à l'histoire du Moyen-Dahomey'. 3 vols. *Etudes Dahoméennes*, XIX, XX, XXI, IFAN, Porto-Novo.
Elbée (d')	1671	*Journal de voyage du Sieur d'Elbée, commissaire général de la Marine, aux îles de la coste de Guynée; pour l'établissement du commerce dans ces pays en l'année 1669 et la présente, avec la description particulière du royaume d'Ardres.* 2 vols. Paris.
Foà, E.	1895	*Le Dahomey—Histoire, géographie, mœurs, coutumes, commerce, industrie (1831–1854).* Paris.
Forbes, F. E.	1851	*Dahomey and the Dahomans*. London.
Herskovits, M. J.	1938	*Dahomey. An Ancient West African Kingdom*. 2 vols. New York.

Labouret, H. et Rivet, P. (Eds.)   1929   *Le royaume d'Ardra ou Allada et son évangélisation au XVIIe siècle*, Travaux et Mémoires de l'Institut d'Ethnologie, VII. Paris.

le Herissé, A.   1911   *L'ancien royaume du Dahomey*. Paris.

Macleod, J.   1820   *A Voyage to Africa*. London.

Newbury, C. W.   1961   *The Western Slave Coast and its Rulers*. Oxford.

Norris, R.   1790   *Mémoires du règne de Bossa Ahadee, roi de Dahomé, état situé dans l'intérieur de la Guinée, et voyage de l'auteur à Abomé, qui est la capitale* (tr. from the English). Paris.

Répin, A.   1863   'Voyage au Dahomey', *Le Tour du Monde*, Nos. 162 and 163. Paris.

Skertchly, J. A.   1874   *Dahomey as It Is*. London.

Smith, W.   1744   *A New Voyage to Guinea*. London.

Snelgrave, W.   1734   *A New Account of Some Parts of Guinea and the Slave Trade*. London.

A HAUSA KINGDOM: MARADI UNDER DAN BASKORE, 1854-75

M. G. Smith

I

When the Fulani under Umaru Dallaji finally overcame the Katsina Hausa and took the city after a bitter struggle and protracted siege in 1807, the defeated Hausa ruler, Magajin Halidu, fled with some of his close kin and servants north-eastwards to Tsirkau in Daura territory, where he is said to have thrown himself down a well in a fit of despair (Barth, 1890; Vol. 1, 261; Daniel, *passim*; Urvoy, 1936: 238; Palmer, 1928: Vol. 3, 8). On Magajin Halidu's death, those Katsinawa present immediately selected as their ruler Dan Kasawa, the son of Agawaragi (1752-69), and he made such appointments as were essential for formal continuity of the Katsina state to those positions that had become vacant in the defeat and confusion of flight. This done, the Katsinawa continued north-eastwards to Damagaram, where they met Abdu, the defeated Hausa ruler of Daura. After two years in Zinder, the capital of Damagaram, Dan Kasawa and his entourage moved west and settled at Gafai near the boundary between Damagaram and Maradi (see map). Maradi had formerly been a province of Hausa Katsina, but, following Fulani victory, came under Fulani rule. During the next eight or ten years, while Dan Kasawa remained at Gafai, the defeated Hausa of Gobir regrouped themselves under Salihu, Gumki, and finally Ali (1817-35), and continued the struggle against the Fulani. Meanwhile many Katsina Hausa withdrew to Gafai; but there is no evidence of counter-attacks by Dan Kasawa. He was evidently too weak to mount them.

The province of Maradi was then under the Fulani official, Mani, who lived at Maradi and administered the district directly on behalf of the Sarkin Suleibawa of Katsina. This territory stretched westward from the borders of Damagaram towards Tsibiri. On its south-eastern limits lay Daura, then under Fulani control,

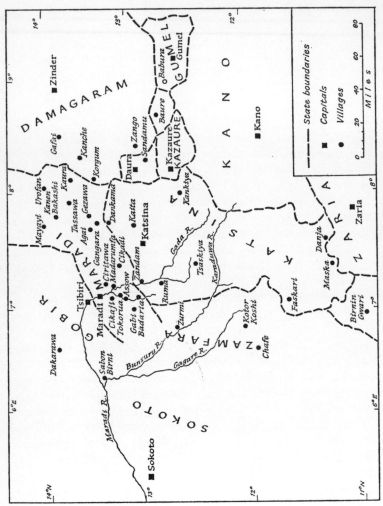

Sketch Map of Maradi

directly south lay Fulani Katsina. Most of the indigenous people were pagans who worshipped spirits (*iskoki, bori*) by sacrificial rites, which included possession. These pagans (*arna*) were grouped in settlements under resident local headmen (*masugari*, s. *maigari*). Maradi itself, the largest settlement in the territory, was fenced with a stockade and had long been administered under the Hausa kings of Katsina by a Hausa lineage from Rano, in whom the title of Maradi was vested. The then holder of this office, Maradi Wagaza, had retained his post despite Fulani conquest and administration. Some time after Dan Kasawa's move to Gafai, Wagaza conspired with him to overthrow the local Fulani, and invited him to come to Maradi as its ruler. Dan Kasawa, fearing treachery, is said to have demanded Mani's head first. Although the Fulani had disarmed the conquered population and had prohibited the manufacture or use of weapons, Wagaza prepared a successful revolt in secret and took Mani and his men by surprise at night. According to tradition, Mani was beheaded at his prayers, and his head was duly dispatched to Dan Kasawa, who moved to Maradi with some Daura Hausa and a slave escort from Damagaram (Landeroin, 1911: Vol. 2, 461–2; Urvoy, 1936: 280–2).

The revolt organized by Wagaza spread rapidly throughout the district. The Fulani were caught off guard, their rule was overthrown, their property and persons placed at the pleasure of their erstwhile subjects. Umaru Dallaji, the Fulani Emir of Katsina, reported the disaster to Sultan Mamman Bello at Sokoto, who at once led his army to join Dallaji in an attack on Maradi town. With Gobir support, Dan Kasawa won a handsome victory and large booty in two battles near Maradi, following which he counter-attacked and captured Garabi, Maraka, Ruma, and Zandam, thus freeing Maradi and a large section of north-western Fulani Katsina, which had been formerly under the Fulani Sarkin Suleibawa. In these struggles Dan Kasawa enjoyed the sympathy and support of those Katsina Hausa who chafed under Fulani domination, and he also received help from Hausa Gobir, Daura, and the Tegamawa Tuareg under their chief, Tambari Gabda (Périé: 6; Landeroin, 1911: Vol. 2, 462).

When Dan Kasawa died in c. 1831 (Urvoy, 1936: 280–2), about ten years after the Maradi revolt, the Hausa dominion at Maradi was assured; and thus Maradi became the site of the successor-state of Hausa Katsina. In accordance with this, Dan Kasawa and his successors are still entitled Chiefs of Katsina, not of Maradi, which is the town governed by the Rano lineage with that title. By 1830 the allies and the enemies of the successor-state were well defined. With active support from adjacent Gobir and Hausa Daura, and passive support from Zinder, the Katsinawa of Maradi were committed to expel Fulani from Katsina territory and to inflict as much harm as possible on adjacent Fulani dominions such as Daura, Zamfara, and Sokoto (formerly Gobir). The Fulani for their part understood this clearly. Dan Kasawa's successor, Rauda, was slain in 1835 with his ally, Sarkin Gobir Ali, at Gawakuke or Dakarawa by Sultan Mamman Bello in a battle which finally assured Fulani rule in Sokoto and Zamfara (Haj Said: 6; Mission Tilho: Vol. 2, 462). Rauda's successor Dan Mari (1835–43) was constrained to accommodate the defeated Gobirawa in Maradi town, so heavy were their losses (see p. 97). For the next year the Gobir and Katsina Hausa lived at Maradi together, each group subject only to its own ruler and officials. Disputes inevitably arose. The Gobir chief, Bakiri, was replaced by his younger brother Mayaki with Dan Mari's support, and the two rulers then agreed to establish the Gobir remnant in a town of their own near by. Dan Mari and Mayaki turned out their subjects in a joint *corvée* to build the new capital of Gobir at Tsibiri, five miles north-west of Maradi on the same watercourse. This separation preserved the fraternal alliance which co-residence had threatened to destroy.

Dan Mari completed the new palace at Maradi which Rauda had begun, and he also pursued the war against Fulani Katsina and Sokoto. When the Sultan Atiku of Sokoto attacked the new town of Tsibiri to destroy it, Dan Mari assisted Mayaki to a victory at Katuru. Atiku died shortly after (Haj Said: 19–22). Dan Mari then led the most sustained effort to overthrow Fulani rule in Katsina. Moving in strength to the Ruma district between Katsina city and Zamfara, he organized a general revolt against Fulani in the environs (Gowers, 1921: 19; Mission Tilho: Vol. 2, 463). In suppressing this revolt, the Katsina Fulani under their Emir, Sidiku, received support from the Fulani states of Kano, Daura, Sokoto, and Zamfara. Sidiku's revenge was to convert the Ruma district into a wilderness, the *dajin Rubu*, which it has remained until recently, many towns being destroyed and their residents killed rather than enslaved.

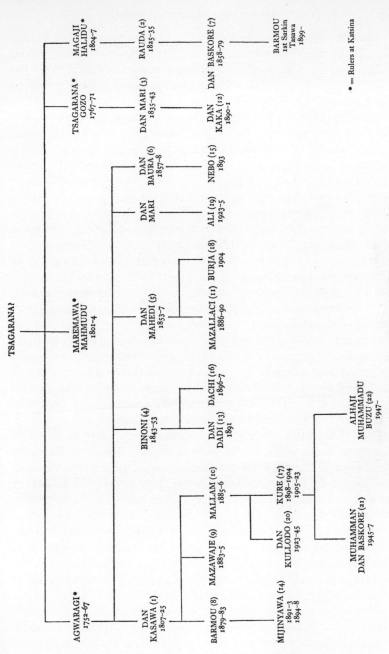

Fig. 4. The rulers of Maradi

Shortly afterwards Sidiku was deposed by the Sultan for contumacy and harshness. He fled to Maradi, where Binoni (1844–1849) had succeeded Dan Mari, and sought help from the Katsina Hausa to recover his Fulani throne. Binoni provided Sidiku with hospitality but little support. Sidiku then moved to Tassawa to seek aid from Damagaram, but was finally persuaded by the Sultan to return to Sokoto, leaving his brother Mamman Bello in charge of Katsina (Haj Said: 31; Daniel: 18–19; Mission Tilho: op. cit.). From Dan Mari's defeat in Ruma until the accession of Rauda's son, Dan Baskore, in 1854, the Sultan of Sokoto, Aliyu Babba (1842–59) bore the brunt of the war with Hausa Gobir and Katsina himself. Aliyu won important victories over the Katsina and Gobir Hausa at Kotor Kwoshi, south of Ruma, and brought that district (Katsina Laka) under temporary Fulani control, but his various efforts to take Tsibiri and Maradi were unsuccessful. The Hausa continued their raids, and so did Fulani, but by 1854 a condition of military stalemate had been reached. While neither side could reduce the other, each was vulnerable to the other's attacks; and these were no longer directed only at vital points, such as the capitals where the contest could be decisive, but also at smaller towns or villages which could be quickly surprised and overrun, and which yielded convenient booty of cattle and slaves. Dan Baskore (1854–75) is credited with eighty-three raids against Fulani Katsina, Zamfara, and Sokoto, including two unsuccessful sieges of Katsina City (Mission Tilho: Vol. 2, 463–4). Thereafter the rulers of Maradi raided farther afield in Kano and Zaria, while the recovery of Katsina remained their aim. For his part, Dan Baskore suffered setbacks, such as the burning of Tassawa by Sultan Ahmadu Rufa'i; but with Gobir assistance he defeated Rufa'i shortly after at Gidan Sarkin Arna in Sokoto (Mission Tilho: Vol. 2, 464).

Dan Baskore's long successful reign marks a watershed in the history of Maradi. At this time the successor-state was most prosperous and fully developed. Its stability, internal and external, seemed assured. Though incapable of much further expansion at Fulani expense, it was apparently too strong for them to overthrow. Its internal organization may also have seemed to assure an orderly future. Dan Baskore had built a large wall around his capital at Maradi. He seems to have ruled his dominions firmly, and maintained effective alliances. Perhaps few then alive could have foreseen the internal dissensions and conflicts by which the Katsinawa of Maradi were repeatedly split in the years between Dan Baskore's death and the French occupation. Since it is not possible to discuss these developments here, I shall describe Maradi under Dan Baskore, three generations after the *jihad*, when its institutions and policies seemed secure.[1] In this account I employ information pertaining to later or earlier periods, where it probably holds true for this period also; but my reconstruction remains preliminary and hypothetical.[2]

II

Unlike its sister successor-states of Abuja and Daura, Katsina-Maradi was able to pursue a vigorous counter-attack on the Fulani rule in its homeland; and, far more than their Gobir allies, the Katsinawa initially expected and met with success. Their conquered home had been weakened by partition among the Fulani. They had at Maradi and Ruma already recovered large sectors of Katsina. Being adjacent to Fulani Katsina, they had excellent information about their enemies' movements and plans. They enjoyed wide support from the Katsina Hausa; and, despite periodic defeats, they undoubtedly had the better of the exchange. For *raison-d'être* their state had one primary objective—the re-establishment of Hausa rule in Katsina, but as a pre-condition Maradi had to maintain its independence and internal order. This internal organization was influenced by its historical antecedents and context; as far as local conditions allowed, it was modelled on the former Hausa kingdom at Katsina.

In eighteenth-century Katsina the four senior titles after the Sarki were the Kaura, Galadima, Yan Daka, and Durbi. Three of these offices were vested in noble patrilineages. The Kaura, a nominal slave, commanded the state's military force and had direct control of its cavalry. He alone resided outside the capital. The Galadima, a eunuch, was the senior civil administrator and supervised the territories south of the Karaduwa River, including the vassal states of Maska, Kogo, and Birnin Gwari. The Yan Daka's territory lay due south-west of Katsina City. The Durbi traced descent from Kumayau and the earliest kings of Katsina. Together these four nobles, the *rukuni*, formed the senior council of state and exercised important checks on the power of the

H

Sarki (chief). The *rukuni* selected and appointed the new Sarki. It is possible that they could also depose him for constitutional breaches, such as refusal to heed their advice, or for certain other faults. Together they may have controlled more military force than the ruler independently. The Sarki and *rukuni* were the mutually indispensable elements of the Hausa Katsina state. Without the Sarki, *rukuni* could not rule; but without *rukuni* neither could the Sarki. For this reason, after his appointment as Sarkin Katsina by the well at Tsirkau, Dan Kasawa is said to have filled these essential offices as best he could. The eunuch Ginga was made Galadima, and the slave Mainasara Dubau, Kaura. Dan Kasawa's Durbi, Kuraye, is said to have been of Kumayau's lineage; his descendant, the present Durbi, has the distinctive facial marks borne only by the Durbawa and the royal lineage. Dan Kasawa's Yan Daka, Muhamman, was a nominal slave of the traditional lineage. Under Dan Kasawa's successors Kaura remained a royal slave office, and the Galadimaship a eunuch office until the time of Dan Baskore.

Territorial Organization

The Katsina Hausa settled at Maradi as liberators resuming their rightful inheritance, with support from the local chiefs. Their initial successes attracted immigrants from Fulani Katsina, and Sidiku's harshness drove many natives of Ruma to Maradi. From farther afield the family and supporters of Alwali, the defeated Hausa king of Kano, came for protection and help. From these immigrants the Katsinawa of Maradi selected persons for the traditional Katsina titles and replicated the official structure of their former state as best they could under the new conditions. Among the principal differences between the original and successor states are territorial arrangements and distributions of titles by status category and descent group.

Even before the Fulani *jihad*, the indigenous pagan population of Maradi was administered by resident chiefs (*hakimai* or *sara-kunan kauye*), each of whom controlled several contiguous villages under local headmen referred to as *masugari* ('owners' of the village). The Hausa reoccupation of Maradi owed much to the initiative and loyalty of these *hakimai* and their subjects. Dan Kasawa and his successors retained them in office as reward, and preserved their former privileges. Most *masugari* and *hakimai* were pagans; all held their office by hereditary right and lived in their administrative areas, rarely visiting the capital unless summoned. All *hakimai*, of whom there were twelve, excluding the Tasar at Tassawa, were placed under the supervision of one or other of the senior Hausa officials. Among the latter were the Kaura, who alone as was customary lived away from the capital, and the Galadima. The ruler's senior slave, Magajin Bakebbi—a title created by Dan Kasawa on his arrival in Maradi—was the channel of communication for the Barazaki in charge of Agai and the Tasar in charge of Tassawa. The history and position of Tasar farther to the east gave him considerable independence. He belongs with the vassals of Maradi rather than with the *hakimai*. In 1851 Barth (1890: Vol. 1, 250) described him as:

'in certain respects an independent prince, though . . . a powerful vassal of the king or chief of Maradi. Every head of a family in his territory pays him three thousand kurdi (cowries) as kurdin-kay, head money or poll tax; besides there is an ample list of penalties (kurdin-laefi), some of them very heavy, for . . . illicit paternity, 100,000 kurdi . . . (for) wilful murder, the whole property of the murderer is forfeited . . . Every village has its own mayor who decides petty matters and is responsible for the tax payable within his jurisdiction. The king or paramount chief has the power of life and death, and there is no appeal from his sentence to the ruler of Maradi. However, he cannot venture to carry into effect any measure of consequence without asking the opinion of his privy council.'

Tassawa (estimated population 15,000 in *c.* 1851) subsequently broke away from Maradi following on dynastic splits at Maradi. Other *hakimai* did not have anything like this degree of freedom. South of Tassawa lay Kworgum, originally claimed by Daura and Katsina, but at this time tributary to Zinder and Maradi (J. F. Schön, 1885: 23–29). Kworgum was supervised by Durbi, and Kwauna by the Sarki through a slave. Maradi town was under the titleholder Maradi (the most senior of the *hakimai*), who had three titled assistants, each in charge of a couple of villages near Maradi town and directly responsible to him. Of these settlements, only Maradi, as capital, was walled (*birni*); much of the country was uninhabited waste through which armies could move freely, water supplies permitting.

The former vassal states of Katsina at Chafe, Kotor Kwoshi, Kwoton Koro, Bena, and Birnin Gwari maintained their allegiance as far as conditions allowed, sending irregular tribute of horses, slaves, and *kyenkyendi* (bales of robes), as well as troops when needed. Most of these distant tributaries communicated through Kaura, and some also paid tribute to another state to avoid molestation. Though dependent and in theory subordinate to Maradi, they remained internally autonomous under hereditary dynasties. The Sarkin Katsina at Maradi levied no tax therein, nor did he exercise any superior or appellate jurisdiction for these areas. The rulers were all appointed locally by their own electoral councils, and were free to fight the Fulani independently. They were only subject to the threat of dismissal or attack from Maradi for disloyalty or treachery, overdue tribute being interpreted in this way. On these occasions the punishment was often severe, as the sack of Chafe *c.* 1897 shows. In return, vassals could call on Maradi for aid against any Fulani attacks, as Birnin Gwari did when raided by Sarkin Kontagora Ibrahim Nagwamatse.

The Sarki and his *rukuni* selected the *hakimai* of Maradi territory from the official lineages, and appointed them formally in Maradi with turban and gown. These *hakimai* lacked jurisdiction in matters punishable by mutilation or imprisonment—that is, crime or serious torts. Each was free to select or dismiss the *masugari* of the various villages they controlled, but only when raided by Fulani could they independently take up arms. Their people were subject to direct taxation and levies from the Sarki, and, when summoned, turned out as bowmen or cavalry to swell his force. These *hakimai* were freely dismissible by the Emir in theory, but in practice he dismissed them only on political grounds of disloyalty or disaffection, choosing a collateral kinsman to replace them. Each *hakimi* appointed his own titled staff (*lawanai*) and held a small court for local cases of divorce, debt, and the like. Each could levy fines for certain offences on his subjects, giving the Sarkin Katsina half. As required, they also supplied the Sarki with *corvée* labour or levies and assisted his tax collectors in gathering various tithes and special taxes. Of these, the *zakka* or grain tithe collected annually in the ruler's name was perhaps the most important. One bundle of guinea-corn or millet in every ten was due the ruler; it was the duty of the *hakìmi* assisted by the ruler's officials to collect this. The bundled grain was then stored in special granaries and recorded by the ruler and the *hakimi* separately. From these stores, the ruler made annual distributions to his officials, in amounts which varied with rank. As secretary, the Magajin Bakebbi recorded the ruler's donations and reserves, the latter being kept as security against famine or loss through war.

Maradi territory also contained bands of nomad pastoral Fulani and immigrant Muslim Hausa. The Fulani were administered through Fulani officials holding the titles of Sarkin Fulani, Yerima, and Hasau, these being drawn from a particular lineage. An older Katsina title, Dan Yusufa, was formerly reserved for Fulani scouts, but this was rarely filled at Maradi. As part of his duties, the Sarkin Fulani mediated between pastoralists and the settled farming population, supervising grazing rights with the local *hakimai* and investigating disputes over damage to crops or beasts. The Sarkin Fulani and his staff also collected the annual cattle tithe (*jangali*) of one beast in ten for the ruler. These officials had powers to settle civil issues of divorce, inheritance, or debt among the Fulani, giving the chief a set portion of the receipts. They were especially required to report all Fulani movements into or out of the territory, and to patrol the cattle routes when required.

A special set of arrangements known as *tarayya* or *tarewa* applied to Hausa Muslims, who were mainly immigrants from Katsina or Daura. On arrival, they either reported to the capital or to the *hakimi* in whose area they had settled. In either event the *rukuni* were notified, and the immigrants were brought to one or other of them. Having identified themselves, the newcomers made allegiance (*chapka*) to the *rukuni* and appealed for protection. He then informed the Council, which discussed suitable placement for the immigrants. From state reserves, the ruler provided such grain, labour, and assistance as was necessary to sustain their families until the following harvest, and the *rukuni* patron then arranged with the relevant *hakimi* for fallow farms and a compound for the strangers.

These provisions were well adapted to accommodate the sporadic movements into Maradi, but they attached Hausa immigrants directly to individual *rukuni* despite their dispersal throughout the country. In consequence, *hakimai* normally administered areas which contained a number of Muslim Hausa subjects of different *rukuni* over whom they exercised no jurisdiction. Such Hausa were directly responsible to their

Muslim patrons at the capital. To these they paid their tax and took their complaints or requests; from them they received instructions and orders. The relations thus instituted were not personal: the immigrant's issue remained and still remain under the jurisdiction of the *rukuni* title. These dispersed Hausa provided their patrons with valuable information about local conditions under the local *hakimai*. Though perfectly free to change residence as they pleased, they could not change their *rukuni* overlord and were obliged to attend his summons and orders directly. In their disputes with local pagans both parties repaired to the *rukuni* at the capital to settle the case. Thus, Muslim Hausa were exempt from local *corvée* and fines, though free to join the local war levy, unless summoned by their lord. Their grain tithe was due to their patron, who could also fine them judicially, retaining the proceeds. As skilled craftsmen and traders, these Muslim immigrants were liable to occupational taxes.

Finally, certain rural towns with predominantly Muslim populations were placed directly under senior Muslim officials. The Galadima administered Galadimci, where there was an official slave estate; the Kaura administered Gezawa, whose population Barth estimated at 10,000 (Barth, 1890: Vol. I, 260). Magajiya, the chief's 'younger sister' administered the village of Liyadi, and the Dan Zambedi, a senior prince, Madarumfa. Thus the territorial organization as a whole combined various methods by which the Katsinawa accommodated to their situation at Maradi.

III

State Offices

Excluding twenty-two titled princes, nine princesses, and nine titled wives and concubines of the ruler, the state of Maradi contained over 130 titled offices (*sarautu*, sing. *sarauta*) distributed as follows: 4 *rukuni* and their official staffs of 45; the chief's free courtiers, 27; his eunuchs and slaves, 34; his territorial chiefs, 12; titled clerics, 9. Of the princes and princesses, two each had administrative roles.

Together these officials represented the main status groups in the kingdom, Muslim and pagan, immigrant and native, free and slave; but the distribution of offices stressed status distinctions mainly significant to the Muslim Hausa, as was the case in Katsina.

Offices were reserved for the dynasty, for the ruler's wives and kinswomen, for his principal councillors and their kin, clients, and slaves, for his eunuchs and civilian or military slave staff, for free clients and Muslim clerics. Even the semi-pagan *hakimai* had their place as a separate rank-order. The *rukuni* were the pillars of the state (*shikashikai*): in local idiom, they supported the ruler as posts a roof. While the chiefship was clearly hereditary, all other offices were divided into two groups, as hereditary (*gado, karda*) or open (*shigege*). The offices of Kaura and Galadima were reserved for royal slaves and eunuchs respectively, and were regarded as *karda*, though in the latter no succession by descent was entailed. Until Dan Baskore's reign, the Galadima at Maradi was always a eunuch; Dan Baskore gave this office to a free man. Some time later the office reverted to eunuchs; and although the last six holders have all been free men, the Galadima is still regarded as a eunuch office.

As the senior eunuch officer, the Galadima was often recruited by promotion from other royal eunuchs, such as Marai, Horoce, and Yari, the last being the probable successor. And perhaps the senior palace slave, Magajin Bakebbi, who was literate in Ajemic and served as the ruler's secretary, was a likely future Kaura. The Durbi title remained hereditary, and so did the Yan Daka's office throughout this period.

Of the *rukuni*, Galadima and Kaura had precedence and most power. Yan Daka was described as 'the Galadima's younger brother'—that is, his deputy, and Durbi's relation to Kaura was the same. Civil and military duties were sharply distinguished and distributed between Galadima and Kaura. As senior civil administrator, Galadima administered the kingdom and capital during the ruler's absence; he was responsible for regulating dynastic affairs, the marriages of princes, their appointments and conduct. The installation of all officials appointed by the ruler took place in the compound of the Galadima and was presided over by the latter's master of ceremonies, Bagalan. Official compounds, with their attached slaves, horses, farms, and other equipment, were provided only for the ruler, the Kaura, and Galadima. The two free *rukuni*, Yan Daka and Durbi, remained in their own family compounds (*gidan talauci*) after appointment, and were installed with turban and gown only, not with an *alkyabba* or mantle such as the ruler, Kaura, and Galadima received. On installation, each *rukuni* made fixed payments to the ruler and his colleagues—one million cowries for Kaura and Galadima, half a million for Yan Daka and Durbi. Shortly afterwards each received a fully caparisoned horse and sword of tempered steel. Together, the *rukuni* and ruler selected individuals to fill vacant *rukuni* posts; the ruler had no authority to fill these independently, nor was he in theory entitled to decide important affairs without the council. Various successors of Dan Baskore were dismissed by *rukuni* with more or less violence for such conduct. No promotion was possible from one *rukuni* office to another. Though the ruler's office was clearly senior, and traditionally dominant, the legitimacy of its power was conditional on support from the council of state. As in eighteenth-century Katsina, the political relations of *rukuni* and ruler formed an important aspect of the political history of Maradi.

The commander of the Maradi forces, Kaura, resided outside the capital at Keffin Kaura, Gezawa, or Madarumfa according to his choice. He was therefore absent from the routine council meetings held on weekdays, and took little part in political decisions about minor civil affairs. However, on the Sabbath, when he greeted the ruler, by tradition Kaura enjoyed the prerogative of a purely private audience from which the other *rukuni* were all excluded. Thus the ruler's position *vis-à-vis* the Galadima, Yan Daka, and Durbi might be strengthened by his private consultations with Kaura, whose deputy, Durbi, had the duty of keeping him informed about council discussions while he was away. With Kaura's support, the ruler could override the council's advice, and if this support was assured he might well be dominant. Conversely, with the council's backing, he could override the Kaura, even in military affairs, the Kaura's province. But, through the good offices of Durbi and his right to attend any councils he wished, the Kaura could also support *rukuni* to overawe the ruler.

In certain spheres the ruler's independence was acknowledged. Though he did not select the Iya or Magajiya independently, he could at his pleasure fill such offices as Maskome, Jesa, Maraya, etc., from the dynasty, the Galadima conducting the appointment; and he also distributed the eight titles reserved for his wives and concubines as he pleased. The ruler selected retainers for appointment to the *shigege* titles reserved for his staff. Hereditary (*karda*) offices at his disposal were filled after canvassing senior men of the lineage in which the title was vested. Again, the Galadima made the formal appointments.

In like fashion, each *rukuni* selected from his own kin, free clients, or slaves, suitable persons for appointment to the titles traditionally reserved for the staff of his office. As a council, the ruler and *rukuni* together selected successors to the three hereditary priestly offices of Maradi—the Limam Juma'a, Magaji Dan Doro, and the Alkali, whose family was settled at Tabarawa. They also chose suitable mallams for *shigege* clerical offices such as Dan Masani. However, the office of Limamin na Kyankyale, who read the Koran to the Palace women during Ramadan, was filled by the ruler's choice.

Independently of the ruler, the *rukuni* distributed princely titles. With few exceptions, these were purely honorific, and entailed neither office nor defined authority. Perhaps as a function of this, they merely conferred an ill-defined and undifferentiated *iko*, recalling the early *imperium* at Rome, but here expressed in *kwace* (appropriation of goods). The main benefits that princes derived from their titles were twofold—public identification as possible chiefs and protection against evil magic (*samau*) through which their Koranic names could be used to injure them. Palpable benefits were otherwise slight.

Of twenty-two princely titles, only two merit notice. When vacant, the Dan Galadima title, whose occupant had formal precedence as the official heir, was always given to a son or brother of the reigning Sarki. Normally, since princes were not dismissible, having no administrative office, this position was often held by a collateral of the chief. Despite its honorific character, the Dan Galadima paid a *kurdin sarauta* of 10,000 cowries and received a turban and robe on installation. But so did the Dan Zambedi, whose office gave him control of Madarumfa, one of the largest towns in the state. Although officially listed as the Crown Prince, the Dan Galadima had no administrative role, and most rulers of Maradi were appointed from other royal titles. Dan Zambedi alone of all princes held administrative office, and thus had the resources with which to canvass his candidacy with the electoral council. Other senior princely titles include Dan Baskore, Binoni, Magaji Halidu, and Mayana. On their accessions, rulers retained these honorifics as shields against magical misfortune.

Of the female titles, only two merit attention, the Iya and the

Magajiya. Iya (Mother), regarded as the Queen Mother, was usually a senior royal kinswoman selected by *rukuni* for her disposition, marital status, and good sense. She presided over all marriages and kinship ceremonials involving girls and women of the royal lineage. She was usually single, though previously married, and was the official head and patron of local prostitutes and devotees of the pre-Islamic cult of spirit worship (*bori*), whom she led in to greet the chief on the Muslim sabbath. She was consulted in all *bori* initiations and public ceremonies, such as market renewal rites. Through her slaves, Iya levied grain from market vendors, and annual taxes from prostitutes and cult specialists. Her compound was an official sanctuary. She had her own clients, horsemen, and attendants attached to the office, whom she equipped with war gear and from whose booty she received a portion. These male clients were not her jural subjects, though privileged by her patronage; and although frequently invoked by *rukuni* to mediate between them and the ruler, she did not directly take part in the council of state.

Magajiya was usually a junior kinswoman of the ruler. She administered the village of Liyadi through her staff and kept the taxes and fines levied there. After Ramadan she led the women's celebrations at the palace. Presumably some Magajiyas might be promoted to the senior title of Iya on the latter's death.

At Maradi most royal title-holders were systematically divorced from administrative responsibility, jural and military power, and economic resources. They were thus dependent on the largesse of senior officials, on gifts (*gaisuwa*), or on appropriations (*kwace*) from commoners. Dan Zambedi, Iya, and Magajiya excepted, none had any subjects; and all princes were under the eunuch Galadima's jurisdiction, their behaviour being reviewed by the *rukuni* critically to select the most suitable successor. *Rukuni* stress the qualities of patience, forbearance, humility, self-reliance, energy, dignity, distance from *talakawa* (commoners), lack of adulterous or other 'un-royal' habits, and respect for the *rukuni* and custom as desiderata in a ruler; but, as the chart on p. 97 shows, from Dan Kasawa to Dan Dadi, the succession passed to a collateral until the senior generation died out. The upheavals at Maradi and Tassawa, which followed the appointment of Mijinyawa as the fourteenth ruler, are linked with the change in the principles regulating succession which his appointment introduced. Under the rule of collateral succession, immediate candidacy had been limited to senior royals. Mijinyawa's appointment seemed to define all titled princes as equally eligible. Thus, *rukuni*, perhaps inadvertently, weakened the chieftaincy.

Together, *rukuni* could and did freely dismiss most of the rulers at Maradi who succeeded Dan Baskore. They also selected their successors. Separately, they formed the electoral council and, with the ruler, the Council of State. The internal politics of Maradi is a history of struggle among *rukuni*, on the one hand, and between *rukuni* and ruler, on the other. In asserting the royal power against local *hakimai*, the ruler could normally rely on support from his *rukuni*, whose interests, though not identical with his, tended to coincide in such cases. The *rukuni* were in no sense popular representatives; rather, in their own and the public eyes, they represented the continuity of Katsina tradition. Together with the dynasty and the ruler's staff, they were the true Katsinawa, the custodians of the greatness and future of the former state, and perhaps its most central institution. Maradi they regarded as a minor province of their legitimate ancestral domains. With their staffs, their *tarayya* subjects, their supervisory roles over vassal chiefs and *hakimai*, their control of the succession, of the princes, and indirectly of appointments to territorial office, they were, if united, undoubtedly more powerful than the Chief; and, given the Katsina tradition, their dissent deprived his acts of legitimacy. In theory and in practice the ruler could dismiss one of the *rukuni* only with the others' consent; and, until the emergence of Kaura Hasau, all *rukuni* died in office. Since in theory they could veto the ruler's plans when they all agreed, the ruler's best chance was to solicit support from Kaura and Galadima, or set them at odds. However, Dan Baskore's dominance was unchallenged.

Each *rukuni* had one or more titled princes who sought his support for the next succession, but, being economically dependent, these princes could only offer promises of future benefit, rather than material gifts, and the position of *rukuni* was already such that their customary prerogatives were not easily enhanced.

It seems that *rukuni* often differed on the candidates they supported for the throne, each having equal powers of nomination. If their discussions revealed agreement the appointment was certain, although the council might pretend dissension in order to strengthen further its hold on the chosen candidate. In the event of disagreement, or even without it, as just shown, they called in the Limamin Juma'a to divine the appropriate choice. The Limam 'measured' (*auna*—weighed) the various candidates by divinatory means in order of their sponsors' seniority without knowing the candidates' names. He would first measure the Kaura's choice, this being unspoken, then the Galadima's, then Durbi's, then Yan Daka's. For this purpose the Limam used either of two divinatory techniques, one with a Muslim rosary, the other with a wooden cube marked with numbers (Mission Tilho: Vol. 2, 467–8). In either case he determined whether the unnamed candidate sponsored by a given councillor was suitable. If the results were positive the selection process stopped; if negative the candidate of the *rukuni* next in seniority was 'weighed'. By withholding the names of their candidates, *rukuni* confined the Limam to a purely technical role, and so prevented him from manipulating the oracle to influence the succession. The Limam's participation lent a certain Muslim sanctity to the proceedings, and his techniques were plainly Islamic.

The selected prince was then installed in an elaborate ceremonial supervised by the Galadima and the *rukuni*. After a ritual bath of henna in the Galadima's compound he was secluded outside the palace in a thatched shed for a week, during which he was instructed by eunuchs in protocol, palace affairs, and chiefly modes of behaviour. News of the accession was meanwhile sent to nearby rulers, who would reply with handsome gifts. Throughout this week of the new ruler's seclusion, he received the allegiance (*cafka*) of his *hakimai* and subordinate officials, and guidance from the *rukuni*. The townsfolk meanwhile celebrated the event with drumming, dancing, and various games. On the seventh day, together with the Sarkin Gobir, the *rukuni* led the new ruler on horseback alone outside the city to a special tree called Kwaru, perhaps a substitute for the old tamarind in Katsina City (Daniel: 2 and fn. 5). This they circled three times, riding in silence, then returned to Maradi, where the ruler received galloping charges of allegiance from all officials of state, as is usual at the two annual Muslim festivals. Next came the *samari* (young men), then drumming, after which the new ruler made a brief speech of thanks and prayer for good fortune before withdrawing to the palace with the *rukuni* to receive the greetings of his officials.

On entering the palace, the new ruler took over many familial roles from his predecessor. Anything the previous ruler had given to his children remained theirs, but all else pertained to the throne under care of the palace eunuchs—Yari, Sarkin Gida, etc. Shortly after entering the palace the new ruler dispatched a properly caparisoned horse to each of his *rukuni* and lesser gifts to other senior officials. Within a fortnight of his installation the new ruler was expected to take the field, irrespective of the season, to *wanka takobi* (blood the sword). Until this was done, the accession was not confirmed. This fortnight was therefore given over to planning the expedition.

On their appointments, turbanned officials received a horse from the person who appointed them, the ruler's kinsmen and senior staff from him, the Kaura's staff from Kaura, and so on. When these officials died their horses and equipment were returned to the superior who had appointed them, as silent evidence. The dead man's successor normally remained in his own compound; but besides Kaura and Galadima, it seems that *hakimai* in the rural areas also had official compounds, one-half the contents of which passed with their office, the remainder going to the ruler.

The ruler's court was the main centre of ceremonial activities, save that installations and princely marriages were held at the Galadima's. The *rukuni* came to greet him daily, except Kaura, who came on Friday or as events required. The *rukuni* would follow the ruler into a special chamber where they met in council. After their departure other courtiers and princes were free to enter and greet the ruler. He might then move to the *zaure* or entrance-hut to hear any law cases awaiting his attention, being screened by his servants with extended robes so that none saw him sitting down; or he might retire to his private rooms within the palace. On the Sabbath and at Muslim festivals there was a more elaborate gathering of officials, with *rukuni, rawuna* (free turbanned officials), slaves, eunuchs, and princes all present, distributed in set positions behind the Galadima and Kaura respectively, on the right and left hand of the ruler. The clerics, titled and untitled, sat directly opposite him, at a distance.

At Maradi the distribution of officials between the right and left hand (*hannun dama da hannun hagu*) seems best to correspond with distinctions between warriors and civil administrators, the princes being grouped with hereditary officials and eunuchs, in contraposition with slaves and *shigege* officials ranged below the Kaura. But various placements were exceptional, and it seems likely that this division, which does not exactly coincide with the *karda-shigege* classification of Maradi, reproduces an older Katsina arrangement rather imperfectly. Behind Galadima and his staff sat Yan Daka, his entourage, the princes, the Maradi and his staff, the Sarkin Fulani, the lesser eunuchs under Dan Karshe, and the *hakimai* and their attendants when present. On the ruler's left, behind the Kaura and his staff, sat Durbi with his, followed by the Magajin Bakebbi and throne slaves, the ruler's craft officials, clients, and titled warriors. No female official, even Iya, took part in this assembly.

Economic Basis of the State

For revenues the state depended on booty, fines, and legal taxes, such as the *zakka* (grain tithe) or the inheritance tithe (*ushira*), tribute from vassals, customary fees paid by office holders on appointment, *corvée* labour, cattle tax paid by Fulani, and on a variety of occupational taxes known oddly as *hurmushi* (the ruler's share of the booty). The ruler also had rights to the skins of any lion or lepoard slain in the territory, to one large civet cat per year from the local civet dealers, and to the larger tusk of local elephant. A charge averaging about 1,200 cowries per year was levied on all occupational specialists such as drummers, praise-singers, fishermen, itinerant traders, leather-workers, tailors, dyers, blacksmiths, barber-doctors, potash traders, haberdashers, weavers, straw-workers, tanners, woodworkers, hut-builders, potters, civet dealers, each item being collected by a separate official. Iya levied her tax on all prostitutes and *bori* dancers. Merchants bringing loads into or through the country paid 500 cowries per camel and 200 per ass. Growers of sweet potatoes, cassava and bambara groundnuts also paid 1,200 cowries per annum.

Each year the ruler's craft officials went on tour with their colleagues who served the *rukuni*, stopping at each *hakimi*'s headquarters, where the local craft heads turned over the tax due from local craftsmen. Presumably the *rukuni*'s representatives collected tax from their lord's Muslim Hausa subjects. On returning to the city, the ruler and *rukuni* appropriated their portion, the collectors keeping the rest. This onerous task was carried out by menial officials, free and slave. Though its direct rewards were probably small, the number of officials involved widened the administrative base, while the method of collection increased the central executive's knowledge of the territory and its population. Indirectly these royal collectors thus helped to supervise the *hakimai*.

In addition, there were numerous customary levies. The gatekeepers of Maradi town, throne slaves, were reimbursed with threshed grain taken from the townswomen, who were required to thresh their grain outside the city walls. Most customary levies were directed at the market, and involved the collection of foodstuffs, antimony, aphrodisiacs, cotton, etc.

Slave officials authorized to collect these levies reported to Masai, the official market head, who then escorted them to the vendors each dealt with. As remuneration, Masai was authorized to levy salt from the Bugaje and Tuareg. He was also empowered to settle any disputes arising in the market. He could select certain vendors in each trade to supervise their colleagues. Through them, market prices were efficiently controlled on instructions from the ruler and *rukuni*.

Some title-holders who lacked subjects or regular means of subsistence exploited the market irregularly according to their needs and opportunities; but such nobles did not confine themselves only to markets. Being mainly of royal descent and without independent means, they exercised this privilege of *kwace* or appropriation with the connivance of the ruling council if not the public; but *rukuni*, despite their independent jurisdictions and means, also periodically practised appropriation. The commoners were the main losers.

Apart from *hurmushi* and *zakka*, commoners were required to perform *corvée* annually after harvest. They were summoned to repair the walls of Maradi or the stockade of their *hakimi*'s town, the mosque and official compounds of the ruler, Kaura and Galadima. During the rainy season they also cultivated the farms of these officials as well as those of Yan Daka and Durbi. The *hakimai* could also levy local *corvée* for farm work and repairs.

Booty taken in war was apportioned roughly according to Maliki Law: one-fifth of the warrior's loot was officially due to the state, and this was collected in the war camp (*sansani*) *en route* to Maradi. At best the rule was interpreted rather stringently; it is said that, if sometimes a warrior captured two cows, the state took one. Special officers of the army commander, usually the ruler or Kaura, attended by staff of other *rukuni*, supervised this collection. Its distribution was limited mainly to *rukuni* and ruler, the Kaura when in command appropriating a portion for himself and his *rukuni* colleagues, and sending the ruler the rest. Much of the ruler's share was distributed to clerics whose charms and imprecations were regarded as indispensable for military success, and who thus received their reward. Those who fought without securing booty received nothing. The *rukuni* and ruler might give some booty to princes, who were prohibited from fighting, but they sold most of it, especially slaves, in nearby markets. Superior captives were sometimes held for ransom.

My informants, the Sarkin Katsina Buzu, the Galadima Kwanyau, Yan Daka Muhamman, and Durbi Ibrahim, all stressed the importance of booty and war in the economy of the Maradi state. It was to these sources and to the irregular tribute from distant vassals or dependent allies that the ruler and nobles looked for the windfalls which validated the militarism of Maradi, and provided occasions for overawing dissident allies or vassals, while mobilizing wide support. None the less, booty alone could not be said to support the state. Its main use was to provide equipment for military forces. Captured horses were distributed to valorous men, who undertook, on receiving them, to turn out whenever summoned. Other booty was used to purchase flintlocks, ammunition, swords, and other gear from nearby Damagaram, where cannons were being made (Mission Tilho: Vol. 2, 444, and Note 2). Arrows, spears, daggers, and inferior iron swords were made at Maradi under the ruler's senior blacksmith by the *corvée* of blacksmiths, the ruler providing large blocks of locally smelted iron.

Court fees and fines provided other sources of income. The ruler's slave, Sarkin Diya, collected a marriage fee of 1,000 cowries from her father on every girl's first marriage. On the death of prosperous Muslims the ruler received as *ushira* one-tenth the value of the movable goods, the inheritance usually being administered by some cleric specially commissioned for the purpose. The ruler received a larger share, between one-third and one-half, of the estates of the deceased and dismissed *hakimai*.

Fines levied by local chiefs were shared equally with the ruler, but besides levying a collective fine of 1,200 cowries per householder in the district in cases of homicide, the Sarkin Katsina imposed a fine of a million cowries on the offender, all of which he retained himself. Substitutes, such as horses, goats, cattle, or slaves, might be accepted. This fine included no compensation to the dead man's kin. Its value was roughly equivalent to the price of twenty camels (Barth, 1890: Vol. 1, 295). The offender's kin were expected to contribute to the payment, under pressure from their *hakimai*. Undue delays were met by confiscation of their property and possible enslavement.

Finally, the ruler received customary fees on the appointment of new men to office. This was the *kurdin sarauta* (money of office), which Shehu dan Fodio also condemned (Hiskett, 1960: 568). On his own accession, the ruler also made similar prestations to the *rukuni* electors.

These official revenues may have touched only a small segment of the Maradi economy, which was primarily committed to subsistence production, with the local market providing necessary services and commodities, such as salt or farm tools. Undoubtedly the most substantial portion of official revenues was the grain tithe (which also applied to locust bean) and *corvée*, and from these the senior officials drew their subsistence. Moreover, given official acceptance of goods in place of cash, the elaborate machinery for collecting cash tax probably served also to increase their incomes in kind. Most Maradi pagans made limited and irregular use of cash; their standard of living is even now typical of a closed household economy.

Judicial Institutions

As formal Muslims, the Katsina Hausa made special provisions for Islam in their government by various observances and appointments; but in many spheres, such as law, Muslim rules were only partially observed. There was an alkali at Maradi, and he was authorized to hear cases between Muslims, but his powers were limited and not unique. Though his jurisdiction covered the Great and Lesser Law (*Shari'a Manya da Karami*), the alkali could only impose fines and whippings. Such fines as he levied were shared with the ruler. In the main, the alkali heard civil issues of divorce, debt, contract, and minor torts. Such cases in rural areas were also

I

tried by *hakimai*, whose jurisdictions included land issues, but as Muslim residents of rural areas were beyond the *hakimi*'s jurisdiction, issues involving them were referred to their respective *rukuni* lords at the capital. I cannot say how the Magajiya and Dan Zambedi, who administered certain villages, handled legal matters, but their position was probably like that of the *hakimai*.

The *rukuni* heard all issues concerning their scattered subjects. They could levy fines and order individual whippings; and thus they could destroy an individual's prosperity. Of the *rukuni*, Galadima acted as jural supervisor of junior officials, especially princes, but not of *hakimai*. In this capacity as a throne eunuch, the Galadima presumably represented the ruler and other *rukuni*. For such matters he employed a special slave official, Dan Negaba, whose police functions at the Galadima's orders were confined entirely to offending officials. Princes who committed adultery, excessive *kwace*, and the like, were summoned by Dan Negaba to Galadima for an admonitory lecture. They were not directly subject to protests by the subjects injured, nor were they liable to fines, whipping, or imprisonment, provided they were politically loyal; but presumably the *rukuni* and ruler might ask Galadima to confine a recidivist prince in his compound as a warning. By such misbehaviour princes forfeited chances of royal favour and further promotion.

The ruler's court could be resorted to for difficult issues between Muslims and pagans. Appeals from lesser courts were rather rare. To the ruler were reserved all offences which merited severe punishments such as 'imprisonment', execution, mutilation, or confiscation—that is, all political offences and any assaults which drew blood or inflicted wounds, as well as theft. Though rare, banishment sometimes occurred in disguised forms as individual flight or sale abroad into slavery. The main issues with which the ruler's court was concerned were *renon ikon sarauta*—literally, rejection of the power (authority) of the office, i.e. treason, subversion. This covered treacherous plotting, breach of customary duties, such as payment of tribute, any tampering with official prerogatives, such as the dead wood which belonged to the Galadima's office, or refusal to execute orders. The ruler also administered estates of dead or dismissed officials. The ruler's court exercised discretionary powers consistent with the Muslim doctrine of *siyasa*, especially as regards the political behaviour of officials. Thus, *hakimai* were liable to dismissal or fine for failure to pass on instructions, to produce the required *corvée* or supplies, to turn out or attend the war levy, to report the movements of immigrants, or to observe the limits of their own *iko* (authority). In extreme cases dissident *hakimai* were lured to Maradi and summarily dispatched along with any free witnesses. When a subject, ordered to carry out some task such as *corvée*, failed to do so he could expect punishment and/or confiscation of his property.

The ruler's palace contained a prison. This was a large pit set deep in the floor of a stoutly walled room well beyond sunlight in a separate courtyard. The royal warders were slave officials: Makama, in charge of arrest, Doka (Law), the executioner, and Dan Tura, who pushed the victims from behind over the edge and into the pit. The last was also in charge of the gates of the city. The prisoner's fall into the pit usually resulted in some injury, but aid, water, or food was withheld, sometimes for a week at a time, unless ordered from above. He shared the pit with others not dead, unless his kinsmen could compound his offence with an acceptable fine. Normally those imprisoned were not expected to survive. No case of female imprisonment is known to me.

Executions were carried out at a special *marke* tree called the Marken Doka by the market-place in Maradi, the head being impaled near by as a public warning. Legislation was also announced in the market and throughout the town by public criers and drummers—the ruler's *maroka* (praise-singers). Such regulations took the following form: 'No one is allowed to cut wood in the marsh. This is an offence. It is forbidden.' Punishments were left unspecified. Orders to assemble for work or war were communicated in similar fashion. The praise-singers were thus town heralds.

Judicial sanctuary was an archaic institution of Maradi, clearly inconsistent with Islam. Whatever their offences, providing it was not political, once offenders touched the walls of the ruler's compound, the Iya's, or any of the *rukuni*'s, they were thereafter immune from trial and punishment. Though I failed to inquire into the subsequent condition of these persons, it seems probable that by such acts they enslaved themselves to the offices which provided reprieve.

Another archaic practice inconsistent with Islam was *kwace*, mentioned above. *Kwace* differs from theft in that it is the open appropriation of an individual's property or labour by a title-holder exercising an ill-defined *iko*. Differences in status are basic to it. The officials most prone to practise *kwace* were *rukuni* and princes, the latter being without regular means of support. *Talakawa* (commoners) were the main losers. On occasion, such a high official as the Durbi simply marched into a pagan's compound and commanded him to deliver so many bundles of grain. If the farmer hesitated he was bound up with ropes and forced to watch its removal. If he demurred he might be whipped. The officials who acted thus held that they were entitled to do so because they lacked subsistence and represented the state. Indeed, there seems to have been a shortage of *rumada* (slave-farming) in Maradi; but late in the last century a dominant Fulani Kaura, Hasau, who controlled an overwhelming force, virtually stopped this practice, to the bitter chagrin of his colleagues, by enforcing restitution of the appropriated goods to the victims. These practices, condemned by Shehu dan Fodio as *kame*, were clearly inconsistent with Islam.

Under Maradi law, owners were liable for offences done by their slaves to the slaves of others. If the offending slaves were alienable—that is, if they were first-generation slaves, captives or purchased—they might be transferred or sold as compensation. If not alienable, failing compensation, offending slaves were delivered to the ruler. If a slave injured a free person further damages or fines were due as though the offender was free. A free man killing another's slave simply furnished an acceptable replacement.

Military Organization

For *rukuni*, war was the purpose of the Maradi state, indiscriminately against Fulani, but especially against Fulani in Katsina. As they phrased it, Maradi was merely their *sansani*, a war camp, in which preparation of new expeditions was the central activity. Though this emphasis may be misleading, their primary interest in war cannot be doubted. To this they looked for changes of fortune, including extra income; and this preoccupation with booty was partly responsible for the redirection of Maradi attacks from Katsina to Kano and Zaria, which offered more loot at less risk.

The main forces of Maradi were cavalry and infantry, the latter including bowmen (*masu-baka*). Nobles, their slave staff, free clients, and a few self-equipped warriors provided the cavalry. *Talakawa* (commoners), especially pagans, supplied the bowmen, and Muslim Hausa youths the infantry (*dakaru*, *'yan karma*). Official scouts, Dan Yusufa and Baita, preceded the army to spy out the route in advance. The ruler maintained storehouses of weapons, with which he equipped his own troops, courtiers, and servants. Others joining an expedition came equipped for the role they wished to play, bringing some food also. Only officials and their immediate staffs were obliged to attend all campaigns.

The ruler and his *rukuni* councillors planned the expedition in secret. Of these, the Galadima always remained at Maradi in charge of the capital and environs during the army's absence. As a eunuch, this was his appropriate role. The remaining *rukuni* were all *tirikai*, that is, officials who could be placed in charge of an expeditionary force. Having selected the target and route, the council calculated the number and types of force necessary, keeping this information to themselves. Officialdom would be mobilized as cavalry; but infantry and bowmen were recruited as needed through the *hakimai*. If necessary, the Gobirawa, Maradi's chief allies, might be invited. The council announced the expedition publicly through their heralds, themselves preparing to join the army at an appointed time and place. On the departure of the expedition, all movements outside or between the various towns of Maradi became subject to official control by the Galadima.

The headquarters of each *hakimi* contained an informal age-grade of young men, *samari*, under a head appointed by the *hakimi*. This head, the Sarkin Samari, was instructed to mobilize a contingent to move to Maradi by a set day. No penalties attached to those youths who did not attend, except ridicule and mockery; but rural chiefs who failed to turn out themselves as well as their forces were culpable.

These contingents of *samari* reported through the supervisor of the *hakimi* to the ruler's Sarkin Karma, who was the Sarkin Samari of the whole territory and captained its infantry. Bowmen were then dispatched to the ruler's Sarkin Baka, in charge of archers. Those lacking equipment who sought this from the ruler's captains were enrolled in the latter's force. Kaura was the permanent captain of the Maradi cavalry. The titleholder Maradi, perhaps as a reward for Wagaza's bravery, but also because

Maradi was the capital, commanded the bowmen under Kaura, the ruler's Sarkin Baka commanding archers in the rear force around the ruler.

The war equipment of Maradi included spears, swords, chain mail, quilted cotton armour, throwing axes, ordinary axes, poisoned arrows, flaming arrows, ankle chains for slaves, cavalry, and muskets purchased from Zinder.

In attacking a town, Maradawa usually adopted one of two plans. Either they relied on darkness and surprise, being excellent night fighters, or they shot burning arrows over the walls to set the thatched huts on fire, thus generating panic, during which they cut foot-rests in the wall for infantry to climb, the archers firing volleys to keep the wall clear. When their own towns were attacked the Maradawa preferred pitched battles to sieges. For this they generally relied on surprise attacks in the enemy's rear or camp. When Maradi or Madarumfa was threatened the forces of Sarkin Gobir or of Kaura at Gezawa had this relieving task.

IV

Despite many omissions, this account adequately represents the kingdom of Maradi during the relatively stable reign of Dan Baskore. To focus attention on its principal features I have simplified the structural details. Its historical background vividly explains the central motifs of Dan Baskore's state, but, as our account shows, the government of Maradi was more elaborate and complex than that of a warrior band. In its overt identification with Islam and its historical derivation from Katsina, we find many institutional features which could not otherwise be accounted for: for example, the positions of *rukuni* and princes and the role of Iya. The organs of state, its councils, offices, procedures, military, judicial, and religious organization are all evident legacies of old Katsina adapted to new conditions. We have seen how this old constitution was accommodated to the circumstances in which Dan Kasawa and his successors found themselves. In turn, these necessary modifications were institutionalized, and so also were later deviations. Though the Kaura and Galadima of old Katsina were free, and are so now, they are still classified as slave and eunuch offices. Thus, some offices classified as hereditary (*karda*) are distributed freely within a given status category. The model to which this classification refers may be that of Katsina before the *jihad*, or Maradi under Dan Kasawa, rather than Dan Baskore and his successors.

In no sense does Maradi or its antecedent Katsina correspond to Weber's patrimonial chiefdom, nor is either government feudal (Weber, 1947: 317 ff.; Goody, 1963). In both states authority and power were vested in the ruling council, and were generally fused in the undifferentiated concept of *iko*, without which various deviations from Islam as well as from Katsina traditions and pagan customs cannot be understood. Dominance oscillated between the ruler and his *rukuni*, and also among the latter. As Muslims ruling a pagan population, the Katsinawa of Maradi administered a plural society held together by external threats and internal symbiosis. Expect for *iko*, the norms of this unit, were uncertain and not inclusive. A strong ruler such as Dan Baskore, by his simple dominance, was tempted to weaken the throne's position, as when he appointed a free official already in charge of the bowmen to the Galadima's office, and gave the office of Maradi to the new Galadima's son, thus concentrating two important and hitherto distinct functions in one family. When Kaura Hasau and Maradi Idi conspired to appoint and depose rulers at will subsequent rulers regretted this innovation.

NOTES

1. No population figures for the state of Maradi in the nineteenth century are available, but in 1938 the Canton of Maradi (in the Niger Colony, now the Republic of Niger) had a population of 48,282 distributed in 144 'villages'.

2. Fieldwork was carried out by the author in Maradi in March 1959, as one phase in a series of Hausa historical studies made during 1958/9.

Since this paper was written, Philippe David's monograph, *Maradi, l'ancien état et l'ancienne ville: site, population histoire* (Documents des études nigériennes, No. 18, IFAN-CNRS, Niger, 1964) has been published.

REFERENCES

Barth, H.   1890   *Travels and Discoveries in North and Central Africa*. Vols. 1 and 2. London.

Daniel, F. de F.   n.d.   *A History of Katsina*. Unpublished MS. in
                    (?1938) Ibadan University Library.

Goody, J.   1963   'Feudalism in Africa?' *J. African History*
                          Vol. IV, No. 1, pp. 1–18.
Gowers, W. F.   1921   *Gazetteer of Kano Province.* London.
Haj Said   n.d.   *History of Sokoto* (trans. Whitting, C. E. J.).
                          Nigeria.
Hiskett, M.   1960   'Kitab al-farq: a Work on the Habe King-
                          doms Attributed to Uthman dan Fodio',
                          Bull. S.O.A.S., Vol. 23, pp. 558–78.
Landeroin, M.   1911   *Documents scientifiques de la Mission Tilho*
                          (*1906–09*). Vol. 2. Paris.
Mission Tilho   See Landeroin, M.
Palmer, H. R.   1928   *Sudanese Memoirs*, Vol. 3. Lagos.
Périé, M.   n.d.   *Cercle de Maradi: histoire complète politique*
                  (?1948) *et administrative des origines à 1940.* Cercle
                          de Maradi.
Schön, J. P.   1885   *Maganar Hausa.* London.
Urvoy, Y.   1936   *Histoire des populations du Soudan Central*
                          (*Colonie du Niger*). Paris.
Weber, M.   1947   *Theory of Social and Economic Organization*
                          (trans. by Henderson, A. M., and Parsons,
                          Talcott). London.

THE KINGDOM OF KOM IN WEST CAMEROON

E. M. CHILVER and P. M. KABERRY

The kingdom of Kom (Bikom, Bekom) is situated in the open country in the mountainous heart of Bamenda, called by its German explorers the 'Grassfields'. It was one of some seventy small states and village chiefdoms with allegedly Tikar or Ndobo-derived dynasties in what is now West Cameroon. In the nineteenth century the Grassfields formed part of a hinterland which included the so-called Bamileke chiefdoms (once included in the Dschang Division), the kingdom of Bamum, and the Tikar chiefdoms proper (Kimi, Bandam, Ngambe, Ditam, etc.), and which was designated by traders of Calabar and the Cameroons coast sometimes as 'Bayong', sometimes as 'Mbudikum' or 'Mbrikum'. It was described to Europeans approaching it from the north across the Katsina Ala River or from the north-east across the Mbam (or Liba) River as 'Bafum' or 'Mbafu' (Barth, 1857: Vol. 2, 631; Zintgraff, 1895: 310; Thorbecke, 1916: Vol. 2, 10). Exploration of the Grassfields from the north was difficult because they lay just south of west of the disorderly march of the rebellious Adamawa governors; Flegel was the first to approach their northern borders in 1884. Between them and the coast lay some two-hundred miles of rain forest. In the end they were first penetrated by Eugen Zintgraff, who reached Bali (a powerful chiefdom with a Chamba dynasty) from the coast in January 1889; later in the year he traversed Kom.[1]

Kom had no further contacts with the Germans until December 1901, when patrols, engaged in a punitive attack on its neighbour and rival Bafut, crossed its border and accepted the submission of two Kom tributary chiefs, those of Mejung and Mejang, erroneously believed to be Bafut vassals. In January 1902 the 'chief of Bekom' is said to have been among the first who complimented Pavel, the commanding officer of the expedition, on his victory over Bafut and gave him gifts and promises to supply labourers for the new imperial military station being established at Bamenda (a name derived from the small chiefdom of Manda

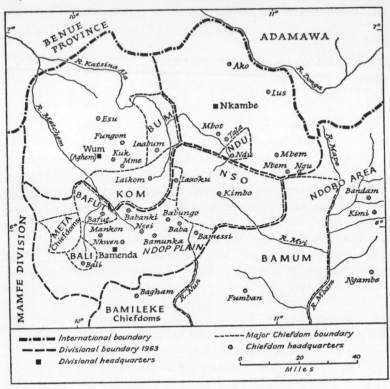

Sketch Map of Bamenda Grassfields

Nkwe, a few miles to the south of Bafut). (D. Kbl.: Vol. 13, 162, 238).[2] A month later Lt. Strümpell visited the chief's palace at Laikom and made the first surveys in the chiefdom. During 1904, when a revolt in the Upper Cross River district was occupying the bulk of the Bamenda garrison, Kom appears to have rejected the Station's demands and is reported as being under military occupation in January–February 1905, when the area was further explored by Lt. Heigelin (D. Kbl.: 16, 557). A head-tax, in fact a tax-quota, began to be applied in 1909, and Kom supplied the porters and station and tax labour demanded of it. It lay rather beyond the sphere of Basel Mission activity, but at the end of the German régime it was being prospected by the Sittard Fathers established in its eastern neighbour Nso in 1913.

The British take-over from the Germans and the policy of

Indirect Rule introduced in 1922 did not present Kom with any overwhelming problems of accommodation. These came rather from the missions, in particular the Roman Catholic Mission, which provided an alternative focus of loyalty. The breakneck speed of political and social change after 1945 caused some convulsions, such as the emergence in 1958 of an antinomian women's movement of protest employing some traditional formulae. Nevertheless, in 1947 many of the traditional kinship, economic, political, and religious institutions remained at the core of social life, and even in 1963 had retained their viability.

In its political institutions Kom resembles many neighbouring kingdoms and village chiefdoms, most of which have dynasties which claim an origin in the region of the Upper Mbam River and its tributaries in what is now East Cameroon. This claim varies in expression: in some cases, for example in Nso, Ntem, Ndu, and Ngu, a direct link is asserted with Kimi (Bankim), the senior Tikar chiefdom, or with its coronation site, Rifum. (In East Cameroon, Bamum, Ditam, Bandam, and Bagham among others also have Kimi-derived dynasties.) In others the claim is more vaguely expressed in terms of origin in 'Tikari' or in 'Ndobo' —a term sometimes specifically applied to the Tikar area north of Fumban and just south of Banyo, or to the people among whom the Tikar dynasts themselves settled after their legendary exodus from the Mbum area on the Ngaundere plateau (Kaberry, 1962: 282-4). The ruler of Kimi still maintains ritual links with Bamum, Bandam, Ditam, Ntem, and Ngu, and has recently revived those with Nso. Kom, Bafut, Nkwen (Bafreng), and a number of chiefdoms in the Ndop Plain, such as Bamunka, Bamessi, and Nsei, claim a 'Ndobo' origin; but there are others, notably Mankon, Babungo, and Mbot, which have similar institutions but which deny a Tikar or Ndobo origin for their dynasties. Linguistic evidence lends no support to the broad theory of migrations put forward in some British assessment and intelligence reports, in which it was postulated that Tikar or Tikarized peoples from the north-east met and mingled with the so-called 'Widekum' peoples of the forested south-west, and were followed by intrusive Chamba, Trans-Donga, and 'Munshi' groups. The bulk of the people of the Grassfields speak Bantoid languages of the group called *Ngkom* by Richardson because they have many of the features of Ngkom, the language of Kom, as

Sketch Map of Kom

described by Bruens (Richardson, 1956: 42; Bruens, 1942-45). Tikar (Tumu, Ndob) dialects are not spoken except in Ngu and a few hamlets bordering the Tikar area proper. The people of Bamum speak a Bamileke type of language. The term Tikar or Ndobo as applied in the Bamenda Grassfields has, then, neither ethnic nor linguistic connotations: it implies, rather, a claim to the legitimacy of political institutions and to their ultimate derivation from a legendary centre which sanctioned their adoption.[3]

In most of the chiefdoms of the Grassfields there was a sacred kingship, a cult of dead kings, a distinction between royals and commoners, certain titles reserved to princes and princesses, state councillors (usually hereditary), and a military organization based on village or ward warrior lodges. A distinctive institution was a regulatory society (known variously as *kwifoyn*, *ngwerong*, *nggumba*, etc.) which had its quarters in the palace precincts and had among its duties the recruitment in boyhood of palace retainers from free-born commoners. (Only in certain chiefdoms were royals admitted to its quarters.) As the executive arm of government, it could therefore be regarded as a body of recruited retainers. But the membership of its inner lodges might be hereditary or appointive or a mixture of both, and it might have advisory, judicial, and ritual functions. It was everywhere a secret society with *sacra* of gongs and named masks. One day in the eight-day week was reserved to it: members met and no one else in the capital might fire a gun or strike a drum on pain of punishment. At important national events or the death of a member the society put on its masked dances. In the execution of its state duties its retainers appeared clothed in net gowns which masked face and body; its authority was of an impersonal kind, and its agents could not be held to account by the populace. It was everywhere seen as supporting the chief; without it there would be disorder (Kaberry, 1962: 287).

During the nineteenth century five kingdoms with Tikar- or Ndobo-derived dynasties—Nso, Kom, Bafut, Bum, and Ndu—extended their boundaries by incorporating and making tributary neighbouring village chiefdoms. Bum though small (population 5,000 in 1953) was important, since it was the entrepôt for the kola trade with Jukun and Hausa in the north-west in the later part of the century. It was on terms of intermittent hostility with its southern neighbour Kom, but had pacts of friendship with Nso and Ndu (population 8,300 in 1953). Nso (population 50,000 in 1953) was for the most part at enmity with Ndu, but had an alliance with Kom; while Kom itself (population 27,000 in 1953) competed with Bafut (population 19,000 in 1953) on its south-western boundary for the allegiance of tiny village chiefdoms. All, with the exception of Kom, had patrilineal dynasties.

Political institutions received their greatest elaboration in Nso, but, as some account of them has been given elsewhere (Kaberry, 1952, 1959, 1962), Kom has been selected for detailed treatment in this essay.[4] In the first place, it can be taken as exemplifying many of the characteristics of other states in the area; secondly, it has, until very recent years, been less affected by direct or indirect colonial pressures as compared, for example, with Bafut, which lay only sixteen miles from administrative headquarters and suffer-ed heavy casualties at the hands of German troops in 1901, 1904/5, and 1907. Thirdly, the recency of the period in which it expanded its borders makes it easier to recover data on its growth as a state; and, finally, it is the largest of the chiefdoms with a matrilineal dynasty. Some of its institutions are very similar to those of the small independent chiefdoms of Mme (Meng), Fungom, Kuk, Nyos, and Kung to the north, which also have matrilineal dynasties; indeed, a number of the larger matrilineal clans of Kom have branches in some of those chiefdoms and are said to derive from them. Other clans, however, claim ancestresses from Oku, Nso, Babungo, Baba, Aghem, and northern Bafut, but they, too, are matrilineal, with the exception of the Kijəm clan, deriving from the former Kijəm chiefdom in what was later to become the southern sector of Kom. Lineage genealogies are shallow in depth, but clan traditions collected in Kom, Bum, and other parts of the Wum Division, together with the marked cultural homogeneity of the area, suggest that a number of the inhabitants of Kom proper and its northern tributary chiefdoms are descended from a population which had long been settled in the northern and central parts of the Grassfields. It is doubtful, however, whether the present dynasty of Kom was established much before the middle of the eighteenth century.

A dateline is provided by Zintgraff's journey through Kom towards the end of 1889, when he received a somewhat hostile reception at the hands of the warriors of its ruler, Yu (Zintgraff, 1895: 317 ff.). There were still, in 1963, individuals living in

Kom who had seen Zintgraff, or who could recall the excitement caused by his visit or who were able to say whether they had been born shortly after that event. If their evidence, including that of Prince Fombang aged about eighty-five and eldest surviving son of Yu, can be accepted, Yu himself had already been on the throne about twenty-five years. Yu was the seventh king (*foyn*) to reign at Laikom, the hilltop capital: he had succeeded as a young married man, possibly in the early 1860s, and he died a very old man in 1912, about three years before the defeat of the Germans by the British. Kom, as it existed at the time of Zintgraff's visit, was largely his creation, and in this it resembled some of its neighbours, where long-lived rulers endowed with intelligence, a gift for innovation, and military leadership consolidated royal control and extended state boundaries.

The Origin and Expansion of the State

The foundation of the dynasty at Laikom is closely associated with three clans—Ekwü, Achaf, and Itinelaa. The kingship became vested in one of the matrilineages of the Ekwü clan, but an Achaf lineage and a Itinelaa lineage provided the enstoolers of kings. (In Mme, Fungom, Kuk, Nyos, and Kung the dynasties all belong to the Achaf clan.) The royal legend of origin brings the ancestor of the royal clan from Ndobo to Bamessi (presumably then in its older location in Bamum), where he settled with his people. Later most of them were destroyed by a trick of the Bamessi chief. The remnant under a new leader crossed Nso to Jottin on its western border; from there they passed to Ajung, where they stayed awhile and entered into an alliance, still commemorated in the royal installation ceremonies. Later Jina, the founder of the Kom dynasty, led his followers to Laikom, where they subsequently displaced the Ndonale clan. The latter moved the seat of their chiefdom to Achain (see p. 133).

The information for the period before Yu's reign is thin, and traditions conflict in the attribution of events, including conquests, to the first rulers. In addition to Ajung and Ake, they controlled a scatter of villages in Abasakom (literally, side or area of Kom) in what is now the northern sector of the kingdom. Within the royal clan of Ekwü there was almost certainly competition for the kingship: one tradition records such an instance following on the

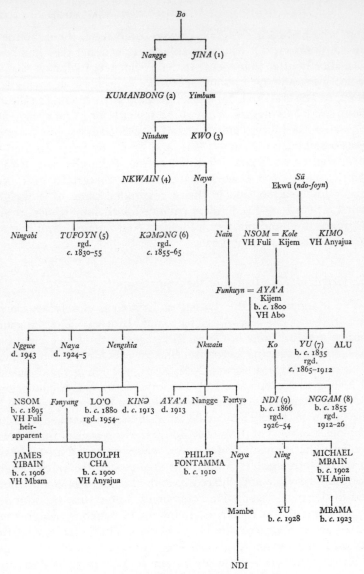

Fig. 5. Genealogy of the Kom dynasty

Limitations of space preclude the inclusion of all members of the generation of Lo'o (the reigning *foyn* in 1963) and all of those of the succeeding generation. Lo'o, tenth ruler of Kom, died in May 1966 and was succeeded by the heir apparent, Nsom

Key: u.c. = males; l.c. = females; italics = deceased; rgd. = reigned; VH = Village Head

death of the second king, Kumanbong. The formalized genealogy
for the early reigns (see p. 130) lacks examples of fraternal succession until the time of Kəməng. This is suspicious, since the
kingship should go to the eldest male in the lineage, but it is
possible that half-brothers were sometimes passed over or else
had died during the reigns of long-lived rulers, such as the fifth
king Tufoyn. The foundation of some settlements south of Abasakom towards the end of the eighteenth century is credited to three
members of the royal lineage who, for one reason or another,
were excluded from the group of likely successors: one of these,
Nsom-Sü, established himself at Fuli, another, Kimo-Sü, at
Anyajua. Later, possibly in the 1820s, Aya'a, who was the son of
Nsom-Sü and a Kijəm woman, founded the neighbouring village
of Abo. These villages gave the royal house a foothold in the fertile
area known as Nggwin-Kijəm (the hunting land of Kijəm). Part
of it, as the name suggests, at one time constituted the chiefdom
of Kijəm, which, in the early decades of the nineteenth century,
had its headquarters near Njinikijəm. Aya'a, in his early manhood,
had lived near his mother's people at Njinikijəm, but in the reign
of Tufoyn—possibly in the 1840s—the Kijəm chief left with
many of his people after his defeat in war by Kom. He eventually
established a successor chiefdom at Kijəm-Kəgu (Babanki) south
of the present Kom border. Although traditions and genealogical
evidence suggest that other people besides the Kijəm were living
in the area, the departure of the Kijəm left lands vacant into which
the Kom proper moved. The king of Kom appointed village
heads (both members of the Itinelaa clan) at Belo and Njir.ikijəm
and placed them in charge of raffia stands.

Tufoyn died a very old man, c. 1850–55, and it seems probable
that his elderly brother Kəməng, who succeeded him, exercised
little effective control over what was now the southern part of the
kingdom, although Aya'a, either in the reign of Nkwain or Tufoyn,
had been given in marriage the princess Funkuyn, who gave
birth to Yu (c. 1830–35) and six other children. Yu, who was the
heir-apparent in Kəməng's reign, left his father's village at Abo
on marriage and built a compound near Belo. Cases were taken to
him for settlement, and this, together with his paternal link with
the former Kijəm chiefdom, may have been regarded as a challenge
to the authority of the aged ruler. Kəməng, at all events, had
him escorted out of the country by *kwifoyn* (the name of the palace

K

regulatory society in Kom (see p. 143), but after two years he re-
called him from banishment for a reconciliation and died shortly
afterwards. Yu, then in his thirties and with a reputation as a warrior, was immediately enthroned and was in a favourable position
to consolidate his position and incorporate Nggwin-Kijəm effectively within the kingdom. He himself had already acquired influence in the area near Belo, his father Aya'a was a man of wealth
and village head in Abo, a few miles to the north-east. Aya'a
was given honours: he was made a titled member in three sections
of *kwifoyn* and was permitted to establish lodges of the two high-
ranking palace societies of *chong* and *achəm*. He was endowed with
slaves and the right to retain one tusk of any elephant killed by
him or his people. By virtue of being father of the Foyn, he was
sent retainers for the clearance of his guinea-corn farms, and he
always received an animal at the distribution of game in the
annual royal hunt. Lastly, it was decreed by Yu and *kwifoyn*
(probably at the instigation of Aya'a himself) that henceforth no
women of the royal matrilineage were to be given in marriage.
They were free to take lovers, but the titular father of all children
born to them was to be the holder of the village headship of Abo.
Aya'a founded the Kijəm patrilineage, in which the village headship is still vested. This conferring of perpetual titular fatherhood
upon the village heads of Abo in relation to the dynastic lineage
gave them a unique position in the Kom polity. It was also, one
suspects, a means by which Yu secured a strong ally in the southern
part of his kingdom.

Yu was ambitious to expand his kingdom: it was said of him
that wars began with him and finished with him, the last being
the battle with the Germans in 1904/5. The mountainous terrain
of Kom protected it to a large extent from external foes and provided sanctuary for refugees, among them the chiefs of Nsei
(Bamessing) and Nkwen (Bafreng), who fled from the mounted
raiders who ravaged so much of the surrounding area in the mid-
century. Yu revitalized the village military lodges: he gave them
war and some of the profits of war and invited noted warriors to
drink weekly at the palace lodge. The most powerful neighbour
to the south was the conquest state of Bafut, which in the reign
of its king Ambu'mbi (Zintgraff's Gwalem) or just prior to it
was harrying the small village chiefdoms of Mejung, Baicham,
Mbinkas, and Baiso. These sought the protection of Yu, who

incorporated them into his kingdom, but permitted them to retain their hereditary chiefs. He raided Bafut for slaves, but did not, apparently, seek to extend his control in the area to the west, where palm-oil was produced and where chiefdoms were miniscule. They were within the sphere of influence of Aghem (population 9,700 in 1953), to whom they gave renders of oil, and Yu may have thought it inexpedient to risk a war with their overlord. He did, however, attack the independent village chiefdom of Mme on the northern boundary of Kom for slaves on at least three occasions.

Kom was on terms of friendship with Oku on its eastern boundary; but the nature of its relations, initially, with Achain and Bum to the north is obscure, and it is not clear whether at that time Achain was already tributary to Kom. Yu waged war against them at least twice: he gained complete control of Achain, but failed to reduce Bum; at a later stage relationships were sufficiently friendly for individuals to engage in trade across the borders. Kom also raided for slaves in the vicinity of Babungo and over towards the south-western boundary of Nso, with whom, however, there was a pact of friendship involving royal gift exchange and the mutual return of run-away wives and slaves.

The Economic Basis of the State

By his policy of raiding, Yu consolidated control along his borders, brought wealth into the country, and strengthened his hold over his own people, not least the members of the dynastic lineage. Nggam, a sister's son to Yu and heir apparent, was made village head of Fuli, was given some two hundred slaves, and was responsible for organizing raids south of the kingdom. Nggam's brother, Ndi, became village head of Mbam in Abasakom, had his own slaves and was responsible for warfare across northern and western frontiers; another sister's son, Kinə-Nengshia, was appointed village head of Anyajua (see genealogy). The palace had a large complement of slaves, but noted warriors and favoured notables received war captives whom they could either use as labourers or trade for guns, gunpowder, and oil. Kom became the main provider of slaves from the Grassfields to the middlemen of the escarpment edge. Kom traders exchanged kola and slaves for Jukun blue stencilled cloth, salt, and beads with Bum; kola for oil with Aghem; slaves, iron goods, and livestock for oil, guns, and gunpowder with Mankon, who, in its turn, obtained oil from Meta chiefdoms to the west and made a middleman's profit. Kom itself also acted as middleman for the distribution of Jukun cloth, obtained from Bum, trading it to Nkwen and some of the villages in the Ndop Plain, who were in touch with the markets of Bagham and Bamendjinda, suppliers of salt and guns (see also, Chilver, 1961).

The economy was a prosperous one. There seems to have been no elaboration of sumptuary laws, such as occurred in Nso, but there were differences in wealth in so far as members of the dynastic lineage, sons of the king, favoured retainers, titled elders of the palace, and some smiths were able to acquire slaves, livestock, oil, cloth, and beads. All men had farms which produced a range of crops—guinea-corn, maize, coco-yams, plantains, and pulses. Kom was fertile and was spared the seasonal periods of shortage which afflicted some of its neighbours. As in many parts of the Grassfields, women were responsible for most of the agriculture, though they received male assistance in the clearing of farms and at harvest. Men built houses, hunted, reared small livestock, grew kola trees, and engaged in trade to obtain salt and oil and to accumulate wealth to pay bride-price, meet their dues to societies, and fulfil ceremonial commitments.

The palace at Laikom was not only a focus of political and ritual activities but a centre of distribution, where notables were in frequent attendance and received gifts of cloth, guns, and wives from the Foyn (king). The Foyn had his own monopolies: herds of dwarf cattle which were killed at festivals and also used to feed the royal household, leopard, lion, and otter skins, tusks of ivory, and the first claim to war captives. The dry season provided the conditions most favourable to the prosecution of hunting and warfare and was inaugurated by the annual ceremony of *ibin* held at the capital at the end of December or early January. The Foyn performed sacrifices to his ancestors; renders of food, fish, oil, wine, and livestock were made by tributary chiefs; and the warriors of village military lodges, equipped with their arms, staged dances in the palace piazza, thus providing a display of the armed strength of the kingdom and its capacity to punish disloyalty. Other sources of royal revenues were a share in fines, levied at the royal court, in fees paid for titles in the palace and *kwifoyn* (see p. 145), and by retainers at the end of their period of service at the palace. There were also royal raffia stands, kola trees, and scattered farms worked by the Foyn's wives. Each village had the duty of building and repairing one or more houses in the palace; skilled carvers and smiths gave their services, but were well rewarded with food, livestock, and sometimes wives.

Rank and Social Categories

There are two main social categories in Kom proper: royals (including not only matrilineal kin but also the children and sons' children of kings) and commoners. Prior to the time of Yu a third category, domestic slaves, was probably of negligible importance, and even during his reign it is doubtful if they numbered more than a few hundreds. As compared with the kingdom of Nso to the east, there was little elaboration of rank in the sense of a hierarchy of hereditary nobles and titled palace retainers. Apart from four hereditary priests who were in charge of the state cults at the capital and who were chosen from four clans, Achaf, Itinelaa, Ekwü, and Egayn, the men regularly employed at the palace and its precincts as officers of *kwifoyn*, as chamberlains and envoys, were all appointees of the king. There was no constituted council of advisers, but all village and compound heads who had paid a fee could assist in the judging of cases in the king's court, *etwi*. Among these a few won the favour of the king, were appointed leading elders in *kwifoyn*, and became his confidential advisers. To a very great extent access to the king's counsels and the exercise of political influence depended on services rendered to the throne, ability, and wealth, though sons of the king who had intelligence and had won his trust enjoyed an initial advantage by virtue of their birth and the freedom of access it gave them to all parts of the palace and familiarity with its affairs.

Clans were not ranked. Ekwü occupied a special position in that the kingship was vested in one of its component matrilineages. It might therefore be regarded as a royal clan, but, unless members belonged to the dynastic lineage, they enjoyed no particular prestige in anyone's eyes but their own, and it would, we think, be a distortion of local attitudes to speak of them as collateral royals. The dynastic matrilineage was called *ndo-foyn* (house of the Foyn), sometimes *ndo-Funkuyn* (Funkuyn being the mother of Yu), or *ndo-Bo*, after the mother of the founder of the dynasty at Laikom. Its membership must always have been small: in 1963 there were eight males and six females still alive; of the latter two were past child-bearing. Members, regardless of generation, were referred to as *woynjemtefoyn* (sisters' children of the Foyn); during their childhood and early adolescence girls lived at the palace. Soon after puberty they underwent a ceremony of emergence called 'washing away the camwood of the palace'; they then lived in houses built round the main piazza and were free to take lovers from among the notables who visited the capital. When a princess formed a permanent relationship with a lover she either went to live in his compound or established one of her own nearby and was endowed with female retainers and sometimes slaves by the Foyn. At her death she was buried in one of the royal burial grounds at the capital or in the village of Kukfini (in Nggwin-Kijəm), and her compound was inherited by her eldest son. Among princesses, the *nafoyn* (queen-mother) enjoyed a rank second only to that of Foyn. She formerly resided in the royal grave shrine (*efum*) at Laikom, watched over the children of the palace, and received visitors.[5] She had no sacrificial or political role, but was in a position to advise the Foyn privately. On her death the Foyn appointed the eldest woman in the matrilineage as *nafoyn*, and she was installed and instructed in her duties by the *bobe-kwifoyn*, the resident officer of *kwifoyn*.

The eldest of the princes of the blood was the heir apparent and, with one exception, has always been village head of Fuli. Other princes in order of seniority of age usually succeeded to particular village headships, where the office since the time of Yu, and before in some cases, had been vested in the dynastic lineage. This device maintained the prestige of the royal house and gave royal incumbents an opportunity to acquire skill in the art of government. The heir apparent acted as the Foyn's deputy in the Nggwin-Kijəm sector, in so far as cases were referred to him for judgement which could not be settled at the village level. But rarely were he and other princes of the blood permitted to become leading elders in the lodges of *kwifoyn*, since this would have placed them in a position where they might threaten the Foyn's authority.

The prince of the blood who succeeded to the kingship was set apart from others by a ritual of installation which identified him with past kings and brought him into communion with them. A week after the burial of a king the two newly appointed priest-enstoolers each took an arm of the heir apparent and seated him on a stone in front of the *ndo-ntul* (house of Ntul), which was associated with rites of reconciliation and appeasement, and was also said to represent the country of Kom (see p. 146). He was slapped and buffeted for the last time, and was then led to the royal grave shrine, was placed on the installation stool, robed, and rubbed with camwood by the priests in the presence of 'sons of the palace' and chamberlains. There, together with his two enstoolers, he was secluded for eight days, visited by notables, and then ceremonially conducted around the palace. Three or four days after this, with the assistance of his priest-enstoolers, he sacrificed a goat before the grave shrine and invoked the names of his ancestors. Thereafter he was expected to do this regularly; sacrifices were also made from time to time to deceased queen-mothers by the priest-enstoolers.

Children of a Foyn born before his accession, together with those born subsequently, ranked as 'children of the palace' (*woynto*) and were regarded as royals or, to use Richards' apt phrase 'royal ineligibles', since they could neither succeed nor bear heirs to the throne (Richards, 1961: 144). Daughters were given away in marriage to notables by the Foyn, and from among the sons of such women some might be brought back into the palace to act as pages and, in late adolescence, might be appointed to the office of *bobe-kwifoyn*, one of the most influential in the kingdom. Of the six men who served Yu in this capacity, one was his own daughter's son, and another daughter's son of Tufoyn. Foyn's sons had access at all times to the palace, and, as mentioned earlier, some became trusted advisers of the Foyn. The Foyn had the right to appoint a son to each of the two senior lodges of *kwifoyn*. It is significant that in the list of men in the Achaf clan who acted as king-enstoolers, several were sons of Foyns. Informants said this was a coincidence, however frequent, but our evidence shows that some of the key offices in the kingdom were held by 'royal ineligibles' and by sons of king's daughters. It was to the support of such men that the Foyn could look, if need be, against the pretensions of princes of the blood.

Territorial Organization

Much of Kom (*c.* 280 square miles in area) occupies a high mountain terrain at an average height of 5,000 feet above sea-level; in the heart of the country on a spur at some 6,300 feet is the capital, Laikom, where the Foyn has his palace and there are a few compounds occupied by retainers and priest-elders. In 1953 there were twenty-seven villages in Kom proper, with a total population of 23,626; the ten former tributary chiefdoms accounted for another 3,000. The great majority of villages had populations of less than 1,000, and many of these under 500.

The people of Kom were divided into named dispersed clans. There were no clan heads; the clan (*isasendo*, lit. buttocks of the house) was neither a political nor a ritual unit. Each clan was composed of a number of non-localized sub-clans, among which there were no postulated genealogical links, apart from a belief in common descent from some remote and usually unnamed ancestress. Within the sub-clan (*iku'o*), the most respected and influential elder presided at mortuary and installation ceremonies for compound heads, and might be invited on such occasions to settle outstanding disputes within the sub-clan with the help of elders of its component lineages. The lineage (*ichu'ndo*), usually some three to six generations in depth, was the exogamous unit. Marriage was usually virilocal, and if a man had been assisted by his father in obtaining a wife he would most probably build a compound near him, unless he had representatives of his own lineage in the village with residential and farm land to spare. If he built on his father's land he resided there until an opportunity occurred to inherit the compound of a deceased lineage member; his former compound was then transferred by him to a brother or sister's son. It follows from this pattern of residence that the lineage in terms of its married males was a dispersed unit, but the degree of dispersal depended to a very great extent on whether or not the founder was one of the early settlers in a village and thus able to acquire considerable areas for building and farming. When this had been the case the heads of four or five neighbouring compounds might belong to the same lineage. Provided land was available, plots could be allocated to sons, daughters' husbands, daughters' sons, and even strangers.

All lineage members had potential rights of inheritance to the compounds of other lineage members, preference being given to uterine brothers and next to the sons of uterine sisters of the deceased. A compound consisted of anything from two to ten dwelling-houses, rarely more, and was inhabited by the compound head (*bobe*), his wives, unmarried children, occasionally a brother

and married son. An heir (*nzhindo*, lit. eater of the house) also
inherited farm plots, kola trees, raffia stands, and livestock; but
widows, with certain exceptions, might be inherited by any
members of the sub-clan of the deceased who won their favour.[6]
In matters of inheritance and succession the opinion of the sons
of the deceased was of the greatest importance. They helped to
bury their father, and the eldest took charge of his father's
sacrificial cup and would withhold it if the compound was inherited
by a man once disliked by his father or likely to squander its
resources. If the heir-designate refused the invitation to succeed
he himself could, with the approval of 'sons of the compound'
and lineage members, nominate another heir. Or, if there was no
lineage member of the appropriate age to succeed, one of the sons
acted as caretaker (*wul nchi*), a role retained until his death. If
the dead compound head had been important politically, either
by virtue of holding a village headship or by receiving favours
from the Foyn, the heir sooner or later went to the palace with gifts,
accompanied by his 'sons' rather than by members of his lineage.

Just as the Foyn looked to the 'children of the palace' for
support and assistance, so the compound head looked to his sons.
And just as the Foyn had certain filial duties to his 'father', the
village head of Abo, so, too, commoners had their obligations to
their fathers which were enforced by moral, religious, and legal
sanctions. Again and again we were told: 'I respect and fear my
father more than my mother's brothers'; and, when we asked for
an explanation, were told: 'We are one blood' or 'My father gave
me life, he reared me.' The Kom believe that they receive blood,
flesh, and bone from their fathers, and that their mothers are
merely vessels. Disobedience and failure to render certain services
were believed to be punished by the matrilineal ancestors of the
father. During his father's lifetime a man handed over all game
to him—failure to do so was a legal offence—assisted him in the
clearing and harvest of guinea-corn farms, provided him with
firewood and care in time of sickness, consulted him on all
important matters, and, prior to marriage, gave him his earnings.
When a girl married, her father's consent was essential, and he
received a substantial portion of the bride-price. As far as lay
within his means, he assisted a son to obtain a wife; he contributed entrance fees for societies and entrusted him with the
secrets of his medicines.

The rules governing succession to a village headship were, with the exceptions discussed below, the same as those for a compound headship. In the genealogies we collected the office was normally held in turn by the eldest male in the lineage, but it was sometimes asserted, more particularly by royals, that any village headship lay within the gift of the Foyn. Such claims were no more than an assertion of the Foyn's political paramountcy and were of the same order as his claim to be overlord of all land. He had, of course, the right to veto an unsuitable choice and to remove from office one who had acted treasonably or who had flagrantly and consistently failed in his duties; but interference in succession over the head of a legitimate and worthy heir was criticized as an abuse of power. Where the latter occurred, the Foyn's appointee was frequently succeeded by a man of the appropriate lineage; this was more likely to happen in the reign of the next Foyn, who at the outset, at least, was concerned with maintaining the law and rectifying injustice. In Abo and three other villages, where the headship was vested in Kijəm lineages, succession was patrilineal and went to the eldest male. In the three villages associated with the royal house—Mbam, Fuli, and Anyajua—appointment of princes of the blood was made directly by the Foyn without reference to the wishes of the 'sons' of the previous incumbent.

The compound of the village head (*bontə*) was normally larger than most in the village and contained the house of the village regulatory society, *ndo-akum*. Frequently there was also a particular type of medicine-lodge, *ndo-nggwin*, whose members were responsible for carrying out apotropaic rites to protect the sprouting guinea-corn and avert witchcraft and who also punished persons who maliciously uprooted crops and trees. The annual performance of these rites was initiated by a more elaborate ritual sequence carried out by the Foyn and his priests at the capital and centred on the three shrines called *fechə*, *ndo-ntul*, and *ndo-azhe'a* (a rain shrine).

At the local level the *akum* constituted an important organ of government, in some respects parallel in its function with the palace *kwifoyn*, an analogy often drawn by informants. All male members of the village belonged to its *akum*, the entry fee being a fowl, but older members were expected to make further payments of goats and wine. There were no grades, but such payments conferred prestige and enhanced influence. The *akum* met weekly, wine being provided by members, and on occasion a libation was poured in front of the house and the blessing of the predecessors of the village head invoked. Notice of an extraordinary meeting was given by a son of the village head striking a gong through the village the evening beforehand. Women were not permitted to see this gong; an analogy was drawn between it and the instrument of *kwifoyn*, since it represented authority which must be obeyed. The village head normally presided over meetings, assisted by two or three deputies selected by himself and frequently drawn from different clans. It was rare for him to retain the assistants of his predecessor, though they might be consulted. When the Foyn wanted anything done he sent retainers to the village head, who was then responsible for transmitting instructions. To the *akum* was entrusted communal work, such as road clearing and the repair of houses at the palace, and the conduct of the annual village hunt in April, which followed on the royal hunt organized by *kwifoyn*. *Akum* deliberated village affairs, tried civil cases, and inflicted fines in matters connected with land, minor assault, matrimonial disputes, and failure to share in public work. In the Abasakom sector difficult cases were referred directly to the palace court; in Nggwin-Kijəm they were taken to the residence of the heir apparent and tried by his *akum*; if no settlement was reached they were transferred to the palace.

The *akum* also had a ceremonial role; its maskers and orchestra performed at mortuary ceremonies for important members and notables of the country. Other important men in the village 'owned' associations which also danced at annual or mortuary ceremonies, but these lacked governmental functions. The most important of the women's associations was *afaf*, usually presided over by a sister or senior wife of the village head (Kaberry, 1952: 98–101); but when the women of a village wished to resort to disciplinary action against a man who had committed incest, adultery with his father's wife, beaten his father, mother, a pregnant or nursing woman, shown extreme disrespect to the old or heaped vulgar abuse on a woman, they assembled as *anlu* (-*lu*, to drive away). *Anlu* was greatly feared, and against its ruling there was no appeal. If it refused to pardon the culprit he was forced to leave the country.

Each village had its military lodge or war-club (*njong*), presided over by a *bondonjong* who was elected by members and assisted by untitled lieutenants, among whom were scouts and tricksters called *gwe*, renowned for superior cunning. Each *njong* had its attached boys' *njong*. Unlike the *akum*, which still plays an important part in village affairs, *njong* has not even survived as a drinking club for men. We know that *njong* leaders met at the palace to discuss offensive war; in defence of its area each *njong* seems to have had a good deal of initiative.

The Foyn himself sometimes visited villages and might spend the night in a hut, which thenceforth was referred to as a palace, *nto*, and was reserved for his exclusive use. By this means he acquainted himself directly with affairs in his country and made himself accessible to individuals, who had been unable to penetrate beyond the retainers and pages who hedged his presence at the capital. Village and compounds heads who had matters to report to him were, of course, free to go to the capital, which, at the most, was only a few hours' walking distance from any part of the kingdom. A certain day in the week was set aside for the hearing of cases there, another for the meeting of ceremonial elders in *kwifoyn*, and another for the palace military lodge. These occasions gave people an opportunity to give and hear news; they were also a means by which the Foyn obtained information in addition to that brought to him by retainers and confidential advisers.

Tributary chiefdoms enjoyed a large measure of autonomy under their traditional chiefs, each of whom had his own palace entourage and, usually, his own *kwifoyn*, though he was not permitted to inflict the death penalty or order enslavement. He rendered tribute once a year, made his contribution to the Foyn's *chong* society when it went on circuit in May (see p. 147), and sent his subjects to repair houses at the palace. The choice of his successor was determined by his own dynastic lineage; but, according to one version the Foyn of Kom sent his own *kwifoyn* to act with the local *kwifoyn* in the installation ceremony. With the exception of Achain, all had patrilineal dynasties.

Central Political Institutions

The Foyn's palace, *nto*, was very similar in plan to those in neighbouring chiefdoms and consisted of a large number of dwelling huts, stores, cult lodges, and courtyards. In 1926 there

THE KINGDOM OF KOM IN WEST CAMEROON

were said to be 252 houses, of which 88 were occupied by the Foyn's 109 wives. In 1946 there were over 140 wives. In the pre-German period the palace must have been much larger, providing accommodation for some 300 wives, a retinue of pages, and over 100 retainers in *kwifoyn* quarters. The Foyn's extensive rights to claim women in marriage or to dispose of them to others was one of his most important prerogatives. Young girls were selected by his wives or retainers from among all sections of the population, with the exception of royals and their children. Some were reserved to the Foyn and trained in court etiquette; others were in the care of senior wives or princesses and were later bestowed by the Foyn on his sons, blood royals, and those retainers, pages, and warriors whom he wished to reward. Commoner recipients of wives were expected to send back a son or daughter to the palace; if they had more than one daughter they consulted the Foyn about their marriages.

Among the males attached to the palace in various capacities there were three categories: page-retainers (*nchisɔnto*), *kwifoyn*-retainers (*nchisɔnda*), and messengers or envoys (*woyndanto*). The last were chosen from among youths of promise who were sent to the palace with messages by their fathers or accompanied them and attracted the notice of the Foyn. They lived near the palace and, when proven, were entrusted with carrying confidential messages to notables in the kingdom and to neighbouring chiefs. Inevitably they became men of influence, possessing a number of wives, large compounds, and sometimes membership in one of the senior lodges of *kwifoyn*.

Pages were under the orders of two or three chamberlains, who had graduated from their ranks, married, and established compounds in the capital. Chamberlains supervised the economy of the palace, stored tribute and gifts, presided at distributions, and acted as intermediaries between the Foyn and those who sought audience with him. They received a wife or wives from him, were ceremonial elders in *kwifoyn*, and sometimes members of its inner lodges, *kwifoyn ntu'u* and *kwifoyn nggvu*.

Kwifoyn was the instrument of the Foyn's secular authority and, short of his personal intervention, there was no appeal against its decisions. It could not depose him, as it could in Bafut, but it could fine him and, if he proved recalcitrant, withdraw its services. Its officials constituted an oligarchy without whose support he was largely powerless. Inevitably there were sometimes disputes, and rivalry between them and his own sons or those of his predecessor. Nevertheless, compared with the situation in many other Bamenda chiefdoms, the Foyn exercised a very large measure of direct control over *kwifoyn* and its lodges through his right to appoint and remove officers. In many chiefdoms the chief was referred to as the 'son of *kwifoyn*', and although senior appointments in the chiefdom were made in his name after consultation, effective power was wielded by its officials. This was the case in Bafut, and in the chiefdoms of the Ndop Plain, where the chief's hereditary councillors acted as the inner college of *kwifoyn* (Kaberry, 1962). In Kom the Foyn was sometimes described as the 'father of *kwifoyn*', with the implication of the overriding authority associated with fatherhood.

The *nchisɔnda* were the palace retainers who were the members of *kwifoyn*, which had its quarters to the rear of the Foyn's apartments. These were recruited by its officers from nearly all sections of the population just before the age of puberty and served for a period of six to nine years. It was only in exceptional circumstances that a man could 'buy off' a son selected for service. When the time came for a retainer to leave *kwifoyn* compound his father, assisted by kin, brought goats, food, and wine to the palace. Connexion with the palace was maintained through attendance at the weekly drinking sessions of *kwifoyn* and by his continued liability to be employed on palace business. A favoured retainer might be endowed with a wife by the Foyn.

While in residence in *kwifoyn* compound, retainers were under the orders of a resident *bobe-kwifoyn* (lit. 'father of the compound of *kwifoyn*'), who was appointed by the Foyn from among the oldest in their ranks or brought in from outside. He was in charge of its *sacra* and its masks, which were brought out for the mortuary ceremonies of its own members and senior royals. After leaving *kwifoyn* compound he retained his title, became an influential elder in *kwifoyn*, including its two senior lodges, and sat in the Foyn's court of justice.

When orders were to be transmitted to the people or new regulations enacted it was *kwifoyn* who made the announcement in the Foyn's name. Its members kept the peace, and inflicted penalties ordered by the Foyn's court. *Kwifoyn's* function as a regulator of certain economic activities also symbolized its role as guardian of the Foyn's pre-eminence. It inaugurated the guinea-corn harvest by playing its instruments all night on the eve of the first day on which harvesting was permitted. In this way the Foyn's influence over the productiveness of the land and the staple crop was emphasized. Premature harvesting was penalized by a fine payable to *kwifoyn*. *Kwifoyn* also organized the royal hunt in April. This was the occasion on which the Foyn's titular father, the village head of Abo, received a headless antelope as a mark of the Foyn's filial obligation. A week after the royal hunt each village head through his own *akum* arranged a local hunt; on this occasion successful hunters presented game to their own fathers, while the Foyn received only the royal animals.

There were two lodges in *kwifoyn's* precincts. The *ndo-nggvu* (house of sasswood) was an ordeal lodge, as it was elsewhere, and also seems to have been used for the elimination of suspected traitors. It was headed by the Foyn (who was *ex officio* head of all associations in the country) and all *bobe-kwifoyns*. Other members were appointed by the Foyn and paid a heavy entry fee of twenty goats and wine. They invariably included an elder son of the Foyn, the village head of Abo, one or two chamberlains, and a few notables. The other lodge, *kwifoyn ntu'u* (*kwifoyn* of the night), was said to be even more important. The nature of its activities was kept a closely guarded secret, but were believed to involve the execution of lawbreakers at night. Its membership was small and included all *bobe-kwifoyns*. In addition, the Foyn appointed one of his own sons, a senior chamberlain, and the village head of Abo. Lastly, there was a much larger group of prominent men, the *nggangsɔ-kwifoyn* (ceremonial elders of *kwifoyn*), who had access to its quarters, met weekly to drink wine, shared in the heavy fees of new members and in the offerings made to *kwifoyn* on occasions of attendance at mortuary ceremonies.

The Foyn was not assisted by a constituted council, although the king-enstoolers and officials of *kwifoyn* formed the nucleus of those he called upon for advice. Magistral duties were performed by them and by other notables who had *tang nto*, that is, paid the fee of two goats and two drums of wine, which entitled them to judge serious cases at the circle of stones called *etwi* once a week at the palace. Village heads on accession were automatically invited to join this group known collectively as *ichü-ɔsɔnto* (elders of the palace). A further payment, again made on the invitation of a smaller group, entitled a man on the Foyn's summons to sit in the Foyn's own drinking hall and take part in private discussions with him. There was one further privilege restricted to a very few notables—the right to greet the Foyn by clapping hands. The priest-enstoolers had it by virtue of their office, but the Foyn gave it to three or four notables outstanding for their wisdom and probity who had served him well as a prince or after his accession. The privilege was not hereditary, and, although its enjoyment required payment of very heavy fees, character, and not wealth, determined the Foyn's choice.

Etwi was the highest court of appeal, but much civil litigation was, as we have shown, handled at the village level. The Foyn alone had the right to order the death penalty or enslavement, and certain cases could be tried only by him and his court: adultery with royal wives, suspected witchcraft, treason, refusal to hand over royal perquisites, murder, grievous assault, selling a Kom person in slavery, and infractions of *kwifoyn* injunctions. The enforcement of judgement was the duty of *kwifoyn*, which was also responsible for keeping the peace in land and property disputes by placing injunction sticks (which turned a private into a public dispute subject to its rules) and summoning contestants to *etwi*.

State Rites and Ceremonies

The cult of the royal ancestors was one of the central institutions of Kom. The Foyn was a sacred king performing both secular and priestly functions. Through legitimate succession (that is, descent from the ancestress Bo, the mother of the founder of the Laikom dynasty, and installation at the palace), he was able to bring peace and prosperity to his people. Usurpation, on the other hand, was believed to bring drought and failure of crops in the country, as instanced in the tradition of the events which preceded the succession of Kwo. The royal grave shrine, which was also used as a dwelling hut, lay within the palace precincts and was the first hut to be rebuilt in the event of fire. Here the Foyn was enstooled and remained for a week in seclusion with his two priest-enstoolers, here he performed sacrifices to his predecessors, here the queen-mother resided.

The other important cult at the palace, centred on the *ndo-ntul*, was associated with peace, reconciliation, and the warding off of evil power. Any male, by paying a fowl, had the right of entry and thereby became *nggang-ntul*, but when a sacrifice was to be performed all left the lodge except the Foyn and the Achaf priest. There were two main occasions for sacrifice: one towards the end of February or early March, another in May at the new moon when it formed part of a sequence of rites, *fachu*, inaugurating the planting of guinea-corn. A week later all those villages which possessed *nggwin* (see p. 140) performed sacrifices and distributed apotropaic medicines. Everyone was then free to plant guinea-corn, but the Foyn's farm was sown first. For the next five weeks village heads and other notables who possessed the two friction-drum societies, *acham* and *chong*, performed dances weekly in their respective villages; the palace *chong*, under an elder son of the Foyn, made its circuit of all Kom, collecting goats and fowls which were later shared between the Foyn and members.

Conclusions

External economic influences favoured the emergence of Kom as a powerful state. During the second half of the nineteenth century the supply of dane guns increased;[8] there was a growing demand for slaves in the palm-oil-producing areas in the south; to the north there was the extension of the Hausa trading frontier to the Central Cameroons and, with it, new opportunities for the acquisition of goods in exchange for kola, ivory, and slaves. Kom, like other Grassfields states, took advantage of these developments, but there is no evidence, for example, that its wars with Bum were aimed at superseding that chiefdom as a kola entrepôt. Although Kom was a purveyor of slaves, we could find no evidence that its institutions were affected by this role, except indirectly. This is in contrast to the city state of Mankon, where the theme of the purchase and capture of slaves recurs in any account given of the workings of government. Nor are there any signs that the palace in Kom was creating an extensive system of royal trade monopolies such as happened in Bamum; nor was there much development of the role of the king as entrepreneur in putting up capital for trading journeys, as, for example, there was in Nso, Oku, and Bafut (Chilver, 1961: 241–2). Rather, the palace obtained a share of private wealth for its own consumption and redistribution by means of payments made by notables for privileged entry to sections within it or to its associations. Perhaps Yu's main contribution to the consolidation of Kom was not only military

L

leadership but also the mobilization of a system of prestige-seeking focused on himself.

The kingship was something more than a village headship writ large. Royal wives were sacrosanct, access to the palace was hedged about with strict rules; as in other Grassfields kingdoms, the Foyn was approached with set gestures and addressed by praise names exclusive to him. Certain animals were royal monopolies. The beneficent and protective aspect of kingship was manifested in its priestly and ceremonial role, which was held to bring peace, fertility, and prosperity to the kingdom; the more terrifying aspect of kingship associated with the enforcement of law and with punishment was represented by its instrument *kwifoyn*. In this, too, Kom resembled many of the surrounding chiefdoms; indeed, if we were to single out a distinguishing feature of Bamenda Grassfields political systems we would locate it in this institution, recruiting its ordinary membership from freeborn commoners, who thereafter were categorized as 'guardians of the palace', and maintained their connexion and had particular ties of loyalty to the palace.

On the whole, Kom central political institutions were relatively simple. Unlike Nso, it had no hereditary retainer group, hereditary palace stewards, and hereditary councillors (Kaberry, 1959). In this it resembled the village chiefdoms to the north, which had matrilineal dynasties. But whereas in those chiefdoms the chief's advisers were so by virtue of their positions as ward and compound heads, in Kom a distinction was beginning to emerge between the general advisory body of village notables and those privy to the king's counsel and given special privileges by him. The latter consisted of men appointed to the inner lodges of *kwifoyn* and those who had the right to greet him by clapping hands. There was no sign, however, that such privileges were becoming hereditary. A distinction had also emerged between village headships filled by the descendants of their founders in accordance with the wishes of the deceased and the approval of his sons, and those village headships which, even when founded by princes of the blood, lay within the gift of the king and were becoming royal appendages and epicentres of national government.

NOTES

1. The documentary materials for any historical reconstruction in the Bamenda Grassfields in the mid-century are exceedingly slender. Such as they are, they record one significant series of events—the invasion of the trans-Mbam region by the Bali (mixed bands of Chamba-led raiders) c. 1820–45, the beginnings of Bamum expansion in their wake (these can be derived from linguistic notes by Clarke, 1849, and Koelle, 1854), and the plundering of 'Mbafu' by Ardo Sambo of Tibati, dated by Barth to the dry season of 1848/49 (Barth, op. cit.: 626). They also record the presence of long-distance traders on the northern borders, and the existence of well-defined slave-trading routes to Duala and Calabar. There are, however, no firmly identifiable mentions of Kom; and, according to oral traditions, Kom itself suffered only one major mounted raid round about the mid-century.

2. Bamenda was also the name of the *Bezirk*, which included the Grassfields, Bamum, parts of the Bamileke region, Kentu, and western Gashaka. Under British administration the name was first used for the Division, and later the Province. In 1954 Bamenda Province was divided into three Divisions—Bamenda, Nkambe, and Wum (see map) —but the term Bamenda still has currency for the wider area.

3. A detailed analysis of traditions of settlement and social institutions is given by the authors in *Notes and Draft Sections for Chapter on the Western Grassfields* (for *L'Histoire des peuples and des civilisations du Cameroun*), mimeog., 1964. Further historical and ethnographic details are contained in an expanded mimeographed version of this paper, circulated locally and deposited in the International African Institute.

4. This essay incorporates part of the material collected by one of us (P.M.K.) during four weeks in 1946/47, and by both of us during three weeks in 1963, when we enjoyed the hospitality of the Cameroons Baptist Mission in Belo. Our warm thanks are due to the Government of West Cameroon for its help and active interest. Mrs. Chilver's research was assisted by a travel grant from the Committee of Management of the University of London Institute of Commonwealth Studies, and Dr. Kaberry's by a Hayter Travel Grant.

5. Since the time of Nggam, no *nafoyn* has resided at the capital. The inauguration of his reign was a troubled one. He quarrelled with two princes of the blood, Aya'a Nkwain and Kinə-Nengshia, and several sons of the late Yu. We received conflicting accounts of the causes of the dispute: according to one version, Nggam as a prince had earned their enmity and, fearing opposition to his rule, accused them of treason to the Germans, who put them to death at Mamfe. Some of Yu's widows

committed suicide on learning of the death of their sons; the *nafoyn* Naya fled the country and, when she eventually returned, refused to live at Laikom.

6. A woman, for whom bride-price had been paid by her husband's father, was inherited by her husband's uterine brother or, failing him, a member of the matrilineage of her husband's father.

The rules governing membership and inheritance in Kijəm lineages presented certain anomalies. A man, whose father was Kijəm and whose mother belonged to one of the matriclans, had potential rights to inheritance in the lineages of both his parents. But, if his father belonged to a matriclan and his mother to Kijəm, he had neither rights of inheritance in his father's lineage nor in the Kijəm lineage of his mother; nevertheless, he ranked as a member of the Kijəm clan and potential founder of a lineage within it. He would, on marriage, obtain from a kinsman or village head a site for a compound, and this might subsequently be inherited by his male descendents.

7. The *ntul* cult occurs in a number of chiefdoms in the Wum Division. In Bum it is controlled by the ruler, a princess, and a college of nine hereditary members, who act as one of the two groups of state councillors, the most senior of whom is also king-enstooler. Ritually it is concerned with success in hunting, fertility, and sacrifices of atonement for those who have accidentally shed blood. As in Kom, leopards brought to the palace are skinned in front of the *ntul* lodge.

8. Dane guns had reached the Upper Cross River area by 1842, but, to judge from datings derived from dynastic genealogies, were not numerous in the forties and fifties in the Grassfields.

REFERENCES

Barth, H.	1857	*Travels and Discoveries in North and Central Africa.* Vol. 2. London.
Bruens, A.	1942– 45	'The Structure of Nkom and its Relations to Bantu and Sudanic', *Anthropos*, Tome 37–40.
Chilver, E. M.	1961	'Nineteenth Century Trade in the Bamenda Grassfields, Southern Cameroons', *Afrika und Übersee*, Bd. xlv/4.
Clarke, J.	1849	*Specimens of Dialects.*
D.Kbl.	—	*Das Deutsche Kolonialblatt.*
Kaberry, P. M.	1952	*Women of the Grassfields*, Col. Res. Pubs. No. 14, H.M.S.O.
	1959	'Traditional Politics in Nsaw (Nso)', *Africa*, Vol. XXIX, 4.

1962 'Retainers and Royal Households in the Cameroons Grassfields', *Cahiers d'études africaines*, Vol. III–ii (No. 10).

Koelle, S.   1854 *Polyglotta Africana.* London.

Richards, A. I.   1961 'African Kings and their Royal Relatives', *J. Roy. Anth. Inst.*, Vol. 91, Pt. 2.

Richardson, I.   1956 *Linguistic Survey of the Northern Bantu Borderland.* Vol. I. London.

Thorbecke, F.   1916 *Im Hochland von Mittel-Kamerun.* Hamburg. Vol. 2.

Zintgraff, E.   1895 *Nord-Kamerun.* Berlin.

ADDITIONAL SOURCES

Evans, G. V.   1927 *An Assessment Report on the Kom (Bikom) Clan, Bamenda*, MS.

Jeffreys, M. D. W.   1951 'Some Notes on the Bikom', *Eastern Anthropologist*, Vol. IV, No. 2.

       1952 'Some Notes on the Bikom Blacksmiths', *Man*, Vol. LII, 75.

Kwain, F. and Briggs, W.   1958 'The Kom Legend', *Nigerian Field*, XXIII, 1.

Nkwain, F. I. W.   1963 *Some Reflections on the 'Anlu' organized by the Kom Women in 1958*, MS.

THE MOSSI KINGDOMS

Dominique Zahan

The Upper Volta Republic, which today incorporates the Mossi kingdoms, covers approximately 100,000 square miles. The region is an arid one—dry scrub land in the north with wooded savanna covering the south and centre; famines are not uncommon, and there has been a long tradition of both permanent and temporary migrations. The southern and central districts are characterized by larger aggregates of population; in the north the population is predominantly Fulbe.

The outstanding characteristic of the Mossi states has been the remarkable stability of their political organization over a period of many centuries. Arab historians and early European travellers were all impressed by its complex nature.[1] The king, surrounded by an elaborate court, stood at the top of the hierarchy. His court comprised officials who administered the provinces and who watched zealously every action, every gesture of the royal person. This image of the king and his court was faithfully reproduced by all Mossi chiefs down to the humblest village head. These revolved in the orbit of the king and were linked to him by a network of relations which achieved the cohesion of peoples of diverse origin and condition.

The Mossi, together with the Bura, Birifor, Dagari, Nankana, Gurmantche, Kussassi, Namnam, Tallensi, Wala, Nanumba, Dagomba, and Mamprussi, speak languages belonging to the Gur group. The last two peoples share many features of political organization with the Mossi. According to western historians, some time between the eleventh and thirteenth centuries a Dagomba king called Nedega, who ruled at Gambaga, appeared on the Volta political scene (Delafosse, 1912: 306–12; Tauxier, 1917: 667–77 and 1924: 16–24).[2] Nedega's only daughter Yennenga married Riale, a Mandingo hunter. Ouidiraogo, a son of this union, became the founder of the Mossi dynasty, which was to proliferate in all directions during the ensuing centuries. He himself founded the first kingdom at Tenkodogo in the south. One

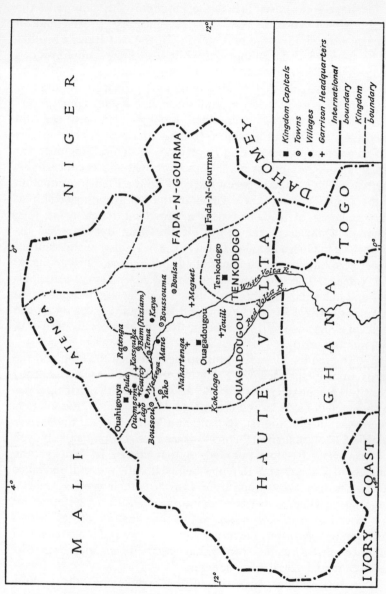

Sketch Map of Mossi Kingdoms

of his sons, Rawa, established the kingdom of Zandoma in the north, which later, under his classificatory great-grandson Yadega, became the state of Yatenga. In the east Rawa's brother Diaba founded Fada n'Gourma, while a nephew Oubri founded Ouagadougou in the west. Within five generations, according to these traditions, the Mossi kingdoms and principalities attained the form they possess today, and since that distant epoch inter-connexions have been maintained among them and are still recognized in terms of kinship (see diagram on p. 155).

The colonial régime, dating from 1897, recognized the different Mossi kingdoms and principalities, but with little concern for any ties which existed between them. With the French occupation of the Upper Volta a new division of the old groupings resulted. The kingdom of Fada n'Gourma remained much as it was, although Tenkodogo, the cradle of the royal dynasty, was in-corporated in Ouagadougou. Thus, at the beginning of this century there were but three kingdoms: Fada n'Gourma, Ouagadougou, and Yatenga. The two latter incorporated several small principal-ities and independent cantons: Zitenga and Ratenga were attached to Yatenga, while Riziam, Yako, and Boussouma came under the aegis of Ouagadougou. Still later, Riziam was incorporated in Yatenga (see map).

Within each kingdom the kinship ties between the king and the heads of principalities were dissimilar, but in each case they constituted a justification for the autonomy of the principalities in their relationship to the capital. In Ouagadougou, the kinglets (*rimnamba*) of Boussouma, Riziam, and Yako regarded themselves as classificatory daughters' sons (*yagenga*) of the king and enjoyed the privileged freedom entailed in that status. In Yatenga the kinglets of Zitenga and Ratenga behaved with the independence of classificatory great-grandfathers towards their great-grandson, the king, at Ouahigouya the capital. It should now be apparent that the degree of autonomy and subordination of the Mossi principalities *vis-à-vis* the great Ouahigouya and Ouagadougou kings entailed a relationship which was quite distinct from that between feudal vassal and suzerain.

It is very difficult to estimate the populations of the three kingdoms in the nineteenth century, although it is certain that Ouagadougou contained the largest, and Fada n'Gourma the smallest. Despite the lack of official statistics, the approximate

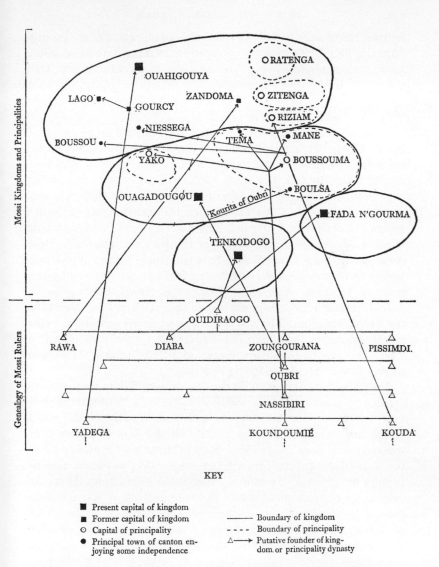

Fig. 6. Kinship links between Mossi kingdoms and principalities

figures today are as follows: Ouagadougou 2,600,000, Yatenga
700,000, and Fada n'Gourma 400,000, making a total of about
3,700,000, reunited since 5 August 1960 in an independent state
called the Upper Volta Republic.

Social Categories

The inhabitants of a Mossi state are not and were never all
'true' Mossi. Strictly speaking, this name applies only to the
nobility (*nakombse*; s. *nakombga*) and to state officials and their
descendants. In fact, the term Mossi refers to a concept which
may best be envisaged in the form of a pyramid. In the uppermost
section are contained the lineages of the descendants of former
rulers (*nakombse*); in a second, larger, section are the descendants
of state officials. Nearer the base of the pyramid are those Mossi
commoners (*talse*; s. *talga*) who bear the family names of *nakombse*
and state officials but whose lineages in fact include very heterogeneous elements—foreigners (*zemba*) or freed slaves who for
various reasons have become associated with the aristocrats of
the Mossi kingdom. The *nakombse* and the state officials are constantly recruiting new families within their sphere of influence.
These are given Mossi patronymics and thus become Mossi, soon
to lose former family and religious ties.

No statistics will ever settle the question of Mossi numbers and
residence, although the *nakombse* and descendants of state officials
may be counted, since they are grouped in villages and wards
which are usually under the control of the Mossi cavalry commander, *widi-naba*. With these facts in mind one begins to query
the traditional explanation of the origin of the Mossi empire:
foreign conquest of a peaceful indigenous population. There are
even more difficult questions to answer: how many warriors were
needed to dominate whole populations and regions in the course
of a few generations? According to early writers, the invaders
were a tiny proportion of the population; even today the *nakombse*
are a small minority in the Mossi state, compared with the large
Foulse, Nyionyiose, Samogo, Dogon, Rhimaibe, Fulbe, Silmi-
Mossi, Yarse, Dioula, Maranse, and blacksmith populations.
At a guess, the Mossi proper comprised no more than 10 per cent
of the total.

From the sociological point of view the disparity in numbers
becomes unimportant: the social functioning of the Mossi kingdom

was assured by the co-operation of all its member groups. In this way the 'true' Mossi, the possessors of *nam* (political authority), were the power equivalent of the priests of the Earth, the *tengasobanamba* (s. *tengasoba*), the possessors of *tengasobundo*. The people themselves differentiated these two controlling powers as far as possible. *Nam* and *tengasobundo* were assigned to well-differentiated lineages, *nakombse* and *tengabisi* (children of the Earth). The terms expressed the essence of the two major social categories in Mossi society, defined the essential cleavage within their social organization, and expressed the interrelation between political chiefs and priests of the Earth. *Tengasobundo* was deemed the more ancient, and hence the *tengabisi* were thought to have an historic priority over *nanamse* (political chiefs). In kinship terms the *tengasoba* was like the elder brother, the *naba* (chief) like the younger brother.[3] The former played an indispensable role at a chief's funeral: he wrapped the chief in a shroud and conducted the ritual; he also provided a newly installed chief with eating utensils. But the concept of *tengasobundo* also included some notion of *nam* in so far as a priest of the Earth was in some ways regarded as a chief responsible for the affairs of his group. When he was appointed he received insignia of office and rode a horse, an activity formerly denied him and all others not endowed with *nam*. On the other hand, *nam* contained no element of *tengasobundo*, since a political chief might exercise the functions of an Earth priest only if he was ritually invested with this right upon his accession to office. Among the Mossi it was rare to find this doubling of roles, though it was of common occurrence among other Gur-speaking peoples.

Each of the two social categories fulfilled important and complementary functions within the global society. Were the king and the *nakombse* to fail in the execution of their *filiga* (New Year rites) in Yatenga, the *tengabisi* would have felt that their association with those invisible powers controlling the rain and harvest had been undermined. And were the *tengabisi* not to conduct the important *bega* ritual which led the spirit of the millet across the kingdom, the king and the *nakombse* would have felt their subsistence threatened. There were other integrating factors. The king made his presence felt at all important *tengabisi* rituals either through his agents or by symbolic prestations.

The Mossi Economy

The Mossi were subsistence farmers cultivating a variety of cereals, roots, and legumes. Most households produced enough for their own needs, but those which lacked sufficient labour were assisted by the village co-operative association formed of young men and women. This association (*Nam*, not to be confused with *nam* meaning political power) was organized along the lines of a state system; it had its 'paramount chief', 'ministers', and subordinate 'officials'.

Within this household-based economy there was some specialization. Blacksmiths provided agricultural tools in return for subsistence products. Weavers, on the other hand, had their own farms, but spent the slack season manufacturing cotton lengths, which were sold in all Mossi markets. In some Yatenga villages entire wards specialized in this activity. Before the French conquest there were few large markets: there were only six in the whole of Yatenga, but nine years later Captain Noiré counted forty-seven. This phenomenon could be partly attributed to the pacification of the country and partly to the increased demand for goods. Village markets, occurring every three days, assured the circulation of goods outside the domestic economy (Zahan, 1954). Markets were under the aegis of both political and priest chiefs. It was the *naba* who authorized the establishment of a new market, but it was *tengasoba* who sacralized the place by pouring libations on the market shrine. A market chief policed the market and collected dues on the *naba*'s behalf. This was not a tax, but rather a countergift to him for the benefit conferred by the market.

At the turn of the century, and certainly before that, the Voltaic kingdoms enjoyed an extensive foreign trade. To the south the network of exchanges included the Gold Coast, Dahomey, and the Ivory Coast; to the north, Bandiagara, Jenne, Mopti, Dori, Timbuktu; to the west, San, Segou, Bamako, and Koury. Bars of salt were imported from the north, kola nuts and cowries from the south. Horses, cattle, donkeys, and sheep were exported to the south. Copper bars and coloured native cottons came in from Oual-Oualé. Farm implements and axes, manufactured in large quantities by the Mossi, were exported almost exclusively to the south; slaves were also sent south (Binger, 1892, 1: 480–506; II: 50–56; Noiré, 1904).

One important aspect of the Mossi economy was the practice of making prestations to the king. These gifts possessed a symbolic significance which must preclude their being termed tribute. It was the chief's right to receive gifts from his subjects, and it was his subjects' duty to make them. Every *naba* and *tengasoba* received these prestations, but it was of course the king's treasury which benefited primarily. Any subject seeking a favour from the king accompanied his plea with a gift. During the New Year festival of *filiga* all the village chiefs and notables brought millet, chickens, and cowries to the palace, the millet being for the king's horses. The chiefs of Riziam, Zitenga, Ratenga, Boussou, and Niessega (independent principalities) each sent a child with a gift of a sheep and cowries. During the *kom-filiga* (a military ceremony) the four army chiefs (Oula, Kossouka, Lago, and Gourcy) each offered a sheep to the Yatenga king. Upon the death of each 'canton' chief (*kombere-naba*) and each provincial chief (minister), the king was entitled to receive their horse, a donkey, an ox, some goats and sheep, and thousands of cowries. The birth of twin foals was a happy event to be shared with the king by presenting one of them to him. The king thus enjoyed many material advantages, though we must remember the return prestations he was obliged to make on many occasions.

The king's revenues were supplemented by his 'clients'. Of these the main category consisted of his slaves, those persons who had renounced their personal liberty in exchange for the king's protection. In former times they constituted his greatest source of wealth. They were distinguished from other slaves by the terms *bagare* and *kanbonse* and were lodged in the outer palace at Ouahigouya and Ouagadougou. The former were of Fulbe provenance, the latter were from Ashanti.

Traders, whether Dioula, Yarse, Maranse, or even Mossi, must also be included among the king's 'clients'. Their security along the trading routes depended on protection, and the king accordingly levied a toll on all goods in transit through his country. We possess scant information on these dues, but they must have been considerable; Noiré gives some account of the character of goods exchanged in 1903 and a glimpse of the clandestine nature of much of the trade. The pastoral Fulbe constituted another category of royal 'clients'. Dues were paid in cattle and given to the king during the traditional ceremonies. Others, enjoying certain independence, were raided by Mossi warriors in order to obtain beasts for sacrifices.

The royal 'clients' were thus of diverse origin, and their status was the result of centuries of Mossi rule. The Mossi were past masters in the art of incorporating diverse groupings into their politico-religious system; they were also experts in drawing together all the invisible threads of the economy to the centre of their kingdom—the king. Indeed, the well-being of the economy was closely associated with the well-being of the king. The market, for example, was not simply a place for the exchange of goods; it was an area of security and order, the equivalent of the world. This explains why at the death of the king the peace of the market was violently disturbed by armed retainers from the palace. The market was transferred elsewhere and did not resume until a new king had been installed.

Mossi kings kept, through their market chiefs, an account of the country's wealth and the extent to which it could be drawn upon in time of emergency. In Yatenga a gift passed through many hands before reaching the *Baloum-Naba* (see p. 168), who received at the palace all prestations on behalf of the king. But payments were supervised by a complex hierarchy of treasury clerks, and there was little opportunity for any diversion of funds. Each king had his own treasurer (*Rassam-Naba*), who was responsible for the actual control of royal revenues.

The Administrative System

Although the king was the hub, of the political system, the Mossi state was a decentralized one, and the country was, for the most part, administered without any direct intervention on his part. The framework of the Mossi state system will be best understood if it is envisaged as a grouping together of five patrilineal groupings or categories (*budu*). The term *budu* is used by the Mossi for a collectivity of persons and things which share a common characteristic; in some contexts, and according to scale, it may be translated as clan or lineage. The five major *budu* are the *nakombse*; the *teng-abisi*, the blacksmiths; the *buguba* (called *tibsobandemba* in Ouagadougou), who are responsible for millet rites (see p. 166), and a grouping of Fulbe, Yarse, Dioula, and all others considered marginal to the functioning of the kingdom. From a political and religious point of view these *budu* differed in importance according to their origin and the degree of domination they were able to exercise over others in their area (Zahan, 1961), but only two of them have always played an important political role—the *tengabisi* and the *nakombse*.

Today these *budu* have an appearance of marked segmentation, but this is unequal. In Yatenga the *nakombse* and *buguba* are the least segmented, the blacksmiths more so, and the *tengabisi* the most highly. At the present stage of our studies it appears that the relative degree of segmentation has some connexion with functional importance; within the system generational depth confers primacy.

Any small section of a Mossi kingdom revealed a confusion of *budu* segments, each with the characteristics described above. But in this kaleidoscopic picture it was possible to delineate coherent entities. The smallest group was the ward (*saka*, pl. *sakse*); several wards constituted a village (*tenga*). The *tenga* was part of the 'canton' (*kombere*), which was part of a province (*solum*), which again was contained within the kingdom (*rim*). For Europeans these terms have spatial connotations, but not for a Mossi. The etymology of the words points to their true meanings. *Rim* contains the root *ri*, which means to eat; one may say of the king *a ri nam*—'he who eats the kingdom'. *Solum* implies the notion of ownership in its widest sense. *Kombere* signifies people placed side by side; *tenga* is associated with the earth in its mystical aspect, and *saka* expresses the idea of 'extraction'.

Strictly speaking, a *saka* included those men who belong to the same *budu* (here meaning a lineage segment), plus their wives and children; its head was always the eldest of the group, and he was responsible for the group shrines. He was assisted in this duty by lineage elders. It was rare to find two or more contiguous *sakse* who were of the same *budu*, although it sometimes occurred with blacksmith and *tengabisi* lineages, in which wards were grouped into villages, even if they were some distance apart.[4] In a sense a village was a miniature state, a political unit patterned along the lines of the *rim*. In each village one ward played a leading political role: it might be the ward with the longest traditions of settlement; more often it was the ward of the highest ranking category which had political precedence. Most villages might be assigned to one of three types: those consisting solely of *nakombse sakse*, those containing some *nakombse* segments, and those with no *nakombse sakse.* In the first category the longest-established ward ranked highest: in the second the *nakombse* ward took precedence and automatically provided the village chief. In the third category the longest established and socially superior lineage, the *tengabisi*, took precedence over the blacksmith and marginal lineages.

The village chief (*tenga naba*) and his retinue faithfully reflected the image of the king and his court. He had his 'ministers' and his pages, although in the Yatenga kingdom there was no *Rassam-Naba* (treasurer). He had his own tribunal and settled civil disputes within the village. He was installed in office at the residence of the 'canton' chief (*kombere-naba*) in a ceremony similar to that for a Mossi king. The office might become hereditary and pass from elder to younger brother.[5] Almost every village had a *tengabisi* segment whose head was responsible for farm ritual. Rites which concerned the village as a whole, such as New Year renewal rites, were the responsibility of both the village chief and the priest of the Earth, and were carried out exactly along the lines of the same ceremony at the capital.

On a higher level lineage segments were grouped into what the French have called 'cantons' (*kombemba*). The Mossi administrator, however, was not concerned with territoriality, but with groupings of human beings, the segments of *budu* dispersed in wards and villages. Tauxier (1917: 344) gets to the bottom of it: 'The cantons are composed of a certain number of villages, but one should not imagine that the whole of Yatenga is divided into regular territorial districts with all the inhabitants of a district subject to the canton chief. On the map, in effect, there is an inextricable interlacing of groupings, and it would be an impossible feat to draw an exact political map of Yatenga. Each canton impinges on others; frequently a village apparently situated in one canton owes allegiance to a neighbouring or even far distant one.'

The *kombere-naba* was, then, a chief of an aggregation of lineages grouped into a 'canton' or principality. He did not have to belong to the largest lineage; in fact, he mostly belonged to a *nakombse* lineage. This situation did not imply any wish on the part of the *nakombse* for hegemony over other lineages. All admitted that *nakombse* were ideally suited to rule, incarnating the best qualities of leadership. They were traditionally vested with *nam*. It is from this point of view that one should consider inter-lineage disputes. The *nakombse* indulged in inter-group warfare in order to validate the rights of the more ancient lineages to a first rank in Mossi society. The independence maintained by certain principalities *vis-à-vis* the central government is best seen in these terms. It also explains the autonomy of the Mossi kingdoms in relation to Dagomba, whence Ouidiraogo, the founder of the Mossi dynasty, and daughter's son to its ruler, derived (see p. 152). In Mossi ideology, autonomy was the privilege of the daughter's son; 'parallel cousins' were placed on a footing of equality. The formation of the Mossi kingdoms and their so-called 'vassal' kingdoms can best be understood in terms of this kinship idiom. Kinship regulated relations between individual principalities; it also regulated the relationship between them and the central government.

A 'canton' chief was selected by the 'ministers' of the royal court from among candidates in the lineage in which the office was vested. His prerogatives were numerous and important, since his authority often approached that of the king. He was, however, powerless to free slaves. For this reason, too, he had no official called the *Rassam-Naba*, since he formerly had no throne slaves (*bingoremba*) for whom the *Rassam-Naba* was responsible (see p. 164). This official, however, existed at the independent courts of Boussou, Niessega, Zitenga, Riziam, and Ratenga.

But if these were the principles which determined the organization of the Mossi kingdom on the 'canton' level, we are still in the dark as to the rules regulating the distribution of 'lineages' among the various 'cantons'. The French administration completely disrupted the system before it was understood, and it is unlikely that we shall ever have complete details of the exact composition of the Mossi kingdoms, of the relations between 'lineages', and of those between subjects and rulers. However, if we compare the 'cantons' and the *solumse* ('provinces') it is clear that the former grouped lineages according to kinship links, while the latter organized lineages according to the harmonious functioning of the global society. The title of *solum-naba* ('provincial chief') throws light on this subject. The French administration dubbed him a 'minister', but the Mossi term is *nensomba* (pl. *nensombanamba*), which means literally 'a person who is good (just, honest)'. The name nicely reflects the functional nature of the province (*solum*), which was created to ensure peaceful relations between heterogeneous elements in the population.

M

The 'minister' was the mainspring of the Mossi state system: his function was to integrate individual lineages into the global society. He had to be not only 'good, honest, and just', but to possess a profound working knowledge of inter-lineage relationships. Ministers were not chosen from *nakombse* lineages. The king appointed whomsoever he wished, and the office was not hereditary.[6] In Yatenga the four ministers were the *Widi-Naba*, the *Baloum-Naba*, the *Togo-Naba*, and the *Rassam-Naba*. They had well-defined roles at court and also acted as intermediaries between the king and his subjects. They were said to 'command' certain lineages.

The *Widi-Naba* was responsible for most of the *nakombse* lineages, although illustrious descendants of past kings and the successors of important military chiefs were exempt from this control. The *nakombse* of Dougouri, Rega, Ninga, Zogore, and Sogode came directly under the Yatenga king. A section of the Samogo also came under the *Widi-Naba*.

The *Rassam-Naba* was responsible for the Kouroumba, the Dioula merchants, blacksmiths, former slave villages of the Yatenga king, and the Torombe branch of Fulbe.

The *Baloum-Naba* was the intermediary between the king and a section of military chiefs (*tapsobanamba*); the principalities of Riziam, Zitenga, Kossouka, Boussou, and Gourcy; the Dialoube and Fitobe branches of the Fulbe, a section of the Samogo, and the Yarse.

The *Togo-Naba* was responsible for those villages which depended directly on the king—former capitals and royal mausoleums (Ziga, Binsigay, Sissamba, Rassogoma, Bougounam, Gourcy, Lago, Kossouka, and Somniaga), where the wives of former kings resided. In addition, all villages ruled by a priest of Earth, the 'canton' of Ratenga, and three *nakombse* lineages of Kalsaka, Tougou, and Bema, came under the *Togo-Naba*.

The complex nature of provincial administration precludes their delineation on a map. The four provincial ministers often exercised authority within the same 'canton'; occasionally the authority of the king and his ministers coincided within one village. In Ouagadougou the situation was basically similar, although there was one extra minister. Precedence at the king's court was as follows: the *Widi-Naba*, *Larale-Naba*, *Gounga-Naba*, *Baloum-Naba*, and *Kamsaogo-Naba*.[7]

In the political hierarchy of a Mossi kingdom the 'canton' chief ranked below the minister; in reality he was more important, since he was a veritable king (*rima*) in his own 'canton' and was often the descendant of a former ruler of the state. The minister, on the other hand, exercised little positive authority and acted rather as a liaison officer between the king and his subjects. Ministers were often base-born and could be non-Mossi (Dim Delobsom, 1933: 52). A recent *Rassam-Naba* at Ouahigouya was of Dogon origin.

In the course of history certain principalities had acquired a prestige which enabled them to cast off (sometimes by force, sometimes by peaceful means) the ties which bound them to the king. Although the French administration had reduced them all to the rank of 'cantons', those of Boussouma, Konquizitenga, Yako, Riziam, and Ratenga were formerly small independent principalities. The autonomy of these can be explained by the classificatory ties of kinship linking all lineages vested with *nam*. On one generational level all the collateral male descendants of a single ancestor are grouped together. Today, for example, all the descendants of the brothers of Ouidiraogo are designated by the same term used for him. All Oubri's collateral male descendants are called by the same kinship term as Oubri. Thus in the Mossi kingdoms we have superimposed layers of kin linked vertically and horizontally, a structure which elucidates the order of precedence among chiefs. It also explains why the Ouagadougou and Yatenga kings called Tenkodogo (the nuclear kingdom) *ba-iri* (my father's house), and the king of Tenkodogo is considered a 'father' exactly like the Dagomba king at Yendi. The same kings call the Mamprussi district of Naleregou 'my grandfather's house' (*yabiri*), while Yendi and Tenkodogo people call it *ba-iri*.

For *nakombse* the consequence of these kinship links are as follows. All the members of the same generation avoid violent dispute; even in the case of proximate generations, only the senior imposes his will on another. All kin vested with *nam* enjoy special prerogatives; this explains why the Yatenga principalities of Boussou and Niessega once enjoyed the same privileges as Riziam. They are all 'parallel cousins', descendants of King Yadega and his brother King Kouda (see p. 155). It also throws light on the relationship between the king and certain 'cantons'. The king grants special privileges to his daughter's son *yagenga*, classificatory or not, if he is invested with *nam*. He would never nominate any of his own sons to a chiefdom where his *yagenga* is a title-holder.

Relations between *tengabisi* lineages are no less intricate. Briefly, in the Yatenga kingdom the *tengabisi* lineage of Ronga (north of the capital) is responsible for all rites concerned with holes, caves, and hollows. A *tengabisi* lineage in Bougoure is responsible for rites dealing with fruits of the earth, mainly millet, while a lineage in Gambo village controls all rites concerning hills and mountains. For the important farming rites the *tengabisi* are divided into five groups, each named after a month in the Mossi calendar. The main role is the performance of the *bega*, an impressive ritual which lasts five months and serves to conduct the spirit of the millet across the Mossi kingdom as far as Giw (south-east of Yatenga). There the *Giw-sad-naba* has a trial sowing to obtain prognostications for the forthcoming crop. The spirit of the millet is thereby returned to the soil and the cereal is assured of renewed vigour. The *bega* originates in the village of Gambo during the month of the same name. After a month the rite passes to Ouomsom, a month later to Bougoure, then to Gourcy, and finally to Koundouba. Six months after the Mossi New Year sowing begins throughout the kingdom.

The constituent of the *bega*, which serves as a vehicle for the spirit of the millet is the yeast plant, which ferments millet beer (*bega ram*). The Earth priests use this beer for libations at the earth shrines. During these five months all the villages under the aegis of the priests of the Earth pass from one to another the yeast plant of the *bega ram*. The *bega* is further complicated by the *tido* ritual, which is the responsibility of the *buguba* (s. *bugo*) in the last month of the Mossi year. The *buguba* have their own organization and a paramount chief who resides at Lougouri. They are responsible for the 'funeral rites' of the millet. In theory each priest of the Earth has his own *bugo*, whom he treats as his superior.

Finally, as we have already pointed out (p. 157), the Mossi conceive of the relationship between political chief and priest of the Earth as that between two brothers, the former being junior to the latter. Both work within the same system for the same ends and without any conflict.

The Palace

A Mossi kingdom was equated with the world, and the centre of the world was the royal palace. At the palace of the Yatenga king at Ouahigouya the two major cardinal points were incorporated into the construction of the palace by the two main entrances. The east doorway was known either as the *pande-nore*—the door of force—or *bingo-nore*—the slaves' door. It was used by women, commoners, and strangers. The west door (*zanga-nore*), with its vestibule, was used solely by men. The centre of the kingdom was the *soko*, the king's sleeping quarters, whence the kingdom was governed. The *zaka-yanga* (east of the house) was separated from the *zaka tawre* (west of the house) by a north-south wall. The former was the domain of the women and contained the old women's huts and those of the young women, among whom the king chose his concubines. This half of the palace was associated with darkness, the past, and death. In the outer courtyard were the quarters of slaves and their chief, the *Rassam-Naba* (one of the king's ministers), and the king's blacksmiths and jewellers. Strangers, such as Hausa, Bambara, Samogo, and Bobo, also had their quarters there.

The other half of the palace, the western, was reserved to the king and his personal retainers. The latter were lodged in the southern corner. The king's sleeping quarters and the rooms of the king's favourites among the women (*rumnamba*) were found here. The western part of the palace was associated with the life and well-being of the kingdom: here the king lived and procreated, here lived the royal horse, an animal inseparable from the king's soul.

The outer courtyard (*samande*) was an extension of the western section of the palace. The west wall, which divided these two courtyards, had a special significance.[8] The outer wall was opened only once during the king's reign, when his corpse was carried out of the palace. South of the west door the wall had the following details: a small doorway, a circular mud hut embedded in the actual wall, and another small entrance blocked up by mud bricks and called the 'golden door'. This section of the wall was in effect the figuration and projection of the sun's position in its progress between the tropics. The first door represented the southern tropic; the round hut marked the equator, the golden door connoted the sun's zenith. The side door which gave access to the vestibule symbolized the northern tropic.

The outer courtyard symbolized the ever-increasing nature of the kingdom and the illimitable Mossi domain of conquest and power. It comprised all that the king had before him as he turned his back to the rising sun and, on horseback, gazed westwards. It was here that the king daily received greetings from his subjects. The image of an all-conquering king was in effect that of the sun (who rules the universe), daily spanning his world from east to west.[9]

The King's Court

The Mossi state was a constellation of minor kings revolving in the orbit of the supreme ruler. The latter's enthronement, his daily life, and his death were all occasions for elaborate ceremony reflecting the Mossi ideology of kingship. His functions were eternal; it was inconceivable to a Mossi that a king should die. Such an occurrence would presage the end of the kingdom, the end of the world.

The king's court consisted of a number of officials, each of whom specialized in some aspect of palace activities. First in precedence were the four 'ministers' or provincial chiefs, whose role as officials in Yatenga will now be discussed.

The *Baloum-Naba* was head of all the male servants employed inside the palace, including the king's personal retainers. He introduced visitors to the king's apartments and received all gifts sent to the king; he also handed out the food and drink which the king made available on certain occasions. The servants (*sogonekamba*) under his control lived in his ward when their period of service at court was over.[10]

The *Togo-Naba* was the king's herald and spokesman; he also officially announced the king's death and the name of his successor. Intimately connected with all matters of death at the court, the *Togo-Naba* controlled those former capitals of the kingdom which were traditionally given to the wives of dead kings. (The word *togo* is derived from the root *togse*—to imitate or reproduce the words of someone.)

The *Widi-Naba* supervised the royal grooms, and looked after the king's horses and those horses belonging to dead nobles. On the king's death he looked after the late king's saddle until the accession of his successor; he also led the king's horse to Gambaga to be sacrificed on the grave of Yennenga, progenetrix of the Mossi dynasty.

The *Rassam-Naba* was the royal treasurer and responsible for the throne slaves (*bingoremba*), who resided in special quarters behind the palace. He was also chief executioner. His name derives from *raogo* (male) and *saga* (beautiful). *Ra-samse* (s. *ra-saga*) were the group of young men who formed the *corps d'élite* in the Mossi army and were commanded by the *Rassam-Naba*.

Besides the four ministers, there were numerous other officials. The *Samande-Naba* was chief of the outer court and responsible for those retainers who were not allowed access to the palace proper. He played an important role during the king's accession ceremonies, and he also deputized for the *Togo-Naba* when the latter was indisposed. There were two *Soba-Naba*: one deputized for the *Baloum-Naba* in case of sickness, the other (a dependant of the *Rassam*) supervised the labourers on the king's farms. The *Bugure-Naba*, who also supervised the royal farm labourers, was responsible for the king's bodyguard.

The two *Kom-Naba*, one a dependant of the *Rassam*, the other of the *Togo*, were responsible for the children and wives of the king. The former dealt with the ailments of royal wives, who were treated outside the palace, since nobody was allowed to lie ill in bed or die in the royal residence—the centre of life. The latter gave shelter to royal wives during childbirth and cared for the younger royal children. The *Poe-Naba* came to the palace every seven days to act as judge in cases concerning the royal wives and pages.

The *Bagare-Naba* was in charge of the *bagare* ward, where the king's herdsmen resided: he supplied the king with beasts for food, feasts, and sacrifices. The *Zaka-Naba* was in charge of all sacrifices at court, and he came under the *Rassam-Naba*. Also under the latter was the *Saba-Naba*, responsible for all the palace smiths. *Bend-Naba* was head of the royal drummers. The *Raga-Naba* acted as chief of the market at the capital and supervised all other markets in the kingdom. The *Tom-Naba* was the keeper of the *tom-vadogo*, a small hole in the outer court filled with sand. Newly appointed 'canton' chiefs and those selected directly by the king appeared before the hole and placed dust on the head of the *Tom-Naba*.

Apart from these officials, each with his specific function, there was a large number of retainers divided into three categories. Firstly, the *balembiyo* or *sogone*, who were pages with access to the inner palace. The eldest, *sogonekasega*, was their head and, with the *Baloum-Naba* and *Zaka-Naba*, was guardian of the royal fire, which was never extinguished during the king's lifetime. Secondly, there were the *widikimba*, who were in charge of the royal horse; thirdly, there were the *samankoamba* or *zankoamba*, who cleaned the outer court and kept the king's apartments in repair. All retainers of the king were unmarried. The *sogone* dressed their hair like women and wore women's copper bracelets on their wrists and ankles.

In Ouagadougou the organization of the court was basically similar, but there were five ministers: the *Widi-Naba* and *Baloum-Naba* had the same duties as their counterparts in Yatenga, the *Larale-Naba* was in charge of the royal mausoleums, the *Gounga-Naba* was chief of the infantry, and the *Kamsaogo-Naba* was chief of the palace eunuchs. A remarkable feature of the system was the precise positioning of the dwellings of important courtiers around the palace; another was the strict protocol which allocated to each minister and dignitary his exact position in the outer court when they assembled to pay their respects to the king each morning. In this courtyard there was a semicircle of stone seats, and the personnel of the court was called *kugzidiba*, 'titled men with stone seats'.

Judicial Institutions

Tribunals were graded according to the political divisions within the kingdom. The lowest court was that of the ward head, who dealt with all cases concerning the lineage segment under his authority. The village head, with his 'ministers' and ward heads, constituted the next grade and also heard appeals from the courts of ward heads. The court of the 'canton' chief dealt with inter-village disputes. The court of a 'provincial' chief (palace minister) was concerned with disputes between the Fulbe, Yarse, Dioula, and others (see p. 160), and between these and the Mossi proper. He also examined appeals from the lower courts. Supreme judicial authority was vested in the king, although in practice he only gave judgement in criminal cases, such as homicide, and cases which proved too difficult for subordinate tribunals. He also constituted the only court qualified to try *nakombse*.

These five types of tribunals were constituted on the same hierarchical pattern as the administration of the kingdom, with no distinction between the judiciary and the executive. Since they had jurisdiction in all civil suits, the judges' competence was very wide indeed and only limited by the social ranking of the parties concerned.

Military Organization

European travellers have often recounted the warlike exploits of the Mossi, yet no study of their military organization has been made. There was never a regular Mossi army, although there were, of course, permanent military chiefs. All adult men were liable for military service and were mobilized in times of war. A small body of regular soldiers at the king's court acted as his armed bodyguard (*kambose*), maintained order in the palace but never went to war.

Nevertheless, a military substructure existed. The army consisted of two divisions: the infantry under the *Tapsoba* (master of the bow) and the cavalry under the *Widi-Naba*. These two divisions were distributed in four territorial districts at the four cardinal points of the compass. In Ouagadougou these were Méguet, Kokologo, Nahartenga, and Tuili; this organization was concomitant with, or posterior to, the foundation of the present capital. In Yatenga, on the other hand, the capital of Ouahigouya was geographically outside the four military districts, which were Kossouka (east), Lago (west), Oula (north), and Gourcy (south). Informants explained this anomaly by the fact that the four garrisons were organized like this in the time of Naba Nassodoba (1475–1505, according to Tauxier, 1917: 81), who had his capital at Oumsom, a village now situated in the centre of the military district. Later the capital was removed to the north-east.

A *tapsoba* lived either in one of the four military strongholds or in a separate village; at all events, he was forbidden to have his headquarters in the capital. The *tapsoba* of Ouahigouya resided at Oula. He was ritually put to death at the end of three years' office. The infantry was composed of archers and of musketeers (originally from Ashanti). During mobilization the *tapsobanamba* led the archers, musketeers, and cavalry, although the latter were directly controlled by the *Widi-Naba* at the capital. Other chiefs provided warriors. The *tapsoba* of Oula became commander-in-chief of the entire army in the field and was assisted by three other *tapsobanamba*.

In action the infantry were placed in the centre of the combined forces under the *Samade-Naba*. In Yatenga there were eleven sections: the gunbearers' section was commanded by the *Bugure-Naba* (chief of the powder); the ten other sections were commanded by the two *Kom-Naba* (chiefs of young men), the two *Soba-Naba* (chiefs of Bobo), the *Kom-Naba* and the *Samade-Naba* of Ziga, the *Kom-Naba* and *Samade-Naba* of Binsigay, and the *Kom-Naba* and *Samade-Naba* of Sissimba. These last three towns were former capitals of the kingdom. The cavalry under the *Widi-Naba* and his adjutant, the chief of the royal stables, was placed on the two wings of the infantry. Army chiefs and captains kept in the rear during the fighting, protected by their bodyguards, whose role it was to prevent them from falling into enemy hands.

The musketeers and archers began an attack with the cavalry supporting the action and taking prisoners. It appears there was no commissariat; the troops either carried their own food or lived off the land, raiding villages they passed. Long sieges were not common. Most territorial conquests consisted of a military rampage to which the peaceable populations submitted with little show of resistance.

In Ouagadougou the organization of the army showed little variation from the above description, except that the *tapsoba*, commander-in-chief, received the support of four of the king's ministers—the *Widi-Naba*, *Larale-Naba*, *Gounga-Naba*, and the *Kamsaogo-Naba*.[11]

Royal Mortuary and Installation Rites

In Yatenga the king's death was announced seven days after his actual decease. Inside the palace the corpse was guarded by special officials and anointed with shea-butter and sewn into a fresh cowhide. The official announcement was made by striking a special funeral drum, the skin of which was split by the herald once the message had been relayed. Before the burial, the *na-poko* (female chief) was installed. She was the king's eldest daughter and was invested with royal prerogatives during the interregnum. She wore her father's regalia and might even wear his clothes.

This rule also applied to the eldest daughter of any deceased Mossi chief, including the Earth priests.

During the mortuary ceremony the *na-poko* immediately preceded the royal bier along the road from Ouahigouya to Somniaga, a village five miles away which was the necropolis of Yatenga kings. Only kings enthroned at Gourcy might be buried there. At the head of the procession the king's eldest son rode the royal horse, without a saddle, and seated so that he faced the tail. At Somniaga the corpse was given over to the guardians of the mausoleum: Ouahigouya people were allowed no farther. The grave-diggers dug two circular pits; ten feet down a horizontal tunnel was channelled between them and the king's body placed in it, reclining and facing east, the usual position adopted in the burial of all Mossi men. Beside him was a bar of salt, a jar of honey, and a jar of millet beer. Traditionally a king's wife and a court jester were buried alive with him, but the modern substitutes for these are a live cat and a cockerel.

The interregnum lasted a complete year, during which the *na-poko* reigned. At the end of this period the second funeral rites ensued. The *na-poko* was dethroned and a *kourita* (lit. '*eater of koure*') was nominated in her place. He was the carrier of the king's soul and was chosen from among the king's descendants: he lived in the palace and enjoyed special prerogatives. The moment the new king was elected the *kourita* immediately left the palace and never let the king set eyes upon him. He was usually made a chief of a distant village.[12]

In Yatenga kingship was not transmitted from father to son but from elder brother to younger brother; failing this, the succession went to the eldest son of the eldest brother of the dead king. Only descendants of the kings installed at Gourcy might lay claim to the throne.[13]

During the enthronement ceremonies the new king visited the three villages of Issigui, Binsigay, and Bogoya, receiving from the chiefs of the Earth those eating utensils he would use for the rest of his life. At the same time he made sacrifices at the shrines of the founder of the present capital. The final ceremony took place at Gourcy three years later. Arriving at the town, the king and his suite mimed an assault on the walls, thus symbolizing his accession to power. The king-elect was placed on the royal stone, underwent a ritual of segregation from ordinary mortals, and received his regalia. For his return to Ouahigouya, he was given wives and personal retainers. Surrounded by the nucleus of his household the king—a creature apart, a sun—arrived at his capital, which he would never again leave during his lifetime.

The rituals of the royal court were elaborate, but only one—the New Year rite of renewal called *basga* in Ouagadougou—will be described here. It corresponded to the *filiga* or *kiwgu* of Ouahigouya and occurred at the time of the winter solstice.

Basga derived from a word meaning separation or desertion, and the rites marked the separation of the old year from the new. In Mossi ideology the dead year was also associated with their ancestors, and thus constituted a cult of the dead. The winter solstice also coincided with the millet harvest, and the ceremony of *basga* thus celebrated the death of the millet. It was through libations of millet beer that the Mossi communicated with their ancestors, and none of the new season's crop might be used until it had been 'tasted' by the ancestors. Closely associated with the *basga* was the idea of renewal. The festival began with the return of the sun from the south to the north tropic. All paths leading to the palace were cleared, huts in the outer court were repaired, and 220 sheaves of millet were brought for presentation to the king. During this time the king played a minor role in the *basga*. This was significant, since the sun's path had first to be opened for the king—that other sun—in order to launch him towards the renewal of his kingdom and the world. During the next stage of the *basga* the king appeared to abandon his palace. Three days before the public festivities which marked the conclusion of the *basga* he left his palace and spent the first night with the *Samada-Naba*, returning to the palace before sunrise. The second night he spent in the *Gounga-Naba*'s quarters, the third with the *Bagre-Naba* (who corresponded to the *Zaka-Naba* of Yatenga). The next day he returned to the palace and performed the important sacrifice in which he himself stabbed the victim and uttered the ritual formulae. The places where the king slept during this ritual were envisaged as three cardinal points, with the palace as the centre. The three nights spent outside the palace represented the renewal of the palace, the kingdom, and the world.

The private, sacred part of the *basga* was now over, and the king's officials congratulated him on his return to the palace. He distributed food and drink to his household. Both the *basga* at Ouagadougou and the *filiga* at Yatenga were rites in the annual cycle which established the vital connexion between *nam* and *tegasobundo*, that is, between political and ritual authority. Through this ritual cycle social distance tended to diminish between the diverse categories of persons composing the kingdom; even strangers, such as the Yarse, Samogo, and Kibissi, occupied important functions at the court and enjoyed special privileges during state festivities.

Conclusions

Down to the present day such terms as feudalism, vassalage, fief, and tribute have been bandied about recklessly. The word 'tribute' has been applied to the prestations made to a Mossi king and viewed as exactions imposed by overlords. Patient inquiry, on the other hand, has revealed that these gifts always returned in one form or another to their point of origin. The focal point of this exchange of goods was, of course, the king. He also had his own sources of wealth, his farms and grain stores. Yet what was produced on his own farms was not for his personal use. Neither he nor his wives might partake of the millet grown there. This was reserved for his subjects, who in turn were expected to feed him. A kind of complementarity was forged between the king and his people.

Our investigations have only begun, and a complete analysis of Mossi social organization will be no light task. This is due to reticence on the part of our Mossi informants, and also to the rapid disintegration of traditional institutions.* Another factor is the infiltration of European patterns of thought into native explanations of the indigenous way of life. None the less, the smallest crumb of authentic information will go far to enrich our knowledge of these people, their neighbours, and their kin.

NOTES

1. Our earliest first-hand knowledge of the Mossi came from Joao de Barros (*Asia de João de Barros, dos factos que os Portugueses fizeram no descobrimento e conquista dos mares e terras do orienta*, Lisbon, 1552–1553, 2 vol. in fol.) and the *Tarikh-es-Soudan*, by Abderhaman es Saadi.

* Fieldwork among the Mossi was carried out by the Author for several months in every year between 1948 and 1958.

The latter work mentions Mossi razzias against Timbuktu and Benka, and Songhai counter-attacks which led to Mossi defeats.

2. Historians of the Mossi are not all in agreement on dates. According to Marc (1909: 131, 136), the founder of the Mossi dynasty (Oubri) appears to have lived about the middle of the fourteenth century. Delafosse (1912: I, 306 ff.) places him in the eleventh century. Tauxier, first of all, suggests the twelfth century (1912: 458 ff.), later the beginning of the fourteenth century (1917: 16 ff.). Recently J. D. Fage ('Reflections on the Early History of the Mossi-Dagomba Group of States' in *The Historian in Tropical Africa*, Eds., J. Vansina, R. Mauny, L. V. Thomas, London, 1964) also proposed the fourteenth century as the date of the origin of the Mossi, Dagomba, and Mamprussi states.

3. Among the Mossi—like some other peoples of Negro Africa—certain dyadic relationships between individuals or between groups, who constitute complementary halves of a social whole, are translated into kinship terms. Thus, the religious hierarchy between the priest of the Earth and the king is shown by the reciprocal use of the kinship terms for elder brother–younger brother. In the kingdom these two dignitaries are envisaged as having a mother's brother–sister's son relationship when it is important to define reciprocal rights and obligations of mutual aid. Legends accounting for the origin of the dynasty frequently use these terms as if the relationship were a real one, thus giving them more consistency.

4. In Yatenga, with a population of 700,000, there are approximately 800 villages (administrative units), thus giving an average village population of 875. Before independence there were 34 districts (cantons) with an average population of 20,500. Skinner (1964: 24), whose study refers mainly to Ouagadougou, estimates the average village population at 500, and the district at 22,500.

5. According to Skinner (1964: 56–59), in Ouagadougou the dead man's eldest son was in a favourable position to succeed his father, although any member of the lineage with a forceful personality might dispute his claim.

6. According to Tauxier (1912: 575), the *Moro-Naba* (king) of Ouagadougou chose the worthiest of the minister's close kin to succeed him. Skinner (1964: 67), on the other hand, says that, except for the *Kamsaogho-Naba*, a minister's office was hereditary.

7. Dim Delobsom (1933: 63) records a legend which states that the *Gounga-Naba* was originally prime minister. For reasons of amity he proposed to King Oubri that the two commoners, the *Widi-Naba* and the *Larale-Naba*, should be prime minister and second minister respectively, retaining for himself the rank of third minister.

8. The description which follows refers to the palace at Ouagadougou where architectural details still exist.

9. The king made two appearances in the morning. In the first he was dressed in red, wore a silver bonnet, held a golden forked stick, and was seated in front of the 'golden door'. He represented the red sun of the rain season, and the ceremony symbolized the sun's path from the north to the south tropic. In his second appearance he was dressed in white, symbolizing the dry season sun. He was seated in front of the circular hut embedded in the wall, and his appearance represented the sun's path from the south to the north tropic.

10. The minister's name probably derived from the root *bagh*, from which comes the word for dog, *bagha*. Among the Dagomba there is a functionary called *balo na*, which, according to Rattray, is derived from *ba logo*, dog (Rattray, *Tribes of the Ashanti Hinterland*, Oxford, 1932, Vol. 2: 572). The derivation given by Bellot seems incorrect (1949: 63). The *Baloum-Naba*'s ward at Ouahigouya is called *balogo*.

11. For further details on this subject, see Skinner (1964: 93 ff.).

12. According to Dim Delobsom (1933: 126) and Skinner (1964: 51), the *kourita* was the dead king's child. Dim Delobsom refers to several chiefdoms with *kourita*-chiefs: Boulsa, Poa, and Koupela. The *kourita* institution resembles that of the Dogon *nani*. It is of immense interest for the understanding of the chiefdom, whose major characteristic is its perennity.

13. In Ouagadougou succession to the throne went from father to son. This principle, however, was not absolutely rigorous, since, as Skinner observed (1964: 36–7), one-third at least of the thirty-four kings succeeded their brothers. Tauxier (1912: 576) holds that the rule of lineal succession, which is now in force on all levels of Mossi chiefdoms, replaced the 'true patriarchal principle' of collateral succession after the conquest of Dagomba and Mossi by the original invaders.

REFERENCES

Bellot, R. P.	1949	'Etude sur la toponymie des quartiers de Ouagadougou', *Notes Africaines*, No. 42, Avril.
Binger, L. G.	1892	*Du Niger au Golfe de Guinée*. 2 vols. Paris.
Delafosse, M.	1912	*Haut-Sénégal-Niger*. 2 vols. Paris.
Delobsom, A. A. Dim	1933	*L'Empire du Mogho-Naba*. Paris.
Marc, L. A.	1909	*Le Pays Mossi*. Paris.
Noiré, Capt.	1904	*Monographie du Cercle de Ouahigouya*, MS.
Skinner, E. P	1964	*The Mossi of the Upper Volta: the political development of a Sudanese people*. Stanford, California.

Tauxier, L.

1912   *Le Noir du Soudan.* Paris, Larose.

1917   *Le Noir du Yatenga.* Paris, Larose.

1924   *Nouvelles Notes sur les Mossi et les Gourounsi.* Paris, Larose.

Zahan, D.

1954   'Notes sur les marchés mossi du Yatenga', *Africa*, Vol. XXIV, No. 4.

1961   'Pour une histoire des Mossi du Yatenga', *L'Homme*, t.I. No. 2. Mai–Août.

THE OVER-KINGDOM OF GONJA

Jack Goody

The study of indigenous African states has been held back by two main factors. Those European-trained historians who have thought it worth while to pay more than a casual glance at these societies do not always show much understanding of such social systems and become easily mesmerized by dates and events. On the other hand, those sociologists who have made a serious attempt to collect from contemporary sources the material necessary to analyse these societies and their change over time are often led astray by their involvement in the present. For when a state succumbs to conquest by a colonizing power the governmental system immediately undergoes a serious of rapid and far-reaching changes, in function, if not form. So that fieldwork in a post-conquest state, carried out along strictly synchronic, functionalist lines, will give a picture of a kingdom very different from that of earlier times.

A study of the dynasty itself has always provided some counterweight to the tendency of fieldworkers to make assumptions of continuity, to project the present back into the past. The collection of royal genealogies and lists of kings has given some overall view of a ruling group existing, and changing, in time. It is probably in the fields of economic and external relations that the most serious discrepancies arise. In external relations, because fieldworkers have inevitably concentrated on the within rather than the without; in economics, because commercial exchanges have often altered as radically as government but with less noise.

Certainly one cannot understand nineteenth-century Gonja without knowing something of its external as well as its internal relations. So I begin by describing its position with regard to neighbouring peoples, the economic system, which stretched far beyond its boundaries, and the historical framework of outside contacts.[1]

N

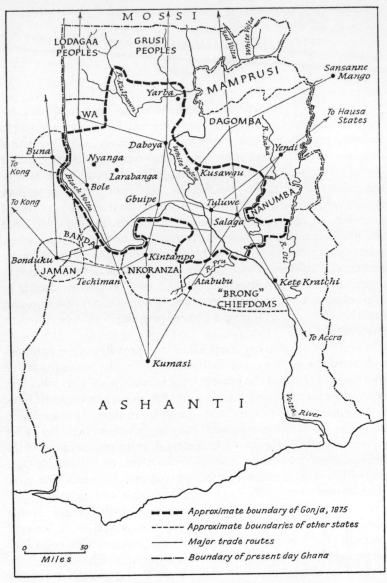

The State of Gonja and its Neighbours (1875)

Gonja and its Neighbours

Gonja lay to the north of the wide bend made by the Black Volta, as the river swings eastward from one side of the present state of Ghana to the other (p. 180). The kingdom stretched across the full width of the country, some 200 miles in all, and rarely less than 90 miles in depth. It covered a total area of some 15,000 square miles, which in 1960 had a population of 118,000. Immediately tò the north-east lay the kingdom of Dagomba and, beyond that again, those of Mamprusi and Mossi—all ruled by branches of the same dynasty; to the east was the Nanumba State, a smaller offshoot of the Dagomba group. South of Nanumba, on the hilly eastern flank of Gonja, there were a number of small-scale, stateless societies, whose inhabitants spoke an array of different languages belonging to the Guang, Gur, and the Togo Remnant families. In the south-east was the Guang-speaking town of Krachi; formerly an important market and religious centre, it commanded access to the upper reaches of the Volta (particularly important in the Ada salt trade from the coast) and engaged in extensive commerce with the countries of the savannah zone.

To the south lay Ashanti, separated not only by the River Volta but also by a *cordon sanitaire* of almost uninhabited country. While there are some physical causes for this 'desert of Ghofe', its emptiness is also a testimony to the effectiveness of the Ashanti armies and a reminder that the economy of many kingdoms of West Africa, Nupe, and Hausa, as well as Ashanti, was bolstered by trade in human as well as material goods, and by production based on a kind of plantation slavery. To the south-west lay the market towns of Banda and Bonduku, Wenchi and Kintampo, which were either anciently established or successors to older towns, such as the legendary Begho. These forest margins formed the key area in the exchange of Ashanti gold and kola nuts with the products of the Niger bend—the region of the great medieval empires of Ghana, Mali, and the other states centred on towns such as Timbuktu, Djenne, Segou, and Gao. For it was here in the gap between the Volta and the forest that primary products from the south were exchanged for the salt and manufactured goods brought down by the trans-Saharan caravans. As a result of trade and conquest, the population of the Banda area became very mixed; and it was probably through here (or somewhat to the north) that the ruling elements of Gonja came on their journey from Mande.

The western boundary of Gonja was formed by the Black Volta. Across the river lay the small state of Buna, of Mande and Dagomba origin, set amidst a number of non-centralized, Gur-speaking peoples, such as the Lobi and the Kulango. To the north-west there was the state of Wa, another offshoot of the Dagomba kingdom. And between Wa and Dagomba lay a belt of stateless tribes, speaking languages of the Gur group (mainly Grusi but also Mossi languages) that stretched from the LoDagaa in the west, astride the Black Volta, to the Tallensi in the east, close to the White Volta. Like similar peoples of the Ashanti hinterland, their social organization is marked by strong patrilineal descent groups and parishes under the ritual control of an Earth priest.

The distribution of state and stateless societies was of fundamental importance to Gonja. The states represented an ever-present threat. Those to the north could be met by equal force and, although there were both victories and defeats, a rough balance of power existed between Gonja, Dagomba, Wa, and the other states of the Mossi group. They had similar weapons, similar military organization, and the co-operation of all was required in maintaining the trade-routes on which an important sector of their economy depended. But to the south the situation was very different. The Ashanti controlled the routes to the coast, and hence the supplies of European guns and powder. Because they refused to allow these goods to pass beyond their territory, their northern neighbours were at their mercy. After a successful expedition in 1744, eastern Gonja and Dagomba were held to pay an annual tribute to the Ashanti, who kept representatives in the main trading towns of Salaga and Yendi. Their interests were in the collection of tribute (mainly in slaves) and in trade with the Hausa (mainly in kola, cloth, and livestock).

The non-centralized societies to the north and east formed a pool of manpower that the Gonja raided to supply themselves and the Ashanti with slaves. The cavalry of the savannah states was no match for Ashanti firearms, but it could easily dominate people whose only weapons were bows and arrows. How was it that such societies remained outside the jurisdiction of states with such armed forces at their disposal? Partly because they

occupied refuge areas, like the Togo hills, which were difficult
to penetrate. Partly because, like the Lobi and Konkomba, they
put up strong resistance and melted away in defeat. Partly because
the boundaries of states were of a fluctuating kind, since owing to
limitations in communication, the control of the paramount was
inversely proportional to the distance from the capital. At times
peripheral areas like Taleland were loosely linked to a centralized
kingdom, but the nature of the link changed over time as the
influence of particular states waxed and waned. And since the
base of the system was subsistence agriculture, the dynastic
superstructure could be removed, leaving behind a country of
viable farming communities. Finally, such acephalous peoples
formed buffers between states, as well as a pool of human
resources. These areas could be raided by parties of soldiers
without trespassing upon the rights of neighbouring states; they
formed regions of free enterprise for bands of state-controlled
warriors, whose prize lay in people rather than property (of this
there was little except food), who were then sold or used as slaves.

The Economy of Gonja

The towns of Salaga in the east and Bole in the west specialized
in trade with the countries of the north and south; in the centre,
Daboya, Tuluwe, Gbuipe, and Kafaba were also important
centres at different periods. Although Gonja lay outside the forest
zone, it was to these towns that many traders came to exchange
the live-stock, cloth and manufactures of the north with the kola,
gold and other produce of the south. Northern trading communities had been established in Kumasi by the beginning of the nineteenth century, but many travellers preferred to keep away from
both the Ashanti and the rain forest, and to transact their business
in the savannah towns. It was just such exchange facilities that
Gonja provided. The town of Salaga had a number of different
wards inhabited by different groups of strangers, some of whom
specialized in the particular commodities that formed the basis
of the external exchange, the Ligby in gold, the Hausa in horses.
Such trading was a very skilled business in this highly monetized
sector of the economy. And it formed part of a network of commercial relations that linked the trading communities of Gonja
with the hinterland of the states of Dahomey and Yoruba (which,
like Ashanti, controlled the European traffic from the Coast),

as well as with the great market towns of northern Nigeria, to which came merchants from the shores of the Mediterranean (Clapperton, 1829: 68, 75-6, 110, 137-8; Lucas, 1790).

The inhabitants of Gonja gained considerable benefit from the traders who came from near and far. It is clear from the account of early travellers such as Binger that strangers passing through the country were called upon to pay duty to divisional chiefs. This payment was a kind of protection money and, provided the charges were not exorbitant, traders usually preferred to travel in relative security through such kingdoms rather than run the risk of being raided in the country of their chiefless neighbours.

There was also much small-scale trading going on between the settlements; young men from the chiefly and Muslim estates tramped from village to village, carrying cloth, kola, and trinkets. In the larger villages were found craftsmen of various kinds. In Daboya the extraction of salt and the dyeing of cloth formed important activities. In the larger towns lived persons who spent more or less their entire time in smithing (often Numu), in butchering (often Hausa), in weaving, or in magico-religious activities concerned either with the local cults or with Islam. In addition, there were part-time specialists, such as barbers, and others, like drummers, were employed mainly by chiefs.

Despite the trading, raiding, and manufacture, the basis of the productive system was the hoe cultivation of yams and cereals. Gonja farms usually lie at a distance of one to five miles from the village. Binger's account of the region round Salaga shows the existence of farm encampments where men lived with their slaves. Slaves were found in other parts of the country too, and were owned by all members of all estates. The captives taken among the Grushi were not for export only; they were also an important element in the economy, performing both male and female tasks on behalf of the other estates.

The History of Gonja

The tale one most frequently hears about the creation of the Gonja state begins with the migration of a band of warriors from 'Mande' (usually identified as the Mali region of the upper Niger) some time in the sixteenth or seventeenth century. These migrants appear to have followed the trade-route leading from the Niger towns of the Segou–Timbuktu area (the termini of the trans-Saharan caravans) down to the gold-bearing areas of Banda, Jaman, and Buna, situated in the Ashanti hinterland. In this region, just north of the forest, were to be found many of the famous trading towns—Begho and Bonduku, Namasa and Nsoko, Bono-Mansu and Techiman.

The inhabitants of this mixed area included small groups of people who spoke languages of the Mande (Northern-Western) family and had long been settled there; farther west one finds other peoples who speak languages of the second main subdivision of the Mande group (Southern-Eastern) and who seem to be autochthones. But there also appear to have been indigenes who spoke Guang languages such as the ruling estate now speak; and it was possibly here (or farther to the east above Nkoranza) that the newcomers adopted their new language. And it was from here too that they conquered, perhaps were driven to conquer, the land they now occupy. Present-day Gonja was then inhabited by a number of small groups, speaking Gur and Guang languages, under the loose hegemony of the Dagomba and Nanumba kingdoms.

The Gonja invaders were accompanied by Muslims, also of Mande origin, and by some followers of commoner status. They established their rule over the autochthonous groups and created a polyglot empire that stretched across the confluence of the Black and White Volta rivers and straddled trade-routes to Hausa in the cast, the Mossi states in the north, and to Mande in the west.

The major enemies of the new Gonja state were the northern Akan chiefdom of Bono-Mansu and the 'Mossi' kingdoms of Wa, Buna, Nanumba, and Dagomba. In their struggles with these powers the Gonja were most successful. But in the mid-eighteenth century the rising power of Ashanti spread its dominion northward and established tributary relations over Dagomba and parts of Gonja that endured in some form or other from 1744 until the Ashanti themselves were defeated by the British one hundred and thirty years later. The effect of the Ashanti invasion of 1744 was to loosen the links between the eastern and western parts of the country. It was in the east that the Ashanti influence was most strongly felt, since their major interest (apart from tribute) lay in the town of Salaga, which provided an outlet for their kola to the countries of the north-east; the Togo Hills made it essential for traders to cross Gonja and Dagomba to get to Hausaland. The result was that some of the divisions lying to the east of the White Volta tended to look to Kpembe rather than to Nyanga as their capital. The organization of Kpembe seems to reflect this state of affairs, for, unlike other divisions, it has a series of territorial subdivisions, each under the control of a specific 'gate'. In this way it duplicates the form of the state itself and undoubtedly represents the point where fissive tendencies have proceeded the farthest.

The Gonja are acutely interested in their past, which is recorded in drum histories, in Arabic and Hausa manuscripts, and in oral traditions handed down from generation to generation. Most of these traditions are firmly linked to the name of the conquering hero, Jakpa, who is seen as the founding ancestor of the dynasty and the creator of the state. Particularly in oral tradition, all localities and all estates link important and marvellous events to his name. The tangled skein of stories that surrounds him presents the historian with an impossible task, but it gives a sense of unity to a scattered nation which had become highly decentralized in many aspects of its organization.

The Social Estates

This brief account of the history of Gonja is sufficient to indicate the existence of at least three major social groups, the rulers (*NGbanya*), the pagan commoners (*Nyemasi*), and the local Muslim community (*Karamo*), who form a kind of *deuxième état* comprising the congregation as well as the priesthood. In addition, there were strangers (*bfɔ*), many of them Muslims, and slaves (*anye*), most of them pagan.

In each case group membership is primarily determined by paternal filiation, but frequent intermarriage, combined with a strong cognatic emphasis at the domestic level (especially the widespread institution of fostering between kin), gave rise to a measure of concealed mobility. For the Mohammedans, conversion is a legitimate means of entry to the community of believers, but Muslim born and Muslim convert are distinguished from one another in many social contexts, and people always tend to regard the convert as a potential apostate. The Muslim estate (the local hereditary element as distinct from the wider community of believers) is divided into named patronymic units on the Mande pattern, and membership of these 'clans' often influences a man's role within the community. From the standpoint of the political system the body of Muslims is viewed as being recruited primarily on an hereditary basis.

Despite the greater differences that existed in the nineteenth century, styles of life were not markedly distinct from one another, except for particular individuals. Even then, the relative position of the three major groups could not easily be summed up on a single scale, since the Gbanya were interested in holding office, the Muslims in trade and in religious grace, while the commoners had a closer bond with the earth and with its animal and vegetative produce. Each enjoyed a position of some prestige in certain activities and not others, though in most situations the chiefs were clearly more privileged than the rest.

Moreover, the three major social categories differed both in the way they were composed and in the way they conceived of themselves. The ruling estate formed one unit of unilineal descent, all of whose members, both male and female, regarded themselves as descended in the male line from the conquering hero, Ndewura Jakpa, 'Lord of the Towns, Conqueror with the Spears'. The Muslims were divided into a number of descent units, subdivisions of the widely dispersed Mande patriclans (*diammou*). Membership of these units plays some part in matters of succession to Islamic roles and offices, but is of limited significance, except in the case of the Sakpare, who belong to the Mande patriclan known as Kamagte. The Sakpare claim descent from Fati Morukpe, the White One, who supplied Jakpa with supernatural aid in his wars of conquest. Just as the Gbanya fill the major chiefly offices, so the Sakpare usually fill the priestly office of *Limam* that is attached to each division.

The commoners, on the other hand, form a number of more or less distinct groups, each with its own linguistic and cultural traditions. The names by which they know themselves are specific 'tribal' designations, such as Vagella or Anga. But the other estates lump these groups together as *Nyemasi*, commoners. Such unity as they have derives from common submission to the Gbanya, for whom they are simply a residual category of non-Muslims, ineligible for chiefship. But the commoners are not held within the system by force alone. Marriage and ideology are also powerful factors. There is frequent intermarriage between members of different estates. Ideologically, too, the commoners are strongly linked with the other estates. Although the ruling group is not Muslim, many of the state ceremonies are in fact feasts of the Islamic calendar. And in these performances the commoners too participate; although each of the plebeian groups has its distinctive features, a common Gonja culture is to be found in the dances they dance, the songs they sing, and the tales they tell. Intermarriage and co-residence on this scale could permit no other outcome.

The Territorial System

The three major estates are found throughout the length and breadth of the land. The commoners, of course, are mainly concentrated in 'tribal' groups, the Muslims are mostly found in the trading centres, and the ruling estate in the divisional capitals. One of the important features of the Gonja state is the absence of any permanent concentration of the descendants of Jakpa in the national capital. The ruling dynasty is divided into a number of segments, each resident in one of the territorial divisions of the country. There was no primary dynastic segment of this kind in the capital, Nyanga, nor any but temporary representatives of the ruling estate, who went with the paramount on his appointment.

In each territorial division the primary segment of the ruling house was further divided into two or three secondary dynastic segments, which were sometimes identified with particular wards of its capital. In Gonja political theory chiefship of a division passed in rotation from one secondary segment to another. In the same way the paramountcy of all Gonja (the Chiefship of Yagbum) was occupied in turn by the heads of the major divisions of the country—although, even in political theory, this process was recognized as more irregular, as one of oscillation rather than rotation.

In the nineteenth century there were some fifteen divisions of Gonja (p. 189). Although nearly all were ruled by chiefs who claimed agnatic descent from Jakpa, not all of these were deemed eligible for election to the paramountcy. The eligible or 'gate' divisions were by far the largest in terms of population; the dead-end or terminal divisions, whose heads were ineligible for further promotion, were much smaller and often acted as sanctuaries for

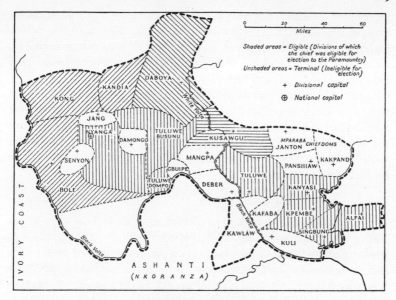

The Divisions of Gonja

men and women fleeing the justice of the other chiefs, or even of the paramount himself.

As the Gonja see their political system, any member of the ruling estate, any agnatic descendant of Jakpa, is a potential occupant of the highest office in the land. How, then, is this idea to be reconciled with the dichotomy between eligible and terminal divisions? The divisional chief who succeeds to the paramountcy had to uproot himself from his natal home in order to go and live in the small and distant village of Nyanga, the nation's capital. Some of his kinsfolk went with him, but the majority stayed behind. Moreover, in moving from his division to the capital a man was apparently exchanging an active command for a ritual and juridical office.

The dispersion of the ruling estate made chiefs reluctant to leave the place they knew best in order to take on the burdens of kingship in a strange area. The Gonja saw the rulers of terminal divisions as the successors of chiefs who in the past had refused the paramountcy when their turn came. Such a view is undoubtedly too simplified. But the reluctance is a fact, and so, too, is the dichotomy between eligible and terminal divisions. In the nineteenth century the eligible divisions appear to have been Bole, Tuluwe, Kong, Kpembe, Kusawgu, and Kandia, while Daboya supplies the present paramount. The terminal divisions were Gbuipe, Mangkpa, Senyon, Kawlaw, Deber, Jang, and Damongo, whose heads were spoken of as the Councillors (*Begbangpo*) of the Yagbum Wura. But it seems highly unlikely that they ever came together to form a council as such. In the first place, their villages were far from the capital; in the second, the chief of Gbuipe, who occupied an important position in the ritual system, was never permitted to see the paramount once he had been installed.

The Organization of a Division

A territorial division is thought of as a collection of villages owing allegiance to its chief, but it also includes the expanse of savannah woodland in which the villages are scattered and which their inhabitants hunt, together with the streams that supply their water and their fish, and that often act as divisional boundaries, watched over by the chief's ferrymen (*ntere*). Village populations range from 50 to 300 persons; the average density in 1960 was 7·5 persons per square mile.

The divisional capital is the focus of political life. It is there that the chief lives, surrounded by subordinates of many kinds. In some divisions the secondary dynastic segments are each linked with separate villages, and in one instance the capital moved from village to village when the chief died. But more usually there is no continuing association between a village and a particular dynastic segment; when a man is appointed to a chiefship he and his family go off to his new post. For a member of the ruling estate, promotion often means yet another move, either to a more important village or else to the divisional capital. If the title carries no village the holder remains in the capital and attends the chief's court. So Gbanya rulers are posted in most villages to administer their affairs, but these chiefs are always assisted by local elders, the Master of the Earth, and shrine priests.

At the annual Damba ceremony chiefs from outlying villages foregather in the divisional capital to pay homage to the chief. The town overflows with visitors, for many villagers go to join the festivities, salute their kin, exchange gossip, and to see their chiefs humbling themselves before their political overlord. This is a favourite time too for those living outside the division to come on a visit to their kin.

The divisional capital usually consists of several wards, each of which is associated with a secondary segment of the dynasty, with the Muslims, or with the commoners. The commoner groups include autochthones, refugees from Ashanti in the south, and nowadays ex-slaves from the north. The autochthones are represented by the Master of the Earth (*Kasaweliwura* in Gbanyito, *Tindaana* in the Mossi languages, *Heu heɲ* in Vagala) and his assistant (*Kupo*), who holds the knife. Refugee groups are represented by two main figures, the *Mbongwura*, the leader of the soldiers, and the *Kagbirwura*, the custodian of important medicine shrines, such as those at Jembito and Chaama; not all soldiers and shrine priests belong to refugee groups, but both guns (which are linked with the Ashanti) and 'medicine shrines' (which are moved about quite freely, in contrast to the static treatment of Earth Shrines) tend to be associated with outsiders.

Muslims have their divisional Limams, who participate in all major ceremonies. And though births, marriages, and burials of the ruling estate are different from those of the Mohammedans, a Muslim is always needed for these major rituals of the life-cycle. But birth is mainly a Gbanya affair, since it defines eligibility for high office, an eligibility which was made manifest in the cicatrices cut on the cheeks of every potential chief at his naming ceremony, seven days after birth. And although each member of the ruling estate has an Islamic name, the Muslims are not called to the ceremony; a messenger is sent to seek the appropriate name and returns with the choice of two.

Nearly all villages had their own chiefs; and the divisional capital contained many such office-holders, including ones with titles that bore the names of villages long since deserted. But it was primarily to people rather than to places that chiefship attached, and a title continued even when everybody had moved to another village and with the passage of time had become the subjects of the local chief. Such titles may still entail ceremonial duties, and they are invaluable counters in chiefly manœuvres.

Whether or not they have subjects, 'administrative chiefs' are of two kinds. Those of the first rank are members of the ruling estate, who may rise to the headship of a division. Those of second rank are the sons of female members of the ruling estate, for the daughters of chiefs no less than the sons belong to the ruling group. In their own right they can become 'female chiefs' (*Wuriche*), a role which came to the fore at rites of passage in both the cosmic and the human cycles—at the annual Damba ceremony, as well as at funerals: upon these and other occasions the *Wuriche* took charge of the affairs of women. They could not themselves hold chiefships involving jurisdiction over males, but they could (in their capacity of 'residual siblings') transmit rights to certain chiefships to their sons, even though these were not members of the ruling estate. These 'sisters' sons' (*eche pibi*) were appointed to the headships of various villages, but they had a more important role in the divisions, which was similar to the part played by the heads of terminal divisions in respect of the paramountcy. At critical junctures, such as interregna, it was they who took precedence in processions, while the potential successors played a relatively minor role.

The installation of a chief of any degree requires the co-operation of both the Muslim and commoner estates: it is their representatives who place the white robe over the chief's head and who admonish him on the duties of a ruler. And it is the non-Gbanya who are in fact the main custodians of Gbanya tradition; the Muslims, with their ability to write, produce histories; the commoners, with drums as their mnemonic, preserve in rhythmic form pithy statements about the Gbanya past. And just as all chiefship is referred to the deeds and descendants of Ndewura Jakpa, so to him too the Muslims refer the traditions of their migrations, and the commoners, often enough, the stories about their shrines.

The Court of the Divisional Chief

The chief held his court in the large round meeting hut (*lembu*), or sometimes in front of his sleeping room. This was where cases were heard, where all serious discussions (*malaga*) took place. It was the main forum of village life. Except in the larger townships, most significant communication passed through the chief. Every Monday and Friday senior men came to pay their respects and give their news; if anyone failed to appear, inquiries were set in motion. All visitors went to greet him with gifts as well as words. Apart from a man's landlord, the chief was the first to see the newly arrived traders, who told him of the state of the road, the happenings of nearby towns, and the affairs of the outside world. What was of great importance, particularly in the smaller, isolated villages, was his position as the gatherer and dispenser of information. The job of the chief was to keep the village 'cool', internally as far as disputes were concerned, externally with regard to strangers and the wider political system. He also protected his village from mystical agencies by means of his chiefly medicine and his knowledge of witchcraft. He was its most powerful inhabitant as well as the centre of its communication system.

The services he gave were repaid by gifts of goats and by the return of services. Visitors to the town, and subjects returning from their travels, brought him food or drink which he shared with those who sat around him (*mpotassibi*). His farms were hoed by the young men (*mberantia*) under the charge of their leader, the *Kaiyerbiwura*. The latter could be either noble or commoner, for in the category of young men were included all persons of any estate who were without office and of less than middle age. It was this same group who organized village dances, cleared paths, and worked in the fields of the village chief, who needed a larger farm to feed not only visitors but also his larger household of wives, children, and dependants. For in this the chief's sons were of limited assistance. The fission of residential units occurs at an early stage in the Gonja developmental cycle; some sons are sent to live with siblings of the parents, some walk about the country or attach themselves to other chiefs, while many of those that remain in their natal village live in another compound and farm on their own. In a rotational system the chief's sons are never his successors; nor under the Gonja mode of inheritance are they the heirs of his property; they have to establish their own position and their own *peculium*. In any case, members of the ruling estate are not always the most enthusiastic of farmers; their military past, the use of slaves, the chiefly tasks and virtues, all militate against too close a dedication to agricultural pursuits.

In addition, the chief benefited from more direct forms of tribute. From raids he received his quota of captives; from the commoners he received livestock at traditional festivals; from traders he collected transit and trading duties; from hunters he got a leg of each animal killed; fishermen sometimes presented him with fish; he received gifts from newly appointed chiefs, and a proportion of all ivory collected and gold mined. He did not, however, attempt to control market activities in the manner of Ashanti kings (Ferguson, 1891). The taking of judicial oaths again brought the chief some return. But these sources of revenue were not destined for the use of the chief alone; the rest of the community expected to share in one way or another.

Apart from receiving additional services and respect, the most obvious way in which a chief differed materially from his fellow villagers was in the number of wives—although here again a certain amount of redistribution in the form of extra-marital affairs often took place. Besides those he had married in the usual way, the chief's wives also consisted of women who had fled to his compound following an unwelcome or unhappy marriage, harsh treatment from parents or foster-parents, accusations of witchcraft, or because they were female twins.

But the expenses of running a large household and of appeasing the in-laws tended to disperse the wealth he accumulated in other ways, while the rotational system inhibited any concentration of property over time in one segment of the ruling estate. Moreover the dynastic segments themselves were gradually increasing in numbers at the expense of the commoner estate, partly through concealed mobility but mainly because of the greater appropriation of sexual services, combined with the marginally better care and diet provided for the children of a chief. And this increase in the ruling estate meant a proportionally wider distribution of privilege through the community as a whole.

The Judicial System: Courts and Sanctuaries

Gonja villages were small and compact. Many disputes were settled by the heads of the domestic groups concerned. Others were ignored until they boiled over into some accusation of witchcraft or sorcery. In many cases leaders of sub-groups would help individuals to reach a settlement. This was especially true of Muslims, whose customs differed from those of other estates and claimed the authority of Islam. Nevertheless, every Gonja had the right to 'seize the chief's leg' and ask him to give a decision. The chief himself could also initiate proceedings. But a chief's meeting hall was like the court of an early medieval king rather than a modern court of law; although it is convenient to describe cases in the language of contemporary jurisprudence, 'trouble cases' were only part of the continuing stream of 'serious discussion' (*malaga*) that flowed through the meeting hall.

The case would be presented by the plaintiff and answered by the defendant. Where necessary, witnesses were called for, either by a sub-chief or by an executive officer, usually the spokesman or *Dogte*, who carried the chief's staff as a sign that the order came from the proper quarter. But the judicial process employed supernatural as well as 'natural' methods, as when one or both parties took an oath to a major shrine in order to establish the truth of the testimony.

In addition to these local jurisdictions, there was appeal to the centre, and asylum at the periphery. Any Gonja could appeal from a divisional to the paramount's court; he would 'seize the leg' of the next highest chief and ask for a reversal of the judgement. If he failed, the payments would be greater, so he increased his risks both ways. This procedure of appeal sometimes involved the swearing of an oath; the formula used could refer to a disastrous event, as in the great oath of Ashanti, or else to the chief's mother. Directly or indirectly, the oath had to come to the ear of a commoner official, known in some parts as the Chief of the Knife (*Kasangwura*) and in others as the Executioner (*Egbangpo*); this man was in charge of the war medicine of the division, which also played a part in other transactions to do with killing, in witchcraft as in palpable homicide.

The capitals of the terminal divisions, and particularly the town of Gbuipe, were sanctuaries for people fleeing the justice of the paramount or other chief. In theory, no one could demand the return of such a fugitive, and this right of asylum is still vigorously asserted. Important shrines and their priests, together with mosques and their Limams, often had a similar function on a more local level. And the function was quite explicit: to provide a breathing space so that tempers could cool and the case be reconsidered.

For the chiefs of these divisions, the role of councillor to the nation is closely linked with the privilege of sanctuary. For like the Islamic and commoner priests, they are inside the state but outside the field of rivalry for high offices; they are both within and without, a position from which they can effectively influence the judgement of the paramount or divisional chief.

o

The Paramount's Court

Until 1944 the residence of the Yagbum Wura was at the village of Nyanga, to which he came at the time of his appointment to the paramountcy. Today Nyanga is a tiny hamlet, but it was probably always small. There is but a passing reference to it in early accounts of Ashanti (Bowdich, 1819: 172), and the first visitors to produce reports overlook the place altogether (Ferguson, 1892).

One reason for the smallness of the capital was the fact that there were few, if any, members of the ruling estate domiciled in Nyanga. The king and certain of his close kin resided there during his tenure of office. Even the local councillors were dispersed in the villages directly attached to the paramountcy, scattered at distances ranging from six to twenty miles. This dispersal was another reason for the relatively small size of the capital. The senior spokesman, known here and in some of the larger divisions as the *Nso'owura* (Leader of Dyula), lived in Nyanga itself. But most of the other advisers were heads of nearby villages, and commoners at that. Some miles away at Kokolassi, lived the Whisperer, who spoke advice into the king's ear and received his murmured instructions. The chief of another village, Sakpa, was guardian of the king's wives and of his eunuchs. The chief of Taari looked after a group of Muslims of the Timite section (*Mbontisua*), who claim to have accompanied Jakpa from the Nkoranza area when he invaded western Gonja. There were two other councillors: the chief of the now vanished village of Konkorompe was a Muslim of the Jabagte section, who are said to have lived in the area before the Gbanya invasion; and the Bia Wura, who is said to have resisted the advances of the Gbanya but then to have joined them, agreeing to guard their left flank against the state of Buna, situated to the west of the Black Volta river. Each of these advisers played a prominent part in the great annual ceremony of Damba. The chief of Sakpa went round the villages to remind them about the gifts for the paramount; the Whisperer supervised the distribution of meat; the chief of Taari collected one hundred kola nuts from his Muslims, to be given to the chief of Bole.[2]

Characteristically, this major festival of the ritual and political year was celebrated by divisional chiefs at their own capitals. At Nyanga the paramount, his entourage, and his villagers performed Damba on their own, although the other chiefs seem to have sent representatives. Indeed, I have been told that divisional chiefs kept in permanent touch with the paramount, placing one of their wives at the now deserted village of Zengpe to look after visitors coming from their area.

While the nation's capital was small and regional autonomy great, Nyanga was nevertheless the hub of the communication system of the state. In the last century, as in this, the Yagbum Wura received a stream of visitors who gave and gathered information about the state of affairs. Difficult trouble cases, particularly those dealing with chiefship, were brought before him (though as arbiter rather than judge); and here, too, came requests for help from divisions threatened from outside.[3]

The paramountcy was also important in the ritual field. While there was no complex system of national ancestor worship, the paramount's predecessors were always implicated in oaths of appeal. Near to Nyanga were sited important national shrines associated with each of the three estates: the Muslim town of Larabanga, the commoner shrine known as Senyon Kupo, and the royal burial place of Mankuma. The most powerful religious objects of the ruling estate, the *Alite*, were kept by one of the king's councillors; these two staves, which had been given by Fatu Morukpe, the priestly aid of Jakpa, to the first Yagbum Wura, were carried into war by the Gonja army, and one at least is said to have been destroyed in 1895 at the battle of Jentilipe, when Samori's forces inflicted a resounding defeat on western Gonja.

When the paramount died, the eldest son sat temporarily in his stead, while the regalia were taken in charge by the Chief of Senyon. The late chief's horse, his staff, and his sandals were sent to the Chief of Gbuipe, as proof that he was indeed dead. A time was then fixed for the major chiefs to meet at the capital under the Chief of Kagbape (near Gbuipe) and install a successor from among their number. In theory, the kingship passed to the head of the next division in line, a claim which had been publicly announced at the previous installation when he (or his predecessor) seized the reins of the new chief's horse and led him from the traditional place of enthronement to the capital itself.

Military Organization

The story of the acquisition and the loss of the *Alite* epitomizes the changes that Gonja underwent during the three centuries that intervened between the original invasion and the coming of colonial rule at the end of the nineteenth century. The Gbanya invaders were clearly an efficient fighting force. From their base south of the Black Volta they attacked the three main commercial centres in the savannah country across the river: in the west the Bole area, on the road to Buna, Wa, and the north-east; in the middle the Gbuipe–Deber region near the confluence of the two Voltas, on the road to Daboya and to the Mossi and Hausa states; in the east the towns of Salaga and Kafaba, where commerce was carried on with Mossi, Hausa, and Ashanti traders.

Gonja rule was established over this area by a powerful force that included cavalry and was feared on both sides of the Volta. The Gbanya still have the ideology of a warrior group. Their myth is one of a conquering hero; the regalia are iron lance-heads and, like other dynasties in the area, they had strong connexions with the horse. The rulers provided an élite force of cavalry armed with spears and swords; the commoners fought with bows and arrows; the Muslims assisted with spells, medicines, and religious grace.

But the very success of the Gbanya led to a weakening of the civil and military organization upon which their power depended. Their extensive conquests were divided out among the ruling dynasty to form a much looser kingdom where force was effectively mobilized only at the divisional level. By the beginning of the nineteenth century there was little central control of military forces, and the divisions appear to have made alliances and conducted wars independently of other parts of the country.

In the nineteenth century the main enemy was the Ashanti, and although they fought various engagements, the Gonja always suffered defeat at the hands of the gunmen from the south. The Gonja had commoner chiefs called *Mbongwura*, *Mbong* being the name for the Akan; here the word referred to the 'war leaders', associated with guns and swords rather than horses, and descended from refugees from the south-west, Grusi slaves from the north, or from other commoner groups. These groups appear to have been recruited in an attempt to counter attacks from the south. But even so, the fire-power of the Gonja was much inferior to that of the Ashanti, who controlled the European trade from the south and strictly forbade the export of guns and powder to the north. The chief of Ashanti told Dupuis that he and his ancestors 'owed all they possessed to the trade they enjoyed with white men'; 'the whites sold him guns and powder; he liked that trade, for his was a *war country*' (1824: 139, 140). As a partial defence, some Gonja made sporadic use of defensive fortifications and guerilla tactics; the people of Bute built a number of strong-points and claim to have thrown the Ashanti raiders into their laterite cisterns; in 1872 the chief of Daboya invited his Ashanti visitors to enter the meeting hall and then ignited the keg of powder on which he himself was sitting;[4] and when the British entered Kumasi in 1874 the inhabitants of Salaga took the knife to the Ashanti residents.

During the nineteenth century the Gonja engaged in other military activities. Various western divisions joined in alliances against the Ashanti: in the west there was a threat from Songhai raiders and a series of battles with Samori's forces; the east was attacked by Dagomba soldiers during the Napo wars. Indeed, around this time the danger of outside attack seems to have led to an attempt to strengthen centralized control, for the paramountcy provided a convenient rallying point around which military co-operation could take place.

Apart from these external wars, armed force was used in struggles over succession and in raids for captives. There was no national army, and it was only on the level of primary and secondary segments that military organization was effective. However, raids on the Grusi brought together men from different divisions, and the booty had then to be shared out at the capital. Aside from the enrobing of a new king, this was one of the few occasions when divisional chiefs went to Nyanga.

If some recent observers of Gonja have had difficulty in reconciling past glories with present status, the discrepancy is due to three main factors. Firstly, the military defeats of the eighteenth and nineteenth centuries. Secondly, the British conquest, which meant there was little point in maintaining a military force, especially when wars and raids were suppressed and trade was passing into other hands. Farming became the mainstay of the economy, a change which was far from welcome to all. Finally, Gonja had herself developed from a colonizing to a tributary and then to a colonized power, not simply because of a lack of guns and powder but because the expansionist phase of the early kingdom led to a decline in the military organization and administrative centralization. In the absence of improvements in the system of communication, more extensive dominions are bound to result in the diffusion of power, which leads to the fission of the state.

Religion, Rite, and Ideology

Given the autonomy of the divisions in all day-to-day affairs, given the dispersion of military power, given the comparative isolation of the capital, it is perhaps surprising that the Gonja state did not split apart altogether.

One of the major factors in maintaining a loose unity, even under the least favourable conditions, was the system of succession by which the paramountcy passed from one division to another. But rotation alone could have done little to counter the powerful tendencies to fission. What gave massive support to national unity was the ideology of common descent held by all the members of a widely dispersed ruling estate who regarded themselves as the offspring of Ndewura Jakpa. Not only members of the ruling estate but also the local Muslims stressed the Jakpa legend and provided it with the sanction of literacy and of a world religion. Even the commoners constantly placed themselves in relation to the coming of the conqueror. Only foreign traders (also Muslims) and foreign slaves remained apart.

Throughout the land, localities associated with the life of Jakpa are revered as shrines and sanctuaries. The greatest of these is, of course, his grave, which is situated at Gbuipe. It is the chief of this small division who has to be informed of the death of every paramount and who then sends a representative to the capital to install his successor. But he himself can never become Yagbum Wura nor can he ever see that chief once he has been enrobed.

The Gbuipe Wura is the most important councillor of the kingdom. His is a town of peace; it has no war leader; no guns should be brought here for the purposes of war; and the local segment of Sakpare Muslims provide the paramount with his Limam. In myth (though there are many variations) the first paramount was Jakpa's eldest son, and the chief of Gbuipe was his youngest: the former represents him in life, the latter in death.

Various sacred spots throughout the kingdom are connected with Jakpa and other paramounts. Near Kpembe in the east, people point to the ruined walls of the house he built of swish and honey; in the middle of the country is the village of Tarkpa, where he was wounded, the grave of his 'father', Manwura, and a shrine for his regalia at Nyangawurape. In the west is the royal burial ground. These dynastic shrines are often guarded by Muslims or commoners rather than by the Gbanya themselves, thus giving all parties a direct interest in their preservation and in their holiness.

As in other parts of West Africa, medicine shrines are found scattered through the country. These differ in the distribution of their altars and in the size of their congregations. The most important of the older shrines are those at Senyon in the west, Jembito in the centre, and Chaama in the east. In addition, subsidiary altars of Dente and Burukung, whose main centres lie to the east of Gonja, in Krachi and Siare, are found in various parts of the country. Of these medicine shrines, the one that Gonja point to most frequently, both in speech and in rite, is the Senyon Kupo, an Earth shrine which has won a national clientele. Usually Earth shrines have only local relevance, although similar customs attach to all localities. But the congregations of medicine shrines vary over time as altars are established in different places. Both sets of shrines are linked to the commoner estate, although Earth shrines are generally associated with autochthones and medicine shrines with immigrants.

Dynastic, Earth, and medicine shrines are propitiated at annual intervals on a community basis and irregularly by individuals and groups in times of affliction. Royal graves are cleared before the grass is burnt in November, while sacrifices to the Earth shrines take place when the rains come, and those to the medicine shrines are made at yearly gatherings where members of the congregation come together.

The Muslims have no shrines, but their influence is strong in the rites that mark out the cycles of yearly growth and of human life. As the Muslim calendar is based upon a lunar calculus, the Islamic year is out of step with the rhythm of the seasons. The major festivals represent not the phases of the productive cycle but of the Prophet's life. As in other universalistic religions, the liturgical year bears the imprint of the critical junctures in the Prophet's life; the main festivals are those celebrated throughout the Western Sudan: Jentige (the fire festival), Damba (the Pro-

phet's birthday), Akisi (Ramadan), and Dongi (when the rams
are slaughtered).[5]

For the Gonja the greatest of these ceremonies is the Damba
festival of Dyula origin and held here upon the day when the
Prophet was named, six days after his birth (18th Rabi'al Awwal).
For on this occasion all Gonja celebrates, not only the Muslims
themselves. The chiefs of outlying villages come into the divisional
capitals with representatives of the other estates. The commoners
provide a cow for sacrifice, the Muslims say prayers for the whole
community, and the chiefs do public obeisance to their overlord.
The medicines and emblems of chiefship are brought out and their
power displayed for all to see. Women and girls get new dresses,
dance, and acquire husbands and lovers. A large meal is jointly
prepared and offered to all comers.

On no occasion are the main features of the social organization
so clearly brought out as at this time of general rejoicing. The
institution of chiefship is reinforced; sub-chiefs are humbled
in their subjects' eyes, and the role of each estate is publicly
re-enacted. So, too, are the ideological bonds which prevented this
locally autonomous state from completely splitting apart. For,
when the meat and cooked food are distributed, the commoner
chief in charge calls out the names of various groups that make up
the nation, including its political divisions. 'People of Tuluwe,'
he shouts, and any person from that division steps forward to
claim his share.

The composition and unity of this scattered kingdom are also
reiterated, for participants and observers alike, in the rites that
celebrate the main stages in the human cycle. Rites of birth (or
naming) tend to be particular to each group, since they are the
ceremonies by which these groups perpetuate themselves. The
Gbanya are given elaborate tribal marks; both they and the
Muslims are circumcised and named seven days after, when a
commoner circumcises and the Limam supplies the proper day
names. Marriage is a composite ceremony, since brides are frequently taken from other estates; there is some ritual but few
transactions of property, although Muslims try to retain a religious
control over their daughters and wives by means of an additional
rite. It is death, however, that demands the participation of all;
Earth priest, Muslim, and chief are each involved, and while
every estate has its own idiosyncratic rituals, the general form of

the mortuary ceremony is the same for all. And on this occasion, as in the annual ceremonies, portions of food are not only distributed through the whole village but are also set aside for the other divisions in the realm.

Summary

The State of Gonja has undergone several transformations in the course of the last three hundred years. The phase of military expansion was followed by one in which the local segments of the kingdom achieved a large degree of autonomy. During this second phase, which lasted until 1874, some divisions of the realm became tributary to the Ashanti. After twenty-five years of uncertain liberation, the British, who had conquered their powerful neighbours, brought them under the control of the central government of the Gold Coast.

In 1933, under the impetus of 'Indirect Rule', the colonial power made a determined effort to re-establish the traditional political structure of the state for purposes of local government. This rebirth was partly effective because the Gbanya saw themselves as a nation even at the end of the nineteenth century when the powers of the king were low, when Samori was attacking from the west and the British advancing from the south. The idea of nationhood continued to exist under such unfavourable conditions for several reasons. Firstly, the country had not depended, since the expansionist period, upon a strong central government. Secondly, the system of rotational succession gave every member of the ruling estate a direct stake in its continuity. Thirdly, in rite, in religion, and in ideology the unity of the state was impressed upon the three main estates, whatever their position.

A state of this kind has some similarities to the continental régimes of the early Middle Ages. This aspect of decentralized power, seen as transitional between the disintegration of one centralized system and the rise of another, Coulbourn sees as the core of 'feudalism'. The position of the ruling estate depended in the last analysis on horsed cavalry, though guns were increasingly important military weapons. But other feudal institutions, such as dependent land tenure, do not occur in Gonja, and it seems best to avoid blanket terms based largely upon the historical experience of Western Europe. We have here a stratified kingdom, where the estates each have their different practices, which in some cases extend to the languages themselves. But the Gonja are bilingual in everything, and local cultures are supplemented by a national culture to which commitment, though it diminishes as one descends the political hierarchy, is always an important factor. Counteracting the centrifugal pull of the locally autonomous state was the centripetal force of a national ideology, reinforced by common rituals, by the sharing of food, the rotation of office, and by frequent visiting.

NOTES

1. This essay presents a first and not a final sketch of the political system. I paid several short visits to the country between 1950 and 1952, and published a brief account of the history of the area and of its language groups. My wife and I carried out fieldwork there in 1956–57 and 1964–66, and the following papers have been published as a result: Esther N. Goody: 'Conjugal Separation and Divorce among the Gonja of Northern Ghana,' in *Marriage in Tribal Societies* (ed. Meyer Fortes), Cambridge Papers in Social Anthropology, No. 3, 1962; Jack Goody: 'Rotational Succession in Gonja,' in *Succession to High Office* (ed. Jack Goody), Cambridge Papers in Social Anthropology, No. 4, 1966. There is very little published work on the social organization of Gonja. It will be noted that the maps, pp. 180, 189, give slightly different boundaries for the state of Gonja. The first represents a reconstruction of the situation in 1875; the second is based upon the administrative district of Gonja at the time of the Independence of Ghana (1957).

2. Just as Kpembe had a special position in the east (due to its distance from the paramount and to the influence of outside forces), so Bole did in the west. Unlike other divisional chiefs, the Bole Wura celebrated Damba at the national capital rather than at his own.

3. Hutchison recounts how a dispute between the senior chiefs in Eastern Gonja was taken before the Asantehene at the Odwera festival (Bowdich, 1819: 397). Relationships with Ashanti clearly varied from division to division and from time to time. The statements of Bowdich and Dupuis concerning western Gonja during the first two decades of the nineteenth century present a picture of a continuing struggle against the Ashanti, in a north-eastern alliance of states that included Kong, Buna, and sometimes Jaman (or Abron, capital Bonduku).

4. Lt.-Col. H. P. Northcott, *Report on the Northern Territories of the Gold Coast*, War Office, London, 1899, p. 13; Ramseyer and Kühne, *Four Years in Ashanti*, London, 1875, p. 231.

5. In addition, there is Achang, the Festival of the Guinea Fowl, held on 27th Rajab. And set firmly within the seasonal cycle is the Yam Festival and other more local ceremonies.

REFERENCES

In a general article of this kind I have largely avoided giving references for my statements, which include manuscript sources, including our field notes. Specific reference is made to the following:

Binger, L. G.   1892   *Du Niger au Golfe de Guinée.* Paris.
Bowdich, T. E.   1819   *Mission from Cape Coast to Ashantee.* London.
Clapperton, H.   1829   *Journal of a Second Expedition into the Interior of Africa.* London.
Coulbourn, R. (ed.) 1956 *Feudalism in History.* Princeton.
Dupuis, J.   1824   *Journal of a Residence in Ashantee.* London.
Ferguson, G. E.   1891   *Report on Mission to Atabubu.* London.
                   1892   *Report of a Mission to the Interior,* 9 December 1892, (CO.96/230, 2199). Public Record Office, London.
Gouldsbury, V. S. 1876   *Report of his Journey into the Interior of the Gold Coast* (CO.96/119, 5162 no. 2).
Lucas   1790   *Proceedings of the Association for Promoting the Discovery of the Interior Parts of Africa.* London.

ASHANTI GOVERNMENT

Ivor Wilks

Introduction

There exists, for the student of Ashanti government in the nineteenth century, an extensive range of documentary source material in Arabic, Danish, Dutch, English, French, German, Hausa, and Twi. The quality of this material is such that the main lines of the development of Ashanti government in that century may be established with reasonable confidence. In an Ashanti context, consequently, the attempt to reconstruct the nineteenth-century situation by inference from the twentieth-century one is unnecessary. It would, moreover, almost certainly be misleading, since the turn of the century was marked by radical changes in Ashanti government brought about by the imposition upon that country of an alien administration functioning primarily as an arm of the Imperial Government in London. It is unfortunate that such a competent and sympathetic observer as Rattray was confronted only with a kingdom in an advanced stage of political decay (Rattray, 1923; 1927; 1929). Many subsequent writers, assuming Rattray's account of twentieth-century Ashanti government to be equally applicable to the preceding century, have been led thereby to overlook the distinctive features of that state in the earlier period.

In this paper[1] I shall try to show that within nineteenth-century Ashanti two distinct systems of government co-existed. At the apex of both was the king, the Asantehene, with his court in Kumasi. The one systematized relations between the king and the rulers of the *amantoɔ*, the group of 'true' Ashanti chiefdoms clustered around Kumasi on all but the west (see p. 208). This system was a segmentary one in which essentially similar powers were exercised by both central and local authorities. A study of it led Rattray to regard decentralization as 'the dominant feature of the Ashanti Constitution', and to suggest extensive analogies with European feudalism. The second system was one which regulated relations between the king and the *amansin* and *mantiase*, the protected or conquered towns and provinces that constituted the greater part of the empire. The characteristic feature of this system was its centralized and largely appointive bureaucracy, capable of exercising a high degree of social control and of organizing the man-power and other resources of the areas under the king's authority. That this feature of Ashanti government has received little attention from scholars is due to the fact that it did not survive the superimposition of the British colonial administration at the beginning of this century. For it was precisely the centralized power of Ashanti government that had to be destroyed if the colonial régime was to consolidate its rule, and the colonial period was in fact ushered in by the arrest and deportation of the Ashanti king, and by the removal from office of many of his senior officials.

The Amantoɔ

The Ashanti are a Twi- or Akan-speaking people in Ghana, and are divided into a number of chiefdoms composed of dispersed matriclans (*mmusua-kese*). Of these Oyoko has been the most prominent, having become the royal clan of Kumasi and of a number of the *amantoɔ* at the time of Ashanti's rise to power. This was in the later seventeenth century. The preceding centuries appear to have been ones in which there occurred a gradual drift northwards of Twi-speaking groups (Bowdich, 1819: 228-9), a series of relatively small and unco-ordinated migrations probably in part at least an outcome of the introduction, via the maritime trade with the Americas, of new food crops. In the later seventeenth century political direction was imparted to this movement by the growth in power—largely through the importation of firearms from the coast—of a combination of matriclan segments that had come under the leadership of Osei Tutu, an Oyoko whose knowledge of statecraft and war had been greatly extended by his stay at the courts of Dankyira and Akwamu, throughout the seventeenth century the two leading powers of the coastal hinterland. By a series of concerted military campaigns Osei Tutu established control over the region around Tafo, an early market town of importance lying on a major north–south gold route (Wilks, 1957: 126-7; 1961: 12-13). Receiving the allegiance of such of the conquered as chose to remain, he built his new capital, Kumasi, only two miles from Tafo. The conquest and pacification

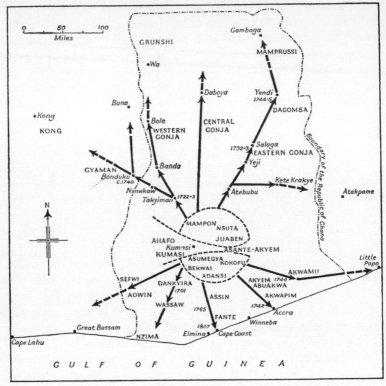

The Ashanti Empire showing Main Lines of Expansion

of the surrounding regions was continued, and a number of associated chiefs established their own towns and dominions, the *amantoɔ*, around the capital. Such were the Beretuo centre of Mampon and the Oyoko centres of Nsuta, Juaben, Bekwai, and Kokofu, none above thirty miles from Kumasi. Of the new Ashanti state Osei Tutu became the first king, the Asantehene. Its unity was symbolized in the institution of the *Sikadwa*, the Golden Stool, which, being without past, was regarded as having descended from the sky. Conversely, older pre-Ashanti symbols of political authority were ritually buried near Kumasi, 'because it was considered improper that any stool in the nation should be regarded as having preceded the Golden Stool'.[2]

The segmentary social organization of the newcomers, in matrilineages, was reflected in the segmentary character of the newly evolved state. The solidarity of Kumasi and the *amantoɔ* was conceived and expressed in genealogical terms. Bowdich, for example, was told that Osei Tutu and the first Juabenhene were sons of sisters—hence their 'common interest, preserved uninterrupted more than a century' (Bowdich, 1819: 232).³ Putative matrilineal ties were supplemented by real affinal ones. The genealogy in Fig. 7 illustrates the close links between the ruling dynasties of Kumasi, Juaben, and Mampon, the latter the most important non-Oyoko division (Agyeman-Duah, 1960).

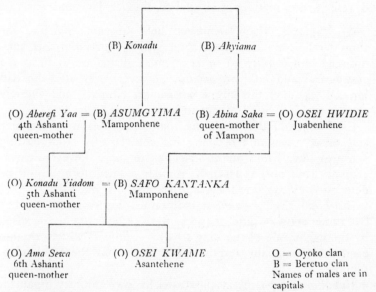

Fig. 7. Links between ruling dynasties of Kumasi, Juaben, and Mampon

The system of government regulating the relationship of the *amantoɔ* to Kumasi was first adequately described by Bowdich, who spent four months in Kumasi in 1817 (Bowdich, 1819; 1821a). It was described more fully a century later, when its main features were clearly unaltered, by Rattray (1929, Chs. xvii–xxiii). Their testimony is further supported by that of such later nineteenth-century observers as Christaller (1875), Ramseyer and Kühne (1875), and Bonnat (Gros, 1884). The chiefs of the *amantoɔ*—the *amanhene* (sing. *omanhene*⁴)—were, it would seem, *de jure* of co-ordinate rank, with the king in Kumasi a *primus inter pares*. Each segment within the system—

each of the *amantoɔ* chiefdoms—constituted a largely autonomous local jurisdiction that in many respects reproduced the higher jurisdiction of the king in Kumasi. Each *omanhene* had his council of hereditary advisers or elders (*mpanyinfo*). Each possessed, as Bowdich saw it, 'palatine privileges' (1819: 296; 1821a: 21), and each had, as Bonnat observed, 'Une cour modelée sur celle du souverain' (Gros. 1884: 188). The nature of such local jurisdictions, which remained in the hands of the matrilineal descendants of their seventeenth-century founders, may be illustrated with reference to matters of allegiance, finance, law, and war.

(i) *Allegiance*. Each *omanhene* held his own *odwira*, the annual religio-political festival at which, *inter alia*, his subordinate chiefs affirmed or reaffirmed allegiance to him. An *omanhene* could hold an *odwira*, however, only after he had himself attended the king's *odwira*, in Kumasi, and thereby confirmed his own allegiance to him.

(ii) *Finance*. Each *omanhene* maintained his own treasury and raised revenue by taxing his subjects, by stool trading ventures, etc. From an *omanhene*'s treasury, however, extraordinary (but not, apparently, regular) contributions could be demanded by the king for use in the national interest.

(iii) *Law*. Each *omanhene* maintained his own courts, but from such courts a right of appeal to the king could be exercised by the use of one of the king's oaths, a process which, though costly, automatically removed the case from the local jurisdiction.

(iv) *War*. An *omanhene* possessed his own military organization and was responsible for its mobilization and demobilization. The king in Kumasi could, however, require the use of an *omanhene*'s forces in the national interest, and could restrict an *omanhene*'s use of his own forces when inimical to the national interest (as, for example, in the case of a conflict between one *omanhene* and another).

Rattray lists other restrictions upon the autonomy of the *amantoɔ*, and clearly none was a twentieth-century innovation. Upon the death of an *omanhene* a death duty, *ayibuadie*, was payable to the king. An *omanhene* could be summoned by the king to Kumasi at any time. Exceptionally, perhaps, an *omanhene* might be removed from office by the king.[5]

The bonds that held Kumasi and the *amantoɔ* together within the segmentary framework of the early Ashanti state derived their strength from a complex substructure of interlocking economic interests. The system would only retain its cohesion so long as these interests remained common ones. In fact, in the course of the eighteenth century the material position of Kumasi changed so greatly *vis-à-vis* that of the *amantoɔ* that the king's continuing relationship to his *amanhene*, as *primus inter pares*, could be maintained, if at all, only as a legal fiction. In a series of brilliantly executed campaigns—Dankyira, 1698–1701; Takyiman, 1722–23; Gonja, 1732–33; Gyaman, *c.* 1740; Akyem and Accra, 1742; Dagomba, 1744–45; Fante, 1765 and 1807, to list some of the more important—the power of Ashanti was extended far beyond the area of the original settlements, and Kumasi, from being in effect only the senior of the *amantoɔ*, found itself the metropolis of a large and sprawling empire. The Asantehene, from being foremost of the *amanhene*, had become the ruler of what was, to at least one early nineteenth-century observer, 'indisputably the greatest and the rising power of western Africa' (Bowdich, 1819: 341).

The Kwadwoan Revolution in Government

Robertson, in the early nineteenth century, remarked on the difficulty of defining the extent of the Ashanti dominions, owing to the peripheral status of many districts, which were loosely associated satellites rather than tributaries, whether conquered or protected (1819: 177). To the north-east, Mamprussi was regarded by Bowdich as 'the boundary of Ashantee authority', though he considered its influence to reach much further (1819: 179). To the north, both central and eastern Gonja lay within the Ashanti orbit (Bowdich, 1819: 236; Dupuis, 1824: xxvi-vii), while in the north-west the Comoe river, between Bonduku and Kong in the Ivory Coast, appears to have marked the effective limit of the king's power (Bowdich, 1819: 182). In the south Ashanti dominated the Guinea Coast at least from Cape Lahu (Ivory Coast) in the west to Little Popo (Togo) in the east (Dupuis, 1824: xli; M'Leod, 1820: 140). On a conservative estimate, Ashanti had established its ascendancy over an area of some 125,000–150,000 square miles, from the southern coasts through the high forest, heartland of the empire, and far into the northern

P

savannahs. Within this area there lived probably between three and five million people.[6] Economically the territory was rich in exploitable natural resources, especially of gold and kola. Along ancient trade-routes to Hausaland in the north-east, and to Timbuktu and Jenne in the north-west, Ashanti commodities could pass into the entrepôts of the Western Sudan and some, by the trans-Saharan caravan trails, on to the greater markets of North Africa. On the southern shores of Ashanti the agents of Danish, Dutch, English, and French companies had established their numerous factories, and vied with each other, and with the northern merchants, for the trade of the interior. Through the ramifications of the distributive trade, the Ashanti economy became linked with those of Europe and North Africa, responsive to the changing patterns of supply and demand in world markets.

The size and complexity of the Ashanti empire in its developed state posed problems of organization of a quite different order from those that had faced the early kings. Government had to be developed *in range*, to embrace regions far distant from the original settlements; *in depth*, to control spheres of activity previously untouched by authority; and *in efficiency*, beyond the abilities of a non-professional administration such as the hereditary chiefs, *mpanyinfo* of the king, and his *amanhene*, upon whom, under the early constitution, responsibility had devolved.

In 1764 Osei Kwadwo succeeded to the throne of Ashanti, and initiated a series of radical political changes—for which reasons I shall speak of the Kwadwoan revolution in government—which were carried forward by his successors, Osei Kwame (1777–c. 1801) and Osei Bonsu (c. 1801–24).[7] The nature of these changes was admirably described by Bowdich in 1817. 'The aristocracy in Ashantee,' he observed, had 'until Sai Cudjo's [Osei Kwadwo's] time, always acquired this dignity by inheritance only', but

'the two or three last kings of Ashantee have artfully enlarged the royal prerogatives, at the expense of the original constitution' (1821a: 21, 54).

The king, he commented, 'raised his favourite captains to the vacant stools', and this process, 'since Sai Cudjo [Osei Kwadwo] pointed out the way', had been a continuing one. Thus Osei Bonsu

'cautiously extends his prerogative, and takes every opportunity of increasing the number of secondary captains, by dignifying the young men brought up about his person, and still retaining them in his immediate service' (1819: 236, 246, 252).

These changes, initially worked out within a Kumasi context, involved the subversion, by a systematic campaign of disgrace and banishment (Bowdich, 1819: 73, 144-5, 255), of the power of the Kumasi hereditary chiefs, and the transfer of the functions of government to a new class of officials controlled by the king and charged with the administration of the affairs of the empire. Instrumental in the achievement of the revolution was the *Ankobia*, a newly created para-military body directly responsible to the king, and deployable at his will. The two most senior posts in this force, the Ankobia stool itself (IAS/AS.2), and the Atipin (IAS/AS.9), were creations of Osei Kwadwo and Osei Kwame respectively. To date (1964), twelve people have been appointed to each, recruited largely from among the male descendants of previous kings, the *ahene-mma*, sons and grandsons of the Golden Stool. Three further stools of the Ankobia, the Anaminako, with ten occupants to date, and the Atene Akoten and Atene Akuapon, each with eight, were all created by Osei Bonsu. Appointees to the first two posts have sometimes been *ahene-mma*, sometimes commoners, while the last was until recently filled by promotion from the lower echelons of court officials (IAS/AS.42, 45, 21). Generally described as the king's personal bodyguard, the Ankobia had the crucial historical role of strengthening the ruler's position *vis-à-vis* that of the hereditary nobility.

By the middle of the reign of Osei Bonsu the preponderance of the old aristocracy in political affairs was completely shattered —in Kumasi, that is, though not as yet in the *amantoɔ*, where the *amanhene* maintained their semi-autonomous status.

A distinctive feature of the new bureaucracy was its appointive character: posts were, as Robertson remarked, 'in the king's gift' (1819: 199). Some appointments were made strictly *ad hominem*, and subsequently allowed to lapse; in this class were the expatriates such as the Frenchman Bonnat, commissioned as co-governor of the Akroso-Yeji area, and that of the Dane Nielsen, employed to enlist Hausa mercenaries in the Ashanti army, and later as envoy to Gyaman.[8] Usually, however, appointment proceeded within an institutionalized framework: there was, that is, not only a bureaucracy but also a bureaucratic class, from which most officials were drawn. Exceptionally, office was vested in a matrilineage, though without prejudice to its ultimate control by the king. Thus, the Butuakwa (spokesman's) stool, created by Osei Bonsu *c.* 1824, while always filled by matrilineal descendants of the first occupant, was none the less abolished by the present Asantehene in 1961. The great majority of appointments, however, were made from among the male descendants of previous occupants of the relevant office. Such posts are known as *mmammadwa*, son's stools,[9] and were vested in patri-centric residential groups, within each of which existed an accumulation of particular administrative skills, and the conditions necessary for their transmission from generation to generation. Rattray paid tribute to the 'remarkably efficient results' obtained from the 'generations of continuity in office, son learning from and succeeding father', and saw in the system a tendency 'to break down the rules governing matrilineal descent and to prepare the way for a patrilineal way of reckoning' (1929: 92, 118). In fact, however, the quasi-patrilineal pattern of succession to office appears to have been without effect upon the continued matrilineal pattern of inheritance of property, a matter of some importance, since only skills, and not capital, tended to accumulate within the patri-group. The bureaucratic class therefore retained its distinctive official character, and showed few signs of transforming itself into an independent and propertied middle class. (Wilks, 1966b: *passim*.)

The Emergent Bureaucracy: Finance

A key position in the emergent bureaucracy was the Gyaasewa stool (IAS/AS.15). The first appointment to this office, that of Asum Adu, would seem to have been made by Osei Kwadwo. Asum Adu was followed by Opoku Frefre (d. 1826), appointed by Osei Kwame 'in exclusion of the family' of his predecessor (Bowdich, 1819: 238). Subsequently the post became vested in the male descendants of Opoku, the present occupant being sixteenth in office (Wilks, 1966b: 221).[10]

The Gyaasewahene was charged with an overall responsibility for the financial affairs of the empire (the *amantoɔ* excepted), and was keeper of the treasury. He exercised a degree of budgetary control over income and expenditure through the machinery of the exchequer court, some of the sessions of which Bowdich attended:

'Apokoo [Opoku Frefre] holds a sort of exchequer court at his own house daily, (when he is attended by two of the King's linguists, and various state insignia,) to decide all cases affecting tribute or revenue, and the appeal to the King is seldom resorted to . . . Several captains, who were his followers, attended this court daily with large suites, and it was not only a crowded, but frequently a splendid scene' (Bowdich, 1819: 296–7).

An increase in state revenue was most easily achieved by adjustment of the general level of taxation—of tributes, poll-taxes, death duties, and tolls. Tributes, levied on conquered provinces and protectorates, were especially subject to review. They were, Bowdich noted,

'in some instances fixed, but more frequently indefinite, being proportioned to the exigencies of the year; indeed, from various conversations with Apokoo and others, and my observations during state palavers, it appeared that the necessities and the designs of the Ashantee government were the superior considerations, and the rule in levying tribute everywhere' (1819: 320).

Tribute was whenever possible demanded in gold. The poor province of Sefwi at one period paid 450 oz. annually, the rich province of Gyaman at another apparently as much as 18,000 oz. (Bowdich, 1819: 321; AGC, 1883: 127). The European trading companies paid what was in Ashanti eyes a tribute of 24 oz. for each of their major establishments. Areas without resources of gold were required to produce cloth, livestock, or slaves (Bowdich, 1819: 321). In the later nineteenth century Dagomba consigned to Kumasi 2,000 slaves annually (Cardinall, 1920: 9), and engaged the services of Zaberima horsemen from the edges of the Sahara to raid for them. Without such assistance the thinly populated divisions of central and eastern Gonja had great difficulty in meeting lower demands (Northcott, 1899: 16). Ashanti requirements, however, could be extremely accommodating, as is apparent from the Assin tribute that arrived in Kumasi on 19 December, 1819: 'several dozens of rum, liqueur, champagne, and some beautiful silk stuffs' (Ramseyer and Kühne, 1875: 107).

Poll-taxes were levied directly by the central government from the subjects of the Kumasi division proper,[11] and also—to judge from Bowdich's reference to areas 'taxed indefinitely by crooms [villages]' (1819: 321)—from any province lacking an effective

revenue-raising machinery of its own. A brief report on the system
as it was in the late nineteenth century describes how, three
months before the annual *odwira* festival, tax officials from the
Gyaasewa visited every village. With the assistance of the *odikro*
(*odekuro*), or village headman, about $\frac{1}{10}$ oz. of gold was collected for
every married man (?family head). The revenue was then divided,
three-sevenths going to the treasury, three-sevenths to the
odikro, and one-seventh to the tax officials as stipend.[12] From
time to time extraordinary taxes, such as an *apeatow*, to meet
the expenses of war, or an *ayitow*, to meet those of state funerals,
were levied.

The level of taxation on personal estates at death appears
likewise to have been adjustable. While a whole estate was,
technically, at the disposal of the king, and could be taken over
by treasury officials, in fact death duty—*ayibuadie*—was imposed
principally on assets in gold, the charge upon the estate varying
with the state of the treasury, on the one hand, and with the
status of the heirs, on the other. Gifts made in the attempt to
evade death duty were liable to seizure.

Tolls constituted the fourth major form of taxation. Bowdich
referred to 'customs paid in gold by all traders returning from
the coast' (1819: 320), and there is evidence for the existence of a
network of toll-collectors throughout the empire. Tolls, it would
seem, were not levied upon a merchant's goods, a form of taxation
certainly not in accord with Osei Bonsu's economic policies
(Dupuis, 1824: 167), but upon the use of specific sections of a
road, their payment to some extent offsetting government
expenditure upon communications.[13]

The Gyaasewahene was also closely involved in the management
of the public sector of the Ashanti economy, namely, in such state
enterprises as mining, trading, and ivory collection. Isert noted
the existence of royal mines, in which the king employed slaves,
each miner being expected to produce 2 oz. of gold daily (1788:
241). For two months in each year, so Dupuis was informed,
between 8,000 and 10,000 slaves were employed in one district
in the north-west of the empire, washing for gold (1824: lvii),
and Bowdich listed such activities as among the principal sources
of state revenue (1819: 319–20). In the commercial sphere the
Gyaasewahene was 'overseer of the King's trade' and 'at liberty
to send the trade where he pleases' (Daendels: 9 Jan. 1817).

Unfortunately, little is known of the ivory industry other than Dupuis' reference to 'hunters of elephants in the king's name' (1824: cviii).

These state enterprises were afforded considerable protection from competition from the private sector. Those producing gold on their own account suffered severe disabilities, for all nuggets— the most lucrative form of return—accrued by law to the state (Horton, 1870: 53; Ellis, 1887: 277). Rattray, likewise, remarked that only official traders were permitted to carry the early kola crop and so to benefit from the out-of-season retail prices (1929: 109–10, 187). A graphic description of state-sponsored activities before 1873 is given by Casely Hayford:

'It was part of the State System of Ashanti to encourage trade. The King, once in every forty days, at the Adai custom, distributed among a number of chiefs various sums of gold dust with a charge to turn the same to good account. These chiefs then sent down to the coast caravans of tradesmen, some of whom would be their slaves, sometimes some two or three hundred strong, to barter ivory for European goods, or buy such goods with gold dust, which the King obtained from the royal alluvial workings . . . . The trade Chiefs would, in due course, render a faithful account to the King's stewards, being allowed to retain a fair portion of the profits' (1903: 95–6).

By the reign of Osei Bonsu bureaucratic control of the complex financial affairs of the empire was highly developed, and the Gyaasewahene was generally recognized to be one of the most powerful men in the kingdom. Control was exercised through a large staff of lesser-ranked officials belonging to different *fekuo* or departments. The Great Chest itself, which was kept in the palace, was the responsibility of the Sana *fekuo*, headed by the Sanahene. The Sana stool was a *mmamma-dwa* (IAS/AS.41). Under the Sanahene were officials concerned with the actual payments into, and out of, the Chest, the *fotuosanfo*, cashiers or 'weighers', and others responsible for the collection of tributes and taxes, the *towgyefo* and *nsumgyefo* (Wilks, 1966b: 222).

The organization of state trading was the function of the Bata *fekuo*, created out of various older groups, including hornblowers, *asokwafo*, and drummers, *akyeremadefo*. Its head was the Batahene, appointed by the king to the Gyaasewa organization, but details of the structure of this *fekuo* are not easily recoverable, the organization having fallen into disuse. More is known, however, of the *nkwansrafo*, the road wardens, an organization essential to the protection of state trade. Posts manned by these officials of the king are known to have been established at numerous points on all the main highways. They exercised a general control over immigration and over the passage of traders—whether public or private—and a specific control over the movement of certain commodities, such as arms and ammunition (Lonsdale, 1882: 79; Gros, 1884: 178).

Essential for the efficient management of financial affairs was the development of a satisfactory records system. Under the Gyaasewahene Opoku Frefre traditional methods of accounting in cowries were still in use, and man-power statistics, important both for taxation and military purposes, were also 'ascertained or preserved in cowries or coin' (Bowdich, 1819: 296, 300). The king's desire to develop an Arabic chancery, however, was remarked upon (Bowdich, 1819: 232; Lee, 1835: 174). Osei Bonsu brought into his service an increasing number of literate Muslims, invested with administrative powers, and also sent members of his household to the Arabic school run by the *shaykh* of the Kumasi Muslims. By 1817 Opoku Frefre himself employed a Muslim secretary, formerly of Oyo, and records of the decisions of the exchequer court seem to have been kept in Arabic (Wilks, 1966a: 328–9).

The Emergent Bureaucracy: the Political Service

It was, Dupuis wrote of Osei Bonsu, 'a maxim associated with the religion he professed, never to appeal to the sword while a path lay open for negociation' (1824: 225–6). The course of Ashanti history in the nineteenth century—not least in the sphere of Anglo-Ashanti relations—bears witness to the lengthy and often costly negotiations that the Ashanti kings felt obliged to conduct before resorting to the use of force. Direction of such negotiations was the function of the political service, the higher levels of which were filled mainly by *akyeame*, spokesmen or 'linguists', and the lower levels by officials drawn from such groups as the *afonasoafo*, the sword-bearers.

The work of this service, however, was not concerned solely with arbitration and conciliation. When the deployment of an army became necessary, whether as an internal security force against rebellious subjects or as a defence force against an external enemy, responsibility for the subsequent settlement fell upon the political service. Thus Bowdich noted:

'one of the king's linguists always accompanies an army of any consequence, to whom all the politics of war are entrusted, and whose talent and intelligence in negotiating, are expected to mature the fruits of the military genius of the generals, and to re-imburse the expense of the war by heavy fines and contributions' (1819: 298).

The growth of the political service followed much the same course as that of other sections of the bureaucracy. The traditional head of the spokesmen, the Domakwaihene, occupies a matrilineal stool, the origin of which reaches back to the early days of the kingdom (IAS/AS.43). During the reign of Osei Kwadwo the Domakwaihene appears to have been forced into semi-retirement: retaining his status, he ceased to play any very active part in the affairs of government.[14] A new linguist was appointed by Osei Kwadwo 'to represent the Domakwaihene at court'. This post became known as the Gyebi and Banahene stool: it is *mmammadwa*. Its second occupant, Owusu Banahene, was killed at Katamanso in 1826 (IAS/AS.46). Senior to the Gyebi and Banahene stool, however, were those occupied at the time of Bowdich by Adusei Kyakya, Agyei, Kwesi Kankam, and Oti Panyin, described as first, second, third, and fourth linguists respectively. All belonged to the new administrative class. Kankam (d. 1826) was second occupant of the Akankade stool in succession to his father, Adu Twum. The post has since been held, with one exception, by male descendants of Adu Twum (IAS/AS.75). Oti Panyin, similarly, was second occupant of the Boakye Yam stool, in succession to his father Boakye Yam, who, in 1814, had 'accompanied the army of Abiniowa in his political capacity, dying at Akrofroom in Aquapim, during the campaign' (Bowdich, 1819: 289). This office, created by Osei Kwame, is vested in the male descendants of Boakye Yam (IAS/AS.73; Wilks, 1966b: 224).

While both Kwesi Kankam and Oti Panyin were from Kumasi, Adusei Kyakya and Agyei were provincials, the former a Denkyira from the south-west, the latter an Akwamu from the south-east. Adusei, as first linguist, appears seldom to have left the capital, where he was responsible for the conduct of political cases transferred there: 'when any palaver comes he settles it at once; but if he is not there, they have to go to council' (Bowdich, 1819: 393). Agyei, by contrast, served as a travelling commissioner; 'he is,' Bowdich noted, 'always employed in difficult foreign palavers' (1819: 249).

The course of Agyei's career, which is known in some detail (Bowdich, 1819: 248-9; Lee, 1835, Ch. v), demonstrates the open character of the bureaucracy in the early nineteenth century. Beginning life as a salt carrier on the Volta between Akwamu and Kete Krakye, he was later taken into the service of Akoto, the Akwamuhene. When charges were brought against Akoto necessitating his appearance before the king in Kumasi, Agyei accompanied him there. Intervening in the proceedings, Agyei made a three hours defence of the Akwamuhene, and secured his acquittal. Osei Bonsu, impressed with Agyei's forensic skill, retained him as a palace servant, and, after a period in which Agyei further proved his worth, appointed him a junior linguist and granted him a house, wives, slaves, and gold. His reputation established as having 'the best head for hard palavers', he was subsequently advanced to the post of second linguist, and granted further property to support the dignity of his office. Thus Agyei,

'continued to advance by his splendid talents, and his firmness in the cause of truth, till he was raised to be the linguist for all foreign palavers, the highest office he could hold which was not hereditary' (Lee, 1835: 168).

A result of the rapid rise of individuals from positions of obscurity to high office within the bureaucracy was the king's particular concern for the public image projected by his servants:

'When the King sends an ambassador, he enriches the splendour of his suite and attire as much as possible; sometimes provides it entirely; but it is all surrendered on the return . . . and forms a sort of public wardrobe' (Bowdich, 1819: 294).

The head of this service was the Abanasehene; the stool, an appointive one, was first invested with responsibility for the state wardrobe by Osei Bonsu (IAS/AS.96).

The importance which the king in general attached to his political service is shown in the scale of the mission that arrived at Cape Coast early in 1820 to inquire into treasonable activities there. The mission 'entered the place with a degree of military splendour unknown there since the conquest of Fantee by the king' Its leader, Owusu Dome, whose precise office is not known, 'had been dignified by his sovereign, with a commission that qualified him to decide for peace or war upon the spot, and to act accordingly'. He was accompanied by several lesser captains, by messengers through whom he maintained contact with the king, and by two Muslim rapporteurs from the Kumasi chancery. Of the remainder of his suite of 1,200 men, 500 were soldiers and the rest bearers and servants. Before the town chiefs, 'drawn up to receive their unwelcome visitors', Owusu Dome opened transactions by demanding the payment of a fine of 1,600 oz. of gold by the townspeople, and the same by the English merchants there (Hutton, 1821: 128-9; 324; Dupuis, 1824, introduction).

The Emergent Bureaucracy: Provincial Administration

The Ashanti system of government of its conquered territories and protectorates was basically one of indirect rule.

'It was no part of Ashantee policy' [observed Cruickshank] 'to alter the government of the conquered country. The chiefs of the different tribes remained in possession of what power the conqueror thought fit to leave them, with the style and rank of a captain of the king; and in that capacity they acted as so many lieutenants, governing the country in the king's name, at the allegiance and service of their own vassals and slaves' (1853: I: 340).

Each subject ruler, however, was 'placed under the immediate care of some Ashantee chief, generally resident in the capital' (Bowdich, 1819: 235), and the Kumasi official served as his *adamfo* or patron at court.[15] Bowdich instances Kwakye Kofi, Akwamuhene of Kumasi, as *adamfo* to the Dankyirahene; Adum Atta, Adumhene, to the Nsutahene (the Nsuta near Takyiman); Opoku, Gyaasewahene, to the Akwahumene; and Owusu Kwantabisa, Adontenhene, to the Wasipewura of Daboya (1819: 235).

As a result of the changes in government brought about by Osei Kwadwo and his successors, this system of clientage was revolutionized by the superimposition of a new structure of provincial administration:

'the king was not content to leave the government entirely in the hands of the native chiefs, who might possibly in the course of time rally the prostrate energies of the country, and combine to throw off his yoke.

In consequence of this suspicion, which ever haunts the minds of usurpers, he appointed pro-consuls of the Ashantee race, men of trust and confidence, to reside with the fallen chiefs, to notify to them the royal will, to exercise a general superintendence over them, and especially to guard against and to spy out any conspiracies that might be formed to recover their independence' (Cruickshank, 1853: I: 340–1).

A network of Ashanti resident commissioners, hierarchically organized at regional and district levels, was thus created throughout the provinces. Its structure, which can be established in some detail for many areas, may be illustrated from the south-eastern provinces.

Tandoh was Ashanti commissioner responsible for the affairs of the large and important tributary of Akyem Abuakwa, his rank such that he moved about

'in great pomp, never going the shortest distance, but in his taffeta hammock, covered with a gorgeous umbrella, and surrounded by flatterers, who even wiped the ground before he trod on it' (Bowdich, 1819: 123).

In 1812 Meredith, governor of the English post at Winneba, remarked how Atta, the natural ruler of Akyem Abuakwa, governed

'in conjunction with Tando . . . and was tributary to the king of Ashantee. He refused obedience to the king's order, by not going [to war] against the Fantees: which produced a dispute between himself and Tando, who drove him out of Akim; and being joined by a number of people hostile to the Ashantee government, he became a respectable, and unsettled, and desperate warrior' (Meredith, 1812: 168–9).

As a result of the revolt, however, Tandoh was retired from his post (and enjoyed 'a long interval of the most luxurious life the capital could afford'), for,

'though Attah was adjudged to be in fault, after the palaver was talked at Coomassie, the Ashantee government thought it politic to displace Tandoh, though he had become disagreeable to the other, only for his vigilance and fidelity' (Bowdich; 1819: 123).

Belonging to lower ranks of the administration than Tandoh were the commissioners at district level, for example the three residents in Accra. Each was responsible for one of the European trading forts—Danish, Dutch, and English—and for the associated Ga wards. Bowdich noted that the first appointments to such posts were made by Osei Kwadwo:

'it was a law of Sai Cudjo . . . which granted to particular captains the honourable patent of receiving the pay of small forts, distinctly, each being responsible for his separate duties to his settlement' (1819: 83).

In fact, at least in the case of Accra, these appointments were made at the end of his reign; in November 1776 three Ashanti officials, with retinues, arrived there to take up their new duties, Boakye being posted to the Dutch quarters, Ankra to the English, and Nkansa to the Danish (*Elmina Journal*: 13 November 1776). These Accra officials appear to have been directly responsible to a more senior commissioner—a 'viceroy of the King of Ashan-tee' as Robertson described him—stationed in Akwapim some twenty miles to the north (1819: 221–2), where, as early as 1788, Biørn noted that 'the King of Ashanti retains a high lieutenant . . . for his subjects' protection from insult' (1788: 204).

The various arms of the Ashanti bureaucracy, three of which have been described, functioned in close interdependence. Thus, a resident commissioner was responsible (*inter alia*) for ensuring that tributes, fixed in the Gyaasewahene's exchequer court in Kumasi, were raised locally. The Sanahene's tax collectors conveyed them to the capital. In the event of a province's refusal, rather than inability, to pay tribute, a resident might request the intervention of an official of the political service, who could, if necessary, transfer the matter to the exchequer court, before which the malcontents would be required to plead.[16] The ultimate sanction of force, always available to the king, was resorted to only following a complete collapse in the machinery of negotiation and conciliation.

The Accumulation of Power

The pivot of government in Ashanti was the office of king, which was vested in a single segment of the Oyoko matriclan, the right of which to supply rulers was never challenged. Its legitimacy was broadly accepted by all classes of Ashanti society. A new king was selected, from among those genealogically qualified, for his moral and physical qualities. Selection of a successor was made by the Queen Mother in consultation with various advisers. There was a clearly established preference for the younger candidate, and the average length of reign tended to be high—for the nineteenth century, about nineteen years.[17] The system of succession was ideally determined by a mother–daughter sequence of *nhemmaa*, 'queen mothers' (see Fig. 8), though in fact, the failure

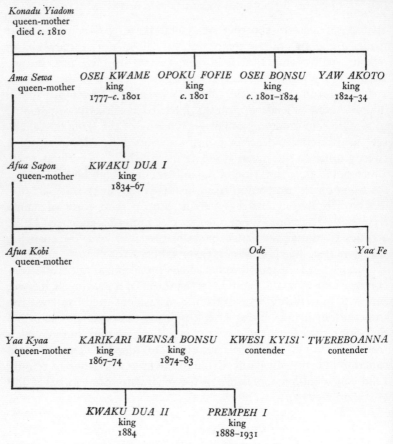

Fig. 8. The system of succession in Ashanti

of any son of queen mother Afua Sapon to become king led, in 1884 and 1888, to contests between daughter's sons and daughter's daughter's sons, resolved on both occasions in favour of the latter. The genealogy illustrates the extreme compactness of the dynastic family. Unsuccessful contenders faded into obscurity, often leaving the capital for remote bush farms; in earlier times they may have been eliminated by death or banishment.[18] This absence of distinct foci of dynastic conflict did much to facilitate the concentration of power in the hands of the king, remarked upon by most nineteenth-century observers (e.g. Dupuis, 1824: xxvi; Gros, 1884: 188).

The power of the king was greatly increased by the emergence of the new bureaucracy, for this marked a transition from a ruling to a controlled administration. Unlike the older aristocracy, the roots of which lay back in pre-Ashanti times, the bureaucracy was totally subservient to the king.

'We are willing to prove to your Majesty' [declared the Gyaase-wahene] 'our devotion to your person by receiving your foot on our necks, and taking the sacred oath that we will perform all your commands. Our gold, our slaves and our lives are yours, and are ready to be delivered up at your command' (Bowdich, 1820).

The careful control exercised over the bureaucracy is exemplified in the case of Tandoh in 1816. In that year Tandoh, the former resident commissioner for Akyem Abuakwa, had been sent by the king to Wassaw to effect the transfer to Kumasi of a number of prisoners of war. Tandoh, having fulfilled his commission, went on to negotiate the settlement of several disputes outstanding between the king and the Wassaws. On his return to Kumasi, Tandoh's settlement was immediately repudiated by the king, not because of its terms, but because 'no man must dare to do good out of his own head', and Tandoh himself was removed from office (Bowdich, 1819: 123; Huydecoper, *passim*). Such *ultra vires* action by an official constituted a usurpation of political authority. Left unchecked, a controlled bureaucracy would by such means transform itself, however gradually, into a ruling one. Many apparently trivial cases of peculation—a tax collector demanding, and retaining, an unauthorized charge; a state trader taking commissions on his own account—were also construed as *ultra vires* actions on the part of the officials in question, and were severely dealt with.

The principle of 'the impotence of the royal messengers in state affairs' was of cardinal importance in the Ashanti conception of government. In so far as the bureaucracy was a dependent one, an instrument of the king's will, it was in the nineteenth-century Ashanti view an acceptable one, since 'the decrees of a monarch have naturally more force with the people, (over whom his power is unlimited)'. In so far as it tended to usurp political functions, it was 'jealously watched by the other parts of the Government' (Bowdich, 1819: 134, 253). As a check upon such dangerous tendencies, the king maintained an elaborate organization of informants, often recruited from the *nseniefo* or heralds and attached to the various divisions of the bureaucracy. 'The King's system of espionage,' remarked Bowdich, 'is much spoken of (for its address and infallibility)' (1819: 294).

While the Ashanti king exercised the closest control over the civil administration, his command of the military resources of the state was less absolute. The *amanhene* of the *amantoɔ*, of course, continued to maintain their own armies. Even the Kumasi forces, however, were in the nature of the case not susceptible to total central direction. The units of military organization were such *asafo* as the *adonten* or centre, the *nifa* or right wing, and the *benkum* or left wing, and each unit was headed by an *ɔsafohene* responsible for the mobilization, when required, of all able-bodied men in his division. The office of senior commander, Krontihene (Kontihene), was the prerogative of the chief of the Bantama ward of Kumasi, and that of deputy commander, Akwamuhene, that of the chief of the Asafo ward. Whether holding old stools, such as the Krontihene, reformed stools, such as the Akwamuhene, or new stools, such as the Ankobiahene,[19] these divisional chiefs jointly constituted a political estate capable of a considerable degree of independent action. Thus, as Bowdich noted, while

'they watch rather than share the *domestic* administration, generally influencing it by their opinion, never appearing to control it from authority',

this was

'in direct contrast to their bold declarations on subjects of war or tribute, which amount to injunction' (Bowdich, 1819: 252).

The constitutional right of such divisional chiefs to intervene in these matters was justified on the grounds that:

'it makes the nation more formidable to its enemies, who feel they cannot provoke with impunity, where there are so many guardians of the military glory' (Bowdich, 1819: 252).

Around 1800 the centralizing policies of Osei Kwame brought him into sharp conflict with his divisional chiefs in Kumasi. Having abolished a number of traditional politico-religious festivals of a particularly sanguinary nature, he was thought to be contemplating radical changes in customary law by the introduction of elements of Islamic law (Wilks, 1966a: 334–5).

'These and other innovations' [commented Dupuis] 'were of a tendency to alarm the great captains; they feared, it is said, that the Moslem religion, which they well know levels all ranks and orders of men, and places them at the arbitrary discretion of the sovereign, might be introduced, whereby they would lose that ascendancy they now enjoy' (1824: 245).

The crisis ended with the dethronement of Osei Kwame. Later nineteenth-century kings, with the downfall of Osei Kwame in mind, embarked upon a programme of military re-organization, creating new formations, directly dependent upon royal patronage, as a counterbalance to the *asafo*. By 1817 Osei Bonsu already possessed his own household troop, 'a guard of foreigners (natives of Coransah)', recruited, so it would seem, from the Muslim Malinke of that area, who were regarded by the Ashantis as 'the best cavalry troops . . . in any part of Sarem' (Bowdich, 1821a: 52; Dupuis, 1824: 124, xxxvii). Half a century later Mensa Bonsu (1874–83) possessed a *corps d'élite* of Hausa troops, and to expand it further offered double rates of pay to trained soldiers to desert the British Gold Coast Constabulary for his service. By 1880 his considerable success in enlisting recruits, in purchasing large numbers of breech-loading rifles from the French, and in securing the services of trained armourers led him to plan the complete reform of the Kumasi fighting forces, and personnel from 'the Ashanti corps of Houssas' were attached to the more conservative *asafo* as musketry instructors (Ellis, 1883: 180–91, 215).

Several nineteenth-century writers noted that the Ashanti king legislated in council. Robertson referred to a 'senate', Bowdich to a 'privy council', Dupuis to a 'cabinet', and Ramseyer and Kühne to a 'Kotoko council'. While it would seem likely that in the eighteenth century this council had been a permanent body of fixed membership, constitutionally limiting the king's power, by the nineteenth century this was no longer the case (Bowdich, 1819: 233). Analysis of the composition of a number of nineteenth-

Q

century councils reveals their *ad hoc* constitution: the king invited the participation of those whose advice he valued and whose support he wanted. Thus, when matters concerning the Muslims of the empire were under review, the Kumasi *shaykhs* were given 'a voice in the senate', and the Imam declared himself 'a member of the king's council in affairs relating to the believers of Sarem and Dagomba' (Dupuis, 1824: 95, 97). A council of 23 March 1820, called to consider the terms of the proposed Anglo-Ashanti commercial treaty, included such interested parties as the Gyaase-wahene and the first and third spokesman; two chiefs of Ashanti towns on the main Cape Coast highway, the Amoafohene and the Dompoasehene, and the resident commissioner for the more southerly Assin province; and a son of Osei Kwame who had been brought up as a ward of the English in Cape Coast, as well as the two senior Kumasi divisional chiefs, the Krontihene and the Akwamuhene, and the head of the state executioners, the Adum-hene (Dupuis, 1824; 166). A council of 17 February 1872, con-cerned with the burning national issue of English encroachment on Ashanti's southern possessions, was correspondingly more broadly based. It included the queen mother; the Gyaasewahene and two linguists; the Kumasi *asafo* chiefs; two *amanhene* in person, the Mamponhene and the Adansehene, and represen-tatives of those of Juaben, Nsuta, and Bekwai (Ramseyer and Kühne, 1875: 157–60). It is thus clear that whatever old patterns of council membership had been destroyed in the course of the Kwadwoan revolution in government, they had not been replaced by new set patterns, and to this extent the king's prerogative had indeed been enlarged.

Applications of Power

In Ashanti the compactness of the dynastic family favoured political stability. A change of ruler, whether necessitated by death or destoolment, could be accomplished with the minimum dislocation of government. The element of choice in the election of kings, with premiums set upon character and youth, permitted the emergence of gifted and energetic leadership. The rise of a controlled bureaucracy, the eclipse of the older traditional authorities, the growth of elaborate organizations of household troops (and palace eunuchs)—all were indicative of the accumula-tion of unchecked power within the ruling dynasty.

The increasingly authoritarian character of Ashanti kingship was mirrored in the increasingly absolutist nature of the Ashanti state. The king, 'one of the busiest men that one could see', so Bonnat noted, extended his administration over matters 'of war, of religion, of commerce, of agriculture, of weights and measures, of prices and tariffs of all kinds, and finally of the exercise of justice, which is not the least of his responsibilities' (Bonnat, 1875). What was significant, however, was not so much the range as the scale of the managerial functions assumed by the state. In 1820 Osei Bonsu proposed to Dupuis a solution to the problem of the Cape Coast people, considered the cause of much of the friction between Ashanti and the English at that town.

'I will' [offered the king] 'bring them all to Coomassy and send another tribe to live among the whites; I will not kill them, but will give them land, and a good governor to make them obedient' (Dupuis, 1824: lxiv).

Such a remedy, to move inland perhaps five thousand people, was well within the competence of the king, for there existed an established machinery for the resettlement on Kumasi lands of prisoners of war, of slaves arriving as tribute, and of free immigrant groups. It was a feature of state policy to increase by this means the population of the metropolitan area, thereby achieving a favourable balance in man-power *vis-à-vis* the provinces and *amantɔɔ*. Such new settlements were often granted to Kumasi officials for the support of their offices. Bowdich, for example, referred to slaves selected

'to create plantations in the more remote and stubborn tracts; from which their labour was first to produce a proportionate supply to the household of their Chief and afterwards an existence for themselves' (1821b: 18).

An upper limit to the intake of stranger groups, whether free or slave, was set by the Ashanti insistence upon absorption and assimilation. Adoption of Ashanti ethical standards and cultural values was not only permitted but enjoined. Communities of slave origin became merged, within a generation or two, with the free Ashanti commoners, and their new status was given full protection in Ashanti law (Bowdich, 1821b: 16–17). *Obi nkyere obi ase*—one does not disclose the origins of another—was described by Rattray as 'a legal maxim of tremendous import in Ashanti' (1929: 40, 82), and Reindorf wrote of an Ashanti 'national law', that:

'Whoever dares tell his son: these people were from such and such a place, conquered and translocated to this or that town, was sure to pay for it with his life. Neither were such people themselves allowed to say where they had been transported from. Considering these captives as real citizens, any rank or honour was conferred freely on them according to merit, but not otherwise' (1895: 51).

By means of the resettlement programme, the organizational resources of the state were deployed to promote a rapid and planned growth in the metropolitan population. By the application of the relevant legal sanctions, the emergence of a class of unassimilated and underprivileged subjects was largely averted.

In comparable ways the growth of a native Ashanti merchant class was inhibited, for it was feared that,

'either from the merchants increasing to a body too formidable for their wishes to be resisted, or too artful from their experience to be detected they might sacrifice the national honour and ambition to their avarice' (Bowdich, 1819: 335).

Furthermore, the revolutionary potential of such a merchant class was clearly recognized: 'the traders growing wealthy and . . . stimulated by reflections they have now too little at risk to originate . . . would unite to repress the arbitrary power' of their chiefs, for which reason, commented Bowdich, the 'government would repress rather than countenance' the private participation of Ashantis in commerce (1819: 336). In pursuance of this policy, the accumulation of the capital necessary for such entrepreneurial activity was restricted by the enforcement of high interest rates on loans, $33\frac{1}{3}$ per cent per month, and by the imposition of a heavy death duty on estates. Strangers, by contrast, were encouraged to establish businesses in the capital, and were granted various privileges, including tax relief: 'I cannot tell them to give me gold,' commented Osei Bonsu, 'when they buy and sell the goods' (Dupuis, 1824: 167). Totally dependent upon the patronage of the king, 'a friend on whom they could always rely for protection', foreign merchants were thought to buttress rather than threaten the régime, and Muslim traders in particular, from as far away as North Africa and the Hijaz, were received in Kumasi as 'the honoured guests of kings and ministers' (Dupuis, 1824: 97, xiv); Wilks, 1966a: 320–2.

Wutwa nkonkonsa a, wusuro Kumase, 'when you spread harmful reports, you should fear Kumasi'. An attendant feature of the trend towards absolutism was the political control exercised over the dissemination of news. Thus, during the Bonduku campaign of 1818–19 the king laid 'an embargo . . . upon the tongues of his trading subjects that they might divulge nothing prejudicial to their sovereign', the failure to observe which was a capital offence (Dupuis, 1824: 211). The border between what could be referred to with impunity and what might be construed as actionable *nkonkonsa,* harmful rumour, was a constantly changing one. In 1817 Bowdich was told of a campaign conducted by Osei Kwame against Banda, and was shown the skull of the defeated Bandahene upon one of the king's ceremonial drums. In 1818–19 the reigning Bandahene gave great military assistance to the king against Bonduku, and in the following year was in Kumasi for the division of the booty. The machinery of censorship came into action: there had been no war against Banda, Dupuis was assured in 1820, and that a Bandahene's skull had been 'placed on the king of Ashantee's great drum, has no foundation whatsoever'.[20]

Basic to such particular systems of control over publication, however, was a more general concern with ideological conformity. Religion was strongly centred upon state cults and expressed through state festivals, the periodical *adae* and the annual *odwira*; independent heterodox cults appear not to have been encouraged. The indoctrination of a new ruler, as an embodiment of Ashanti values, was of cardinal importance, and

'during the minority, or the earlier part of the reign of a monarch, the linguists and oldest counsellors visit him betimes every morning, and repeat, in turn, all the great deeds of his ancestors' (Bowdich, 1819: 296).

The preservation and transmission of sanctioned historical lore was largely institutionalized, and was the responsibility of such trained professional groups as the state drummers, hornblowers, and *kwadwom* singers. The ordinary Ashanti, by contrast, who might incur the death penalty for an out-of-place reference to the demise of a king, remained tactfully 'ignorant and disinterested about researches into past ages' (Dupuis, 1824: lxxxiii; Bowdich, 1819: 228).

The Apogee of Power

The high degree of control established over the patterns of social, economic, and ideological organization produced in Ashanti a combination of institutional features of a kind unusual in West Africa. In the range of its proprietary and managerial functions, over land, man-power, and production, the Ashanti state in the nineteenth century was far removed in character from the 'feudalities' to which many scholars, following Rattray, have inclined to assimilate it. While there existed within Ashanti society gross disparities in the distribution of wealth, yet in its prevention of the consolidation of a slave class, and in the general accessibility of high office to commoners, the Ashanti state was not without its egalitarian aspects. The restrictions upon private Ashanti entrepreneurial activity, moreover, made possible the planned development of the national economy, and in its supervision over the means of production, distribution, and exchange, the bureaucracy faced no serious challenge from a rising bourgeoisie.

Nevertheless, despite the major changes in the power structure effected during the reigns of Osei Kwadwo, Osei Kwame, and Osei Bonsu, one major limitation upon the king's autocracy remained: the amantoɔ still preserved their semi-autonomous status and maintained independent armies, treasuries, courts, and festivals. They constituted states within the state, united in their recognition of the king in Kumasi as overlord, but possessing jurisdiction from which the king's administration was constitutionally excluded. By 1817 it was already apparent that the policy of the central government was directed to the destruction of these anomalous reserved jurisdictions, and to the achievement of a uniform system of administration throughout the empire. 'It is clear,' remarked Bowdich, 'that the King of Ashantee contemplates the reduction of the King of Juaben from an independent ally to a tributary' (1819: 245). The most powerful of the amantoɔ, Juaben, was subjected to increasing pressure: a number of test cases of the king's right of interference in its affairs were neatly contrived, and charges of theft of state property were brought against its omanhene. By 1831 the situation had sufficiently matured for the king to send his forces to occupy the Juaben capital. The Juabenhene and many of his people escaped southwards into Akyem Abuakwa, where they sought and obtained the protection of the British, who, since 1826, had been intruding their jurisdiction into a number of Ashanti's southern provinces. Although most of the Juaben returned to their homeland in 1841, the sequence of events established a pattern of *amantoɔ* response to the centralizing pressures of Kumasi, and provided the British with a strategy for subverting the authority of the Ashanti kings. 'Our policy,' wrote Ellis, should be 'to play off Djuabin against Ashanti, to use the one to keep the other in check' (1883: 181). In 1875 British protection was again extended to the Juaben, in 1888 to the Kokofu, and in 1889 to a section of the Mampon.

In their desire to extend the *Pax Britannica* over Ashanti, however, the British did not eschew more direct methods. In 1874 battalions of the 2nd Rifle Brigade, the 23rd Royal Welch Fusiliers, the Black Watch, and the Naval Brigade, with auxiliaries, fought their way through to Kumasi, burnt an empty town, and blew up an empty palace, and the next day began a retreat to the coast. The blow was absorbed and, under Asantehene Mensa Bonsu, a rapid recovery effected:

'In less than two years from the burning of Coomassie' [wrote Ellis] 'the Ashanti diplomacy had met with such success that Mensah had recovered the whole of the Djuabin territory, repudiated the payment of the war indemnity, re-established the prestige and power of the Ashanti name, and outwitted the Colonial Government upon every point' (1883: 187).

Fifteen years later a new approach to the problem was ventured, when Hull, British Acting Travelling Commissioner, was sent to Kumasi to invite the Ashanti 'to place their country under British protection' and so prevent it 'gradually falling into decay'. Ashanti, observed the king, Prempeh I, in a courteous reply,

'must remain independent as of old, at the same time to be friendly with all white men. I do not write this with a boastful spirit, but in the clear sense of its meaning. Ashanti is an independent kingdom . . . I am happy to inform you, that the cause of Ashanti is progressing and that there is no reason for any Ashantiman to feel alarm at the prospects, or to believe for a single instant that our cause has been driving (*sic*) back by the events of the past hostilities' (see Tordoff, 1962).

How far and to what end the Ashanti cause would have progressed, and in what ways Ashanti would have adapted itself to the demands of the twentieth century, remain matters for speculation. In 1896 a new expeditionary force was dispatched to Kumasi and entered the capital unopposed. The king, unprepared for war, made his submission, but, with various of his relatives and officials, was nevertheless deported, first to Elmina, then to Sierra Leone, and finally to the Seychelles. An unsuccessful but bitterly fought war of independence in 1900 led to the annexation of Ashanti as a British Crown Colony by an Order in Council of 26 September 1901. Its military organization, the basis of resistance, was disbanded and the functions of the bureaucracy were transferred to the new colonial administration. Without its king, without central government, Ashanti reverted to its pre-Kwadwoan segmentary structure, and only with the emergence of the Republic of Ghana in 1961 were some of the fundamental lines of Ashanti development once again to be taken up, adapted to a wider mid-twentieth-century context.

NOTES

1. This paper is a summary of a series of lectures given in the University of Ghana in 1962–64. Within its length it has been impossible to present the evidence for many of the theses argued; this I hope to do in future and more detailed studies. I wish to acknowledge my deep indebtedness to Mr. P. C. Gibbons of the University of Ghana for his assistance in the preparation of this paper. I have also gained much from numerous discussions of Ashanti affairs with Mr. E. F. Collins of the same University, and with Mr. J. Agyeman-Duah of the Kumasi State Council.

2. Statement by the Asantehene, *Daily Graphic* (of Ghana), 24 March 1962.

3. Compare Rattray's remark that 'Bekwai, Kokofu, and Nsuta became powerful, because all their chiefs were 'nephews' of the Asantehene' (1929: 132).

4. *Omanhene*, chief of an *oman* or state. The term *Birempon* is preferred by Rattray (1929: 81, 94–5).

5. For a detailed account of the internal organization of some of the *amantoɔ*, see Rattray (1929) and Busia (1951).

6. For a useful discussion of Ashanti population, the general conclusions of which the writer inclines to accept, see Beecham, 1841: 130–4.

7. In a paper on 'Some Developments in Akan Administrative Practice in the 17th and 18th Centuries', presented to the Historical Society of Ghana in January 1959, I attempted an analysis of these changes in terms of a struggle for power between the Kumasi chiefs and the *amanhene*. This analysis was followed by W. Tordoff in 'The Ashanti Confederacy', *Journal of African History*, Vol. III, 3, 1962. I have since come to regard this approach as unsatisfactory, being only quasi-explanatory. I would now regard an understanding of the emergence of the bureaucracy as fundamental to the political history of the period, and in particular to the struggles between Kumasi and the *amantoɔ* described by Tordoff.

8. Bonnat's Commission dated 31 July 1875, issued by the Asantehene, *L'Explorateur*, III, 1876: 238. For Nielsen, see Ellis, 1883: 1888–91. Dupuis, 1824: 167, records that he himself was offered employment by Osei Bonsu, as a comptroller of trade. Other cases are on record.

9. Of the first hundred stool histories recently collected from Kumasi, in this context at random, over a third are *mmamma-dwa*. An investigation of the positions held by the leading Kumasi chiefs met, 1816–19, by Huydecoper, Bowdich, Hutchison, Dupuis, and others, shows that almost all occupied other than matrilineal stools.

10. This stool has been redesignated the Gyaase stool by the present Asantehene. For a full account of its origins, see Kumasi state archives: proceedings relating to the Gyaasewa stool, 21 December 1939—24 April 1940 (IAS AS/CR.101). Although a civil functionary, the Gyaasewahene was not exempt from military service. Indeed, Opoku Frefre and his son Adu Bofuo, who also held the same post, were two of the most renowned campaigners of the nineteenth century.

11. By the nineteenth century, Kumasi division (as opposed to the provinces administered from Kumasi) included Asante-Akyem to the east and Ahafo to the west. The population of the division probably approximated to ½ million.

12. Kumasi state archives: letter from Asantehene Prempeh I (enstooled 1888) to D. C. Kumasi dated 26 October 1927.

13. The central government assumed responsibility for the construction and maintenance of major roads, see, e.g., Huydecoper: 2 December 1816 *et. seq.*; Freeman, 1843: 18.

14. The stool may subsequently have regained its importance, for half a century later Domakwaihene Poku Agyeman was described as 'head of the linguists, minister of foreign affairs', Ramseyer and Kühne, 1875: 308.

15. For the institution of *adamfo*, see Rattray, 1929: 94–98. Rattray analyses the institution in terms of 'court etiquette', and considers it only within a Kumasi–*amantoɔ* context. The system, however, appears

to have involved a patron in military obligations—to suppress revolt on his client's part—and was universal throughout the empire.

16. An interesting example of a constitutional case transferred from eastern Gonja to Kumasi is given by Hutchison, in Bowdich, 1819: 396–7, 401.

17. Of nineteenth-century kings for whom reliable figures exist, on enthronement Osei Kwame was about 12 years of age, Osei Bonsu about 22, Kwaku Dua I about 30, Karikari about 35, Kwaku Dua II about 20, and Prempeh I 17.

18. The succession dispute following the death of Opoku Ware in 1750 ended, for example, in the slaying of the principals of the unsuccessful party, and in the exile of others (whose descendants are still in Baule, Ivory Coast).

19. The Krontihene occupies a *podua* stool created by Osei Tutu; it is patrilineal (IAS/AS.39, 40). The Akwamuhene (not to be confused with the ruler of the southern province of that name) occupies a stool succession to which was switched from the matri-line to the sons *temp.* Osei Kwadwo, IAS/AS.38. For the Ankobia, see above.

20. Bowdich, 1819: 237. Dupuis, 1824: 79–81, 244. This sort of case suggests the great care necessary, in an Ashanti type context, in the use of traditional material for historical purposes.

REFERENCES

The following works have been cited:

Published

AGC	1883	*Further Correspondence regarding Affairs on the Gold Coast* (House of Commons).
Agyeman-Duah, J.	1960	'Mampong, Ashanti: a traditional history to the reign of Nana Safo Kantanka', *Transactions of the Historical Society of Ghana*, Vol. IV, ii.
	1964	'Ceremony of Enstoolment of Otumfuo Asantehene', *Ghana Notes and Queries*, 7.
Beecham, J.	1841	*Ashantee and the Gold Coast.*
Biørn, A.		'Beretning 1788 om de Danske Forter og Negerier', in *Thaarups Archiv*, III.
Bonnat, J.	1875	'Les Achantis d'après les relations de M. Bonnat' (ed. Gros), in *L'Explorateur*, Vol. I, ii.
Bowdich, T. E.	1819	*Mission from Cape Coast Castle to Ashantee.*

Bowdich, T. E. 1820 *A Reply to the Quarterly Review.*

      1821a *An Essay on the Superstitions, Customs, and Arts common to the Ancient Egyptians, Abyssinians, and Ashantees.*

      1821b *The British and French Expeditions to Teembo.*

Busia, K. A. 1951 *The Position of the Chief in the Modern Political System of Ashanti.*

Cardinall, A. W. 1920 *The Natives of the Northern Territories of the Gold Coast.*

Christaller, J. G. 1875 *Grammar and Dictionary of the Asante and Fanti Language Called Tschi.*

Cruickshank, B. 1853 *Eighteen Years on the Gold Coast of Africa.*

Dupuis, J. 1824 *Journal of a Residence in Ashantee.*

Ellis, A. B. 1883 *The Land of Fetish.*

      1887 *The Tschi-speaking People of the Gold Coast.*

Freeman, T. B. 1843 *Journal of two Visits to the Kingdom of Ashanti.*

Gros, J. 1884 *Voyages, Aventures et Captivité de J. Bonnat chez les Achantis.*

Hayford, Casely 1903 *Gold Coast Native Institutions.*

Horton, A. B. 1870 *Letters on the Political Conditions on the Gold Coast.*

Hutton, W. 1821 *Voyage to Africa.*

Isert, P. 1788 *Reise nach Guinea.*

Lee, Mrs. R. 1835 *Stories of Strange Lands.*

M'Leod, J. 1820 *A Voyage to Africa.*

Meredith, H. 1812 *An Account of the Gold Coast of Africa.*

Northcott, H. P. 1899 *Report on the Northern Territories of the Gold Coast.*

Ramseyer, F.
& Kühne 1875 *Four Years in Ashantee.*

Rattray, R. S. 1923 *Ashanti.*

      1927 *Religion and Art in Ashanti.*

      1929 *Ashanti Law and Constitution.*

Reindorf, C. C. 1895 *History of the Gold Coast.*

Robertson, G. A. 1819 *Notes on Africa.*

Tordoff, W. 1962 'Brandford Griffith's Offer of British Protection to Ashanti (1891)', *Trans. Hist. Soc. Ghana*, Vol. VI.

Wilks, I. 1957 'The Rise of the Akwamu Empire, 1650–1710', *Trans. Hist. Soc. Ghana*, Vol. III. ii.

Wilks, I.   1961   *The Northern Factor in Ashanti History.*
                 1966a 'The Position of Muslims in Metropolitan
                        Ashanti in the early 19th Century', in *The
                        Influence of Islam in Tropical Africa*, ed.
                        I. M. Lewis.
                 1966b 'Aspects of bureaucratization in Ashanti
                        in the nineteenth century', *Journal of Afri-
                        can History*, Vol. VII, No. 2.

Unpublished

General State Archives, The Hague

KvG. Archives of the Dutch Settlements on the Guinea Coast:
        82–167: *Elmina Journals*, 1715–1788.
      349–370: *Journal of the Settlements*, 1815–1870, containing:
                (*a*) Huydecoper: Journal of a Mission to Ashanti,
                1816–17.
                (*b*) Journal of Director-General Daendels.

Public Record Office, London

Lonsdale. Report by R. la T. Lonsdale dated 24 March 1882.
           Parliamentary Papers xlvi, 1882, C.–3386, 42, enc. 2.

Kumasi State Archives

Proceedings of the Kumasi divisional court, used by kind permission of
Otumfuo the Asantehene.

Institute of African Studies, University of Ghana

IAS/AS 1–n. Ashanti stool histories recorded by Mr. J. Agyeman-Duah.
IAS AS/CR 1–n. Transcripts of proceedings of the Kumasi divisional
court.

THE MENDE CHIEFDOMS OF SIERRA LEONE[1]

Kenneth Little

In 1843 Dr. Robert Clarke, assistant surgeon to the Colony, indicated the extension of Mende-land as described by a friend with some twenty years experience of Sierra Leone: 'The Kussoh country appears to lie between the parallels of 7° and 8° 15' north latitude and in a south-east direction, between the degrees of 10°30' and 12° west longitude.' That is to say, east of the River Jong and south of Mongeri. Giving further particulars of Mende-land, Clarke says:

'This country is said to be divided . . . into several principalities or states, or head towns; it is bounded on the north by the Timnehs, on the east and south by tribes of which I have not yet got any account, except that one on the east is said to be the Konah nation; on the west by the Sherbro, Krim, or Kixxum, and the Fye or Vye nations.

'. . . The Sherbro country, commencing at the Ribbie. . . . river on the north, and ending at the sea bar on the south, runs east to the Kussohs' (Kup, 1961: 157).

Nowadays, Mende inhabit a somewhat larger stretch of country which includes the western corner of Liberia as well as a fairly compact area of nearly 12,000 square miles in the central and eastern part of the former Sierra Leone Protectorate. According to the 1921 Sierra Leone census they numbered 557,674 out of a total Protectorate population of 1,672,058. There were some seventy chiefdoms varying widely in area and population: some of the smaller ones had probably no more than 5,000 inhabitants; the largest, Luawa, a Kissi–Mende chiefdom on the border of the then French Guinea, had in 1941 over 26,000 (Little, 1951: 61–2).

Until recent times most of this region consisted of dense rain-forest, and tradition suggests that it was once inhabited by small bands of hunters who followed a semi-nomadic life. Settlement, although sparse, was on peaceful lines, and it is said that the arts of war were either brought to or forced on these people by invaders from the north during a period relatively recent in history. The

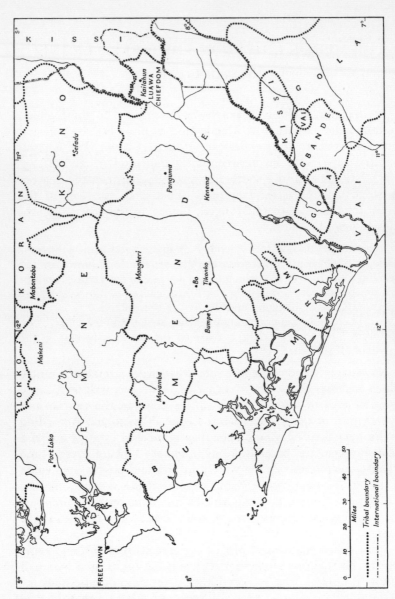

Sketch Map of Southern Sierra Leone

invaders pushed their way into the country and waged war against anyone opposing their right to settle there. They killed any of the local rulers whom they captured, and made slaves of the younger men and women or put them to work on their farms. Their leaders set themselves up as chiefs; but difficulties over boundaries brought them into constant conflict with each other, as well as with any of the neighbouring people who were able to withstand them. This helped to establish warfare as a principal form of activity and institution.

This traditional account is not incompatible with what is known historically about population movements during the seventeenth and eighteenth centuries. Refugees from the former great empires of the western Sudan were streaming into the forests to the south, and much of the Guinea Coast was in turmoil. According to Ogilby, who is the first English author to mention them, one of the groups jockeying for position there were called the Mendi. They are described as subjects of the emperor of Manow and, so far as can be judged, they constituted part of a congeries of closely related peoples inhabiting Quoja, a country inland from Cape Mount. This was at the height of the Atlantic slave trade, and the inhabitants of Quoja acted as middlemen between Manow in the interior and the traders on the Coast, exacting tolls upon everything sent to or brought up from the sea-ports. Came the time, however, when the emperor desired a direct path to the European ships and, being militarily more powerful, he was able to push many of the inhabitants of Quoja aside. As a result of this and of other upheavals a number of tribes with close affinities, including the Mende, were forced westward. At first the Mende did not penetrate deeply into Sierra Leone, but by the end of the eighteenth century their raids had taken them as far as the new British colony in Freetown (Kup, 1961: 152–54). It would appear that their onward march was made by transforming the original settlements into primitive fortresses. In other words, each small town with any strategic value for military or administrative purposes was strongly stockaded. Fighting was carried on partly for the purpose of enhancing prestige, and, even today, it is a matter of pride on the part of a Mende man to lay claim to some big warrior as an ancestor. Stories of the exploits, part historical and part fictional, of famous Mende fighters and chiefs, like Ndawa and Kai Lundo, the founder of the Kissi–Mende chiefdom of Luawa, are the common heritage of the present generation of Mende children.

The main incentive, however, was slaves. Slaves constituted the principal form of wealth and were bartered and exchanged for goods, notably for salt from the Coast and up-country for cattle. A single slave was worth from three to six cows, and a man, woman, or child were all considered as one 'head' of money. This was equivalent later in the century, i.e. 1890, to £3. Slaves also formed an invariable and important part of bridewealth and were deposited as security in the case of debt or any kind of dispute. They provided the basis, in fact, of the social system, and upon their labour as domestics depended very largely whatever agriculture the Mende possessed. It was they who felled and cleared the high virgin forest in preparation for the rice crop, and they were also responsible for the collection and cracking of palm kernels and extraction of oil. Palm kernels were the main commodity supplied to traders from the Colony during the nineteenth century.

Military Organization and Tactics

The fact that personal prestige and affluence, as well as safety, depended almost entirely on success in war led to quite an elaborate military technique, which can be recorded in some detail. The presence of so much thick bush made open fighting a rare occurrence, and rendered the movements of an opponent difficult to detect. This meant that both sides found it convenient to concentrate their principal goods and main defence inside the kind of strongly stockaded town which was the only means of warding off a surprise attack. To make the sudden approach of an enemy difficult, all paths leading to the town were left as narrow and as overgrown as possible, so that progress along them could be made only in single file. Only a single road led into the town itself, and it was so constructed as to be easily blocked, if necessary. The actual gate into the town was so narrow that it would barely admit a man. Inside the town itself the houses were deliberately built close to each other, so as to constitute a veritable maze and make it difficult for attacking warriors to find their way about.

The town itself was encircled and guarded by fences, usually three in number. There was also, as a rule, a further outer fence consisting of a light breastwork of material, piled up between convenient cotton trees and along a bank. This was not regularly defended, and its object was merely to provide a temporary brake on the attack. The next two fences were regularly guarded and defended by war-boys, stationed at intervals behind each one. There was a shed, or guard-house—*golohg boie*—at each point on either fence where the road passed into the town, and four warriors were posted there at night-time. In charge of them was an 'officer'—*Kotulei-mui* (one who passes the stone)—whose duty it was to see that an efficient watch was maintained. A stone was handed to one of the warriors on duty at the guard-house and he carried it along to the next post, whence it was relayed completely round the fence back to the original point. It was then handed to the second man and completed a further circuit. Its return to the third man marked the changing of the guard, and the second two warriors, who had been resting in the meantime, took over from their comrades.

The warriors did two days' duty at a time, and during it they cooked food for themselves, because no women were allowed between the war fences. On campaign only the principal warriors were allowed to take women with them. Every effort was made to effect a surprise attack, and generally one or two individuals were sent on ahead to spy out the way. If possible, they would insinuate themselves inside the town itself, or gain what news and information they could by listening in the nearby bush to women's gossip on the farm or at water places. On the strength of this intelligence the attackers decided on which part of the war-fence to make their assault. The whole body then crept up as stealthily as possible; and, provided the outer fences were reached, the following tactics were then followed.

The primary responsibility rested on a number of special warriors called respectively the *Miji* (the 'needle' or 'jumper down'); the *Fande* ('thread'); the *Kanye* ('wax'); and the *Haka-houmoi* (holder of the ladder). These acted as leaders in the assault, and before it was undertaken the ordinary warriors (*Kugbangaa*) arranged themselves in parties behind each one. There does not appear to have been any definite number to each leader, but perhaps the average would be about twenty, depending, of course, on the size of the force. If the *Miji* thought he had insufficient men to follow him he might choose from those left. If, as was

R

usually the case, the attack was to be made in the dark, two Mende proper names, such as *Vandi* and *Kanga*, were used as watch-words. If two men met and one said 'Vandi' the other would reply 'Kanga'.

Led by the *Miji*, the various parties then swarmed as best they could over the outer fences. If any of the fences proved unsur-mountable the *Hakahoumoi*, or ladder bearer, rushed forward with his ladder to help the *Miji*'s ascent. It was the custom to hand the latter a bottle of very strong palm wine, before he made his leap, to give him extra courage. It was the duty of the *Miji* and his party to overcome all opposition as quickly and as silently as possible between the fences. At the final stockade the *Miji* was expected to call out his name as he jumped into the town itself. He was then followed, in due order, by the *Fande* and the *Kanye* and their men, and then by four warriors known as *koko-yagbla* (drivers from the fence), who immediately split into two couples. The latter went around the inside of the fence, killing all they met and preventing anyone from escaping. It was impossible, of course, for all the warriors to use the same ladder, and the remainder swarmed over the fence by means of poles, once a footing inside had been gained. This more general part of the attack was carried out by two further categories known as *ngo-mbuhubla* (men in the midst of battle) and *gbamai* (ordinary men), who served in reserve. There were also *ko-sokilisia* ('war-spar-rows'), who were young recruits and served as carriers, and might be called upon to fight. The chief himself, who bore the military title of *Ko-mahei*, left everything in the hands of his *Miji* and did not enter the actual fighting unless the day seemed to be going against his men.

Once the inner fence had been forced, the capture of the town was almost certain, and any further resistance was soon overcome. Fugitives, who escaped by the back gate, sometimes scattered ants behind them on the bush path to put their pursuers off the trail. Women and children were shut up in the women's houses during the fighting, and the first warriors to enter the town were allowed to slash the outer walls of these houses with their swords, or leave some other token, such as a sheath, on them. This was a sign that they claimed the inmates as their captives. The remaining warriors were expected to continue the fight until they heard the *Miji* call out twice, '*A-wa-o*' ('All come!'), which was the sign of victory. Then they could join the others in marking houses and securing booty.

Once the assault had been started no quarter was given. The actual combat was practically all hand to hand, with swords and spears as the main equipment, and a species of shield called *kafa-lowoi* (fork of the kafa tree), which was of very hard wood. Strips of iron were placed across the fork, and the whole was used to ward off blows of a sword, to deflect the flight of a spear. Dane guns and muskets were also used, but were of little value after the first volley, as it took too long to reload them. For success, as well as protection, the warrior also relied on numerous charms, mainly procured from '*Mori*-men' (Muslim advisers of chiefs), which he wore all over the body. These were supposed to be proof against even a shot from a gun. Before his departure to war the warrior's family also made offerings on his behalf to their ancestors, and his uncles prayed for him.

When approaching an adversary in the fight the warrior would call out the name of his own war chief, and his opponent would reply in the same way. When the town was entered the unsuccessful defenders might escape detection by climbing into the eaves of the houses or by some secret path out of the town. Warriors captured in the fight were brought forward as a group, and those who had resisted most strongly were put to death. Before executing them the victors danced round the town. The captives were led out and stabbed as they passed through the fences. Their bodies were covered with leaves and left in the bush. For members of the victors' side who had been killed in the fight the usual ceremonies were performed at a fork in the road. The captured women and children, and the plunder, were then brought before the head warrior for division. Out of every four captives, two went as slaves to the chief himself; one to the head warrior, and one to the man who had made the capture.

If the people inside a town knew that an attack was imminent their chief's decision as to whether to resist or sue for peace depended mainly on the forecast of his Muslim adviser, as well as on the prestige of individual warriors among the opposing forces. The presence before a town of a well known fighter, such as Ndawa, is said to have been enough in itself to compel surrender. If the besieged chief decided to call for a truce he would send a woman of light-coloured skin as his ambassador, with a white country cloth, a gun, and some salt. She would probably be his daughter or one of the most valued women he had, and she automatically became the wife of the conqueror. Alternatively, he might appeal for help from neighbouring chiefs by sending them gifts of country cloths and a gown. In the event of it being decided to make a stand, the morale of the defenders would be strengthened by sacrifices carried out by the chief's Muslims, and by war-dancing. A warrior might be stationed at the only exit from the town to cut down any would-be deserters.

The exigencies of this kind of warfare and the practice of putting slaves to work on the land determined both the pattern of settlement and the general political structure. The immediate picture we have is of a large number of small towns, each of which lodged a local chieftain and his company of warriors, or 'war-boys'. The latter acted as his bodyguard and private army. A chief derived his power and authority from his own prowess and that of his followers, and warriors. The latter served him almost entirely in the capacity of mercenaries, and they included young men who came for military training. Some of these mercenaries were allocated farming sites as a reward for their services in addition to a share of the slaves captured.

Since the slaves themselves were housed as close as possible to the fresh tracts of land they cleared on behalf of their masters, this added fresh sections to already existing towns. It meant that the villages inhabited by the slaves were simply an extension into the countryside of the particular kin group to which they appertained. Further land was allowed to warriors who answered a beseiged town's call for help as well as to refugees flying from other wars. Sometimes, also, fresh villages were added through the initiative of individual free men seeking new places to farm and thus settling themselves and their descendants at the sites where the clearing was made. The jurisdiction of the warrior-chief would extend to all these satellite villages established from the town, including the villages which had been established by his warriors. He might also seek to found new towns as outposts. This would involve a similar procedure—the settlement of warriors on the spot chosen and the allocation of portions of virgin forest to them.

Since, in these circumstances, so much depended upon military strength, there was a constant need for military alliance and protection on the part of the weaker chiefdoms. For this reason, but mainly as a result of conquest, there was often a single chief, or 'high chief', whose general leadership was recognized by his neighbours. Each of the latter kept his own administration, but the arbitration of the high chief was accepted in important cases, including disputes between fellow members of the 'confederacy'. Fealty was displayed, sometimes, in the shape of periodical payments of tribute, and it might also involve the provision of military assistance, if the high chief were attacked. He, in return, would go to the aid of chiefs whose towns lay within his sphere of influence, when war threatened them. The alliance was also symbolized by the periodical exchange of customary presents. This kind of paramount role seems to have been played by the chiefs of Panguma, Bumpe, Mongeri, and Tikonko during the latter part of the nineteenth century.

According to Astley's description of Quoja, another important prerogative of the high chief was that of crowning each new chief who succeeded to office in the tributary state. This right probably derived from the original conquest of the chiefdom concerned. it being the custom of the victor to leave one of his warriors in charge. It was then the duty of this viceroy to 'look after the country' on his own chief's behalf. Alternatively, a weaker chiefdom might invite a well-known warrior from outside to serve as its leader. The fact that this political affiliation was continuously confirmed by the high chief's ceremonial right of coronation probably explains a further complication in the system. Thus, it was quite possible for a tributary state situated geographically on the borders of the confederacy to undertake military conquests of its own. This would give rise to an additional pattern of overlordship, but without altering the original relationship of the chiefdom concerned to its own high chief. Finally, a tributary member of the second hegemony might, in its turn, carve out yet a further 'empire', while continuing fealty to its own overlord. It was also possible for a given people to pay homage to more than one high chief at the same time (Astley, Vol. 2: 17 et seq.).

Given this loosely knit system of superordination and subordination, it is tempting to speculate about its operation. Fighting being on a limited scale, it was quite possible for a warrior chief of resource, backed by competent followers, to win one or two quick victories and thus to overawe a whole country within a short space of time. To keep it permanently under control by military methods alone was another matter. Should war break out afresh, his communications with the disaffected area were likely to be impeded not only by forest and rivers but by the presence of fortified towns on the route. He had also to reckon on the possibility of treachery at home should he move his personal bodyguard of trained warriors too far from the capital town. Additional safeguards consisted partly in the measures outlined above. However, the extent to which a puppet ruler could be used was obviously limited, and there was the constant danger of a viceroy's authority being locally usurped or of his becoming too closely associated through intermarriage, or in other ways, with the people under his charge. In other words, some sanction was necessary which could operate more widely and more effectively than mere physical force or traditionally ingrained habits of allegiance.

Poro

It is very likely that this sanction was supplied by the Poro. A belief in the supernatural power of spirits and of medicine seems to have been common to all the peoples of the Guinea Coast, and the Poro supposedly controlled most of these forces. In addition to possessing medicines of great strength, its leading officers claimed to have intercourse with the world of spirits, which they impersonated by the aid of masks. Moreover, since it was virtually compulsory for every youth to be initiated, this meant that most of the younger men were entirely under the society's command as represented by the 'inner circle' of senior members. The latter were fully entitled to place the initiates under Poro oath, and after this everyone was bound to adhere to whatever plans had been decided upon in secret. So far as can be judged, however, there was no permanently existing Poro in the sense of a continuous and uninterrupted round of organized activities. Members were called together at indefinite times for the attainment of specific objects and, when these objects had been attained, the 'poro' broke up or dissolved. Even the periodic initiation school for new members was no exception to this rule or principle. Nor did the Poro possess any centralized form of organization. It was called together and organized locally through the medium of what, for lack of a better term, have been called 'lodges'.

The 'lodges' were quite independent of each other, so far as their administrative and specific activities were concerned. At the same time they operated along lines and carried out rituals and practices which were substantially the same all over Mende country. In other words, if a person had been initiated in one area he would be admitted to a gathering anywhere else and, according to his particular status, might participate fully in whatever was going on in the place visited.

For this reason the Poro as an association was, in all likelihood, the means by which a uniform system of government as well as set of customs was possible among a large number of politically separate and scattered communities. As an arbitrator in chiefdom disputes, the Poro acted through an armed band of its officials, and their intervention was sufficient to overawe any party rejecting the society's decision. Indeed, all warfare had to cease while the society was in session, and prohibitions placed in the name of the Poro on the harvesting of palm fruit or on fishing at certain seasons were ignored only at the greatest peril. The Poro also regulated trading practices and fixed prices at which various commodities should be sold and at which certain services, for instance, a day's load-carrying, should be performed.

It is probable, therefore, that this society and the chieftainship mutually reinforced each other. Since the chief's function as ruler largely derived from his role as director and leader in time of war, his ability to command and to exact obedience was based on physical power and personality and not the mystical sources from which the Poro derived its voice. Nor had the Mende chief any religious or ritual duties to perform which were other than presidential. He was expected to sponsor certain public ceremonies, but not to officiate in them. In fact, any attributes of a religious kind that the chief possessed were merely those which any senior participant in the ancestral cult also shared. He was a purely secular figure.

This apparent lack of religious elements in the business of administration was remedied by the Poro in a number of ways. For example, the society signalized the respect due to secular authority by parading, at the funeral or coronation of a chief, its principal and most sacred spirit, the *Gbeni*, which ordinarily came out in public only on the most important occasions. At the funeral the procedure was for one of the society spirits to go first to the house where the chief was buried, and thence to every house in the town, announcing the chief's death. At each place he was given a present. Another Poro spirit went round the town dancing and was also given money. After this, every Poro man was ordered to the bush so that the *Gbeni* could appear. Amidst great beating of drums, the *Gbeni* proceeded to the burial place and bowed over it. He remained until the chief's family had given him money. A further point was that the chief, when dying, was taken to the Poro bush for medical treatment.

Secular Administration

It is obvious, therefore, that the connexion between this society and political authority was very strong. However, before discussing this complicated question it will be convenient to return to the secular administration of the Mende chiefdom. This was vested primarily in a ruling lineage whose members held most of the principal offices. As already implied, their right to rule hinged mainly on descent from the warrior chief and warriors who first ruled in that part of the country. It had its basis in land ownership of a substantial proportion of the chiefdom and included the dying chief nominating his successor. The name of the person would be kept a secret as long as possible in case of harm befalling him, and his family had to 'beg' the other 'big men' of the chiefdom with gifts of slaves before he was appointed. The successor was usually the first-born, but might be another son of the late chief, if the latter's mother stood in higher favour. In some cases a series of brothers followed each other as chiefs before the son of the first brother was appointed. The idea in this—that the sons of the former chief stood in closer relationship to him than his son's sons—denoted the guiding principle. In default of a suitable successor, there was nothing to prevent a woman, such as a daughter of the late chief, being appointed, and even a daughter's child had a right to succeed in the absence of nearer heirs in the male line. Sometimes a powerful warrior or other person of influence would act as regent chief during the senility of the actual chief, or during the minority of the rightful successor, but this conferred no right either on him or his descendants to inherit the chiefdom.

A number of social insignia and special characteristics of the office marked the chief out from ordinary society. One of these was the wearing of leopard's teeth—a sign of royal rank and of membership of such a family—and other emblems, such as an elephant's tail, were borne by the chief's followers. One of the latter, a trusted attendant, was known as the 'Bearer of the Chief's Life'. He had charge of various special medicines to safeguard the chief's life and health from witchcraft and other misfortunes. There was also the chief's *mori*-man, who acted as special adviser and assisted him to carry out public sacrifices, when the occasion arose. Not only was it contrary to Mende custom to use personal names in addressing a person but, in the case of the chief, a serious offence to mention his name publicly at all. To do so constituted grave disrespect and earned the further suggestion that the person using it was working some medicine against the chief. The approved title of address was *marda*—'grandfather', the title of chief itself—*maha*—being applied more frequently to other leading officials in the chiefdom. A person approaching the chief, including the younger members of his own family, was expected to move towards him with body bent and with hands on knees, and to uncover his head. It was also etiquette for the chief to be accompanied by a crowd of courtiers whenever he walked or moved outside his own compound. Generally, he was carried in a hammock followed by a group of women singers and male drummers, whose duty was to extol his praises. Needless to say, a further important sign of the chief's status was the large number of wives.

The means of upholding this dignity and prestige, as well as discharging the chief's office, were supplied by various customary forms of service and tribute from the chiefdom. The first of these was *ndɔ-yenge*, or chiefdom labour, which meant that the chiefdom, in terms of levies from workers from the individual sections, had the responsibility of making the chief's *manja* (rice) farms. In the same way, the chiefdom supplied labour for the purpose of keeping the chief's compound in good repair, or of building a new one if need be, as well as clearing main roads, etc. In addition, the chief was entitled to a small proportion of the rice and palm-oil produced by every farming household in the chiefdom. This was collected through the sub-chiefs. There were also various customary presents. When the chief visited one of his sub-chiefs the latter was expected to 'put down the chief's hammock'— *mboma hitie*—by offering him a fairly valuable gift, such as a number of cows, and entertaining him and his followers on a lavish scale. The chief also had the right to certain animals killed in the chiefdom, such as the leopard, and could claim, in some cases, a small 'dash' from anyone tapping palm wine. A further and more important source of income was the fees and fines gained in the hearing of court cases.

As already implied, the chief's own primary obligation was as the military protector of his people. He was also responsible for the civil as well as the military administration of the chiefdom, and acted as the principal adjudicator in the case of disputes. In addition to entertaining strangers, he was also expected to keep open house and to succour needy members of his own chiefdom. As already stressed, he had no ritual or religious function.

The second person in the political hierarchy was the Speaker, or *Lavalie*. It was possible that the office originated in the original leader appointing one of his followers as deputy; sometimes it was a sister's son. In any case, the practice seems to have led to the establishment of regular Speakers' 'houses' (just as there were regular chiefs' 'houses') from which the Speaker was invariably chosen.

The Speaker had two principal functions in the chiefdom. First, he was essentially the chief's deputy. He took over these duties whenever the latter was ill, or absent from any public occasion. In such an event the Speaker officiated in full capacity and with entire responsibility for the chiefly office. Secondly, the Speaker was the main intermediary between chief and the chiefdom, and complaints and disputes were brought initially to his notice for transmission, if necessary, to the chief. Part of the Speaker's role, in this respect, was to act as a 'sounding board' to public opinion, on the one hand; and, on the other, to let the people know if the chief should depart, in his actions, from traditional custom and practice.

The Speaker was also responsible for passing the chief's orders and instructions down to subordinate officials, and was essentially, in this respect, as the title of his office (from *la*–mouth) implied, the chief's 'mouthpiece'. The Speaker was therefore supposed to be diplomatic, tactful, and eloquent. The general practice, in the event of any particular command, was for a messenger to set out with a sign of the Speaker's credentials to each sub-chief in turn. It was for each of the latter to see that the message was implemented in his particular section of the chiefdom. Similarly, in the general assembly of the chiefdom council, it was customary for the Speaker first to inform the gathering of the business of the meeting before the chief himself addressed it. The Speaker's duties made him, in fact, a kind of 'chief of staff' in the general business of the chiefdom.

Sub-chiefs, who came next in order of precedence, were also assisted by their own speakers. They not only had similar privileges and duties as the chief but also maintained bodyguards which were used to maintain law and order and for raids. A sub-chief settled disputes brought to him by the people under his jurisdiction, represented them at a chiefdom council, and saw that the decisions of the chief were carried out. Sub-chiefs also gave annual gifts to the chief, a share of the spoils taken in raids, and provided warriors when the need arose. Subordinate to sub-chiefs were town-chiefs and village headmen, who had similar privileges and duties and derived their income from the same sources. Like the other holders of titles, these functionaries were usually descended from or connected with the ruling lineage. It was to the latter officials and to the local elders that quarrels and disputes were taken for settlement. If, however, the principals were persons of consequence the case was taken to the chief for arbitration. In the latter case the chief held court and was assisted by the principal men in the chiefdom. According to an elderly informant, the following was the judicial procedure:

'In the old days, if your wife went to stay with her father's people and became pregnant, you called on them for satisfaction (i.e., "woman damage"). If they did not meet you, you send a "shake hand" (customary present) to some big man in the town, asking him to take the matter up in the Chief's court. The Chief sent his messenger to summon you and the defendant, and the case was heard in his *barri*. Each morning you and the defendant would "awaken" the Court with presents to the courtiers. You, as plaintiff, would be asked to state your case, and to swear on your opponent's medicine. Then the defendant stated his case and was sworn on your medicine. The Chief would ask how much damages you were claiming, and you were required to deposit the amount in a nearby house. It might be forty country cloths and a number of slaves. The defendant was called upon to do likewise, and a kind of "betting match" ensued. If you did not own any slaves, you might offer your sister's son or daughter as a pawn, but not your own son, because you had no right to pawn him. If after pledging your nephew, you lost the case, you had to redeem him. The father and mother of the pawn also had to work to redeem him.

'After the cases of both the plaintiff and the defendant had been heard, the Chief called upon them to name their witnesses. The witnesses were sent for, and would ask the Chief to "introduce them" to the parties concerned, i.e., they required a "hand shake" from both suitors. The witnesses then gave their version of the matter, after being duly sworn, and were asked to withdraw and "hang heads" on it. Providing their verdict was unanimous, the Chief pronounced judgement accordingly. If it was not unanimous the witnesses were fined, and it was left to the Court to bring in a verdict. The plaintiff and the defendant were asked to make a further statement, and the courtiers retired and "hanged heads". On their return, the Chief asked each one on whose side he stood, and the courtiers arranged themselves accordingly. The Chief then gave his verdict according to the majority of opinion.'

A customary method of summoning the court was for the plaintiff to send a quantity of palm wine to the elders. The defendant was expected to do likewise if he wished to contest the claim. Failure to do this was equivalent to an admission of guilt, hence the question which the elders would put to him, *Mba ndoe la hwei lo?*—Will you cross the summons? There was (and still is) a great variety in methods of administering the oath. It might take the form of tapping together two pieces of iron, of stirring a mixture of chopped kola, salt, and water, etc. If the medicine used had to be drunk, the party supplying it had to taste it first himself. The witnesses gave evidence in each others' hearing, and this had the effect of producing closer collaboration, particularly if they had been approached beforehand by either party. The courtiers, including the chief's Speaker (his deputy), might also be bribed, and the latter might intercede on the side in which he was interested by indicating, by movements of his switch, the appropriate answers to questions put by the court. The court members indicated their own allegiance to either of the parties concerned by wearing their caps in a distinctive way. The suitors themselves were permitted to cross-examine each other 'on the bridge'. This meant that they stood directly opposite each other at a close distance, and the one questioned the other with the object of pressing him to admit a certain point. The chief, alone, was supposed to be immune from bribery, as this was one of the specific obligations undertaken at his 'crowning'.

We have, then, in these terms a formal picture of Mende political organization. It is extremely difficult to say how far the system actually functioned in this way because the extent of local sovereignty was obviously variable. Probably, as implied above, there were three types of political units: firstly, a town with its satellite villages; secondly, chiefdoms consisting of several such local groups; and finally, large confederacies. In the first case there is reason to suppose that the chief's administration was personal and was carried on with the aid of his Speaker and of the leading men in the town who were the chief's close relatives or friends. In the second case the chief's own council was enlarged to include all title-holders in the chiefdom. Theoretically, the chief was supposed to consult this body over any measure affecting the chiefdom as a whole, and was responsible to it for his actions. In fact, owing to difficulties of communication and for other reasons, the probability is that it was rarely convened as a full assembly and that the chief ruled with the help of his own council. Undoubtedly, for news and intelligence concerning events and affairs in the chiefdom he would have to rely largely on those most closely about him. These people and those who took care of him by, for example, tasting his food, were known respectively as the chief's 'gossipers'— *nga fa bla*, and as the chief's 'eyes and ears'—*mahei makum gbei bla*. Probably, in the last resort, he depended largely on the support of the Poro society to ensure the maintenance of customary law and behaviour.

The implication of the latter point—that the Poro and the chieftaincy are to be regarded as complementary forces in government— is especially relevant to the confederacies. Normally, political power was balanced between the two institutions. It was the prerogative of the society, as main custodian of tribal tradition, to watch the chief; to ensure that his actions as ruler conformed with customary practice. Among the Sherbro (culturally very akin to the Mende) the Poro supervised his installation. When the new chief was chosen he was put into *kungh*, i.e. remained in seclusion for some weeks, or longer, and during this time he was under the instruction and control of Poro elders (Hall, 1938). Among the Mende themselves not only had questions of succession to be decided in Poro but all important cases affecting the chiefdom at large had also, in theory, to be taken there. The chief, on his part, was expected to hold the Poro in check, and to see that its officials did not take undue advantage of their special privileges by exploiting the people. For example, he could withhold his permission when the society wished to initiate new members. A session which lasted for three years or more was a serious drain on the public wealth. The chief and other big men were also entitled to the labour of Poro initiates on their farms.

The explanation of this relationship is possibly that indigenous government functioned at two levels, not mutually exclusive, but overlapping. The first, which might be termed the civil phase, was concerned with the everyday management of the country and its citizens, common laws governing conduct, etc. This included the external organization of chiefs and minor officials. On the second level, which might be thought of as religious, were the mechanisms for handling the crises and emergencies of life. 'It was in this second level of government, calculated to deal with the hidden spiritual forces, that the (Poro) masks found their special place' (Harley, 1950: viii).

In these terms, therefore, there was a sense in which the Poro was practically supreme in a chiefdom. Discussions affecting both internal affairs and relations with other chiefdoms were held in the Poro council. The chief was a member of that council, but its authority could override him, and the real power lay in the hands of the Poro 'inner circle' (Hall, 1938). However, according to Harley's description of the Mano there was usually one chief in the community who was a peer of the Poro elders. He was something of a king, and had power of life and death over his subjects provided he worked through the Poro, never against it (Harley, 1941: 7). Evidence given to the Royal Commission suggests that certain chiefs in Sierra Leone enjoyed similar prerogatives. Thus, after explaining the practice of placing the whole country under oath, one of Chalmer's witnesses went on:

'The head chief is always at the head. . . . As a rule the porro is brought down to the head chief of the country, who forms a porro bush in his town, and he will then initiate the chiefs of various districts under him, and they, as they call it, buy the porro bed from him, and take it to their own town where they initiate the people . . . Several Head Chiefs may combine in a porro—indeed very rarely is anything attempted by one man. There is always a tribe of several . . . When several Head Chiefs resolved on a war, they would meet and form their porro, then communicate with the Sub-Chiefs, and spread it through the country. A one word porro would mean a one opinion' (Parliamentary Papers, 1899: 489).

This illustrates the way in which the signal could be given for war. Taken in conjunction with the still earlier reports, it may also explain how law and order could be maintained through Poro on an extensive scale. In particular, Lieutenant John Matthews, who lived in Sierra Leone between 1785 and 1787, says that the society had some very summary ways of restraining contending parties once its word had gone out that there should be peace. It sent down a party of forty or fifty men, all armed and disguised. They put to death anyone who was out of doors, and removed as much livestock and provisions as they pleased (1788: 84–5).

What this and additional evidence of Poro's political function suggest is that the larger confederacies and hegemonies may have been held together mainly through the society's control. A great deal depended upon the chief's relationship with Poro, and about his exact position there the information is ambiguous. Provided, however, a head chief was influential in the 'inner council', the attitude of local headmen and chiefs would be less important.[3] He would have at his disposal a body of secret agents, well disciplined and already under oath, to police the particular territory in which they belonged. These agents would keep the head chief continuously informed about what was going on, and he would be able to use them, if need arose, to stamp out disaffection or civil unrest. Furthermore, in addition to mobilizing the country for purposes of military aggression or defence, these local lodges could be employed, in ordinary times, to regulate trade and other economic affairs. They could also be used by the high chief to promulgate legislation. To this should be added the generally wide functions of secret societies in traditional life. The Poro and the Sande societies train respectively the younger men and women for their everyday occupational and other duties and indoctrinate them with tribal values. Other associations exist to regulate sexual conduct, including the laws of marriage, and to operate important social services. They provide, for example, medical treatment and take care of the sick, as well as organizing entertainment and recreation.

In view of all this, there is no reason to object to Eisenstadt's typification of the Mende political system as a monarchy based on associations and secret societies (Eisenstadt, 1959: 10). In other words, we find—following his categorization—a centralized chiefdom in which most political positions are vested in members of hereditary groups and with the additional factor of associations. These perform important political and administrative functions, especially in economic and cultural fields and in the general maintenance of social control. Here is also a greater elaboration of special political and administrative apparatus, some of which is under the control of the high chief and some under the control of the associations. Some degree of personal politics probably also existed in the upper echelons of the secret associations and in relations between the secret associations and the more powerful chiefs.

It seems important to stress the latter considerations because the original arrangements for administering the Sierra Leone Protectorate made use of the chiefs and headmen, but no serious notice was taken of the political function of the secret societies. Only in a negative sense was their influence recognized, as when, in 1897, it was made a criminal offence to employ Poro laws as a means of interfering with trade. Moreover, in adopting for administrative purposes what was believed to represent the indigenous hierarchy, the Government limited itself to individual chiefdoms, putting all the native rulers whom they recognized as 'paramount chiefs' on the same footing. In a number of cases persons were recognized as chiefs whose position and standing was of a very minor and subordinate nature. The status of other native rulers was misrepresented or misunderstood through mistakes, deliberate or otherwise, on the part of interpreters, and, in some instances, too, the chiefly staff of office was awarded to individuals whose only claim to the territory concerned lay in their having agreed to bring in House Tax for it. Again, in the early days the Frontier Police virtually created chiefs out of persons who won their favour or were useful to them.

Analogous circumstances have clouded the reconstruction of pre-Colonial political systems not only in Sierra Leone but also elsewhere in West Africa. One wonders, therefore, if a renewed analysis of some of these earlier kingdoms might perhaps give greater prominence to the associational factor. Yoruba and Dahomey are cases in point, and it may be that this particular specialization of political function was characteristic of a much wider region than the Guinea Coast.

NOTES

1. This essay is substantially based on the account published in the author's book, *The Mende of Sierra Leone: a West African People in Transition*, 1951. (The author is indebted to the publishers for permission to reproduce sections from Chapters 1, 9, and 12.)

2. *Kussoh* or *Kossa* appears to be a Temne word for the Mende. It has developed an impolite meaning, although it occurs in the mid-nineteenth-century treaties signed by the Mende leaders themselves apparently without objection (Kup, 1961: 156).

3. Space does not permit a fuller examination of this complex question, but it is discussed in the author's 'The Political Function of the Poro,' (1965-6).

REFERENCES

Astley, Thomas   1745– *New General Collection of Voyages and*
                         47   *Travels*, Vols. 1–4. London.
Dapper, Oliver   1686   *Description de l'Afrique*, trans. Flamand,
                                 Amsterdam.
Eisenstadt, S. N.   1959   'Primitive Political Systems: a pre-
                                 liminary comparative analysis', *Amer.
                                 Anthr.*, Vol. 61, 2.
Hall, H. U.   1938   *The Sherbro of Sierra Leone*. Pennsyl-
                                 vania.
Harley, G. W.   1941   'Notes on the Poro in Liberia', *Peabody
                                 Museum Papers*, No. 2, Vol. 19.
                         1950   'Masks as Agents of Social Control',
                                 Peabody Museum Papers, No. 2, Vol. 32.
Kup, A. P.   1961   *A History of Sierra Leone: 1400–1787*.
                                 Cambridge.
Little, K. L.   1951   *The Mende of Sierra Leone*.
                         1965– 'The Political Function of the Poro',
                         66   Parts I and II, *Africa*, Vol. xxxv, 4,
                                 pp. 349–65; Vol. xxxvi, 1, pp. 62–72.
Matthews, John   1788   *A Voyage to the River Sierra Leone*.
                                 London.
Ogilby, J.   1696   *Africa, the Regions of Egypt, Barbary
                                 and Billedulgeria*. London.
Parliamentary Papers   1899   *Report on the Insurrection in the Sierra
                                 Leone Protectorate*.

S

THE WOLOF KINGDOM OF KAYOR

VINCENT MONTEIL

The History of Kayor[1]

Kayor, now a province of Senegal, is inhabited mainly by Wolof, an ethnic group speaking a West Atlantic language, who numbered more than a million in 1965. The *Wâlo Chronicle*[2] confirms that they were in their present geographical position by the thirteenth century. Kayor extends 150 miles from south-west to north-east and 80 miles from north to south—between Saint-Louis and Rufisque; it is bounded by Waalo, Dyolof, and Baol. Today the railway cuts across its entire length. The map on p. 261 shows Kayor as it was in 1883; the railway, dating from 1885, is a later addition. The main provinces of Kayor are shown: Dyambur, Mbawar, Sanyokhor, Dyander, and Ghet.[3] Barthélémy (1848: 39) quotes Malte-Brun's estimation of population for Kayor: 100,000 souls. The people of Kayor, unlike other Wolof, are not known by the doubling of the name of their country: i.e. Waalo-Waalo, Baol-Baol, Dyolof-Dyolof, Siin-Siin, and Saalum-Saalum, the two last lying south of Baol. They are called Aadyor or Waadyor—people of the 'dry, red sand' (*dyor*). They live in circular huts 'like beehives' (Mollien, 1820: 103). Their major crops are millet and rice; and groundnuts, introduced from Brazil, but not mentioned by Mollien, 1820, have been systematically cultivated in Kayor and exported since 1849. Gandiole and Rufisque have become important trading centres based on the ports of Gorée and Saint-Louis.[4] At Leybar, the king—or *Damel*—imposed fixed dues on all exports from Kayor to Saint-Louis. In 1850 he demanded seven hundred guineas as his 'custom'—i.e. tribute. Farmers paid him a proportion of their harvest.

Villages, on the average, numbered one hundred and sixty inhabitants. A typical village was formed by a 'square' (*kör*) around a watering-place, shaded by large trees. Elders sat in the centre on a kind of platform (*dat*). In theory, village chiefs, who were often marabouts, were appointed by the Damel. Their main functions were to keep public order and collect tribute for the

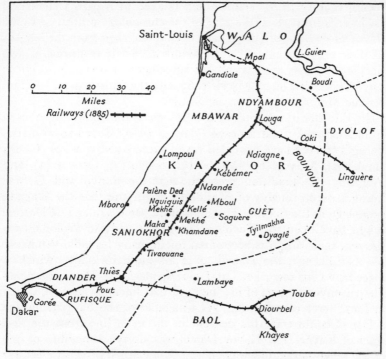

Sketch Map of Kayor (1883)

Damel. Matrilineal descent was formerly important for sucession and inheritance; at the present time, however, under the influence of Islam, patrilineal descent is stressed. In Muslim villages *cadis* (*khaali*) delivered Islamic justice, tempered by customary codes. At the capital the marabout, who advised the king on Islamic affairs, often held a court of final appeal.

Oral traditions indicate that the Wolof originated in Walo about the turn of the twelfth century from a fusion of Serer, Sose (Mandinka), Fulbe, and Tucolor elements. Walo and Dyolof are the oldest Wolof states. According to oral traditions imparted by Yoro Dyaao, chief of Waalo, Kayor remained a vassal state of the Dyolof empire until the sixteenth century. It became independent following the refusal of its Damel to pay tribute: 'Links were snapped and the prickly thorns removed' (Rousseau, 1933 and 1941; Brigaud, 1962: 85–115). By the end of the nineteenth century thirty Damels had reigned in Kayor. Calculating backwards from 1854 (the year of the chronology published in the *Moniteur du Sénégal*), dates have been established from the lengths of their reigns as preserved by tradition. Apart from one or two details the griots are basically in agreement; I was able to check the *Moniteur* list on 21 March 1963 with the famous griot El-Hadj Assane Marokhaya, known as 'Samb'.

In this traditionally matrilineal society the king was chosen from a particular matrilineage (*kheet* or *meen*). Seven royal matrilineages (*garmi*) have provided seven successive dynasties: Geedy (11 kings), Muyoy (6), Dorobê (5), Sonyo (3), Gelwar (2), and Wagadu (1). Tradition recounts that the Sonyo and Gelwar lineages were probably of Mandinka origin and that the Wagadu originated in the Soninke kingdom of the same name. The Dorobê might have been the Tucolor TorodBe. Geedy in Wolof means the sea; their origin is accounted for in many legends. Whatever his matrilineage, the Damel takes his mother's name, which is placed after his own, i.e. Lat-Dyor Ngone-Latir. He is also given the patronymic (*sant*) of his 'belt', or patrilineage (*genyoo*), which in Lat-Dyor's case was Fal. As a member of the Fal patrilineage a Damel could trace his descent in the male line from the first ruler of Kayor. The Kayor Damel was always a member of one of the seven *garmi* and was chosen by a council of great electors: representatives of the nobles, the free-born, slaves, and, later, Muslims.[5] On the whole the history of the Damels was the history of the struggle for power between the seven matrilineages.

Other Wolof kings were called: *Buur* in Sine (Siin) and Salum, *Buur-ba* in Dyolof, *Teeny* in Baol, and *Brak* in Waalo. Eight Damels of Kayor were also Teeny of Baol.

Accession rites were held at Mbul, the capital. Seated on a mound of sand, the king-elect was given a pot of millet seed, and a turban placed on his head. He then retired to the sacred wood, where he was initiated according to indigenous rites. He also underwent a ritual lustration—a custom which originated from the influence of a sixteenth-century Moorish marabout. The entire history of the Damels reveals an intermingling of Islamic and indigenous religious practices.

The Damel was, above all, considered a magician who obtained power only through a recourse to potions. The whereabouts of a

Damel's grave was never divulged, to prevent the manufacture of talismans from his bones.

In the early nineteenth century the Damels showed considerable hostility to Islam: it was a vain boast for the Muslim Emir of the Trarza Moors, Mohammed El-Habib, to swear to 'make his salaam in the Ma-Isa Tende's hut' (1832–55). In 1859 the Muslims of Dyambur province rebelled against the exactions of the Damel's soldiers (*tyeddo*)—drunkards and looters for the most part. The Damels were also noted for their love of alcohol—trade gin and *sibakh*, a beverage made of fermented millet and berries.

The Damels were constantly at war with their neighbours. They also came into conflict with the French. Ma-Kodu (1859–61) was deposed when he attempted to prevent the installation of a telegraph line from Saint-Louis to Gorée. And between 1877 and 1883 Lat-Dyor put up a fierce opposition to the construction of the railway.

The names of the Damels (with their matrilineages) have been given by Yoro Dyao (it is his list which is published in the *Moniteur du Sénégal* in 1864), Faidherbe (1883), Sabatié (?1925), and Duguay-Clédor (1931). These sources were cross-checked by 'Samb' the griot—El Hadj Assane Marokhaya—in 1963. From about 1549 until 1790 twenty-three Damels reigned.

The twenty-fourth king, Amari Ngone-Ndela-Kumba (Geedy), 1790–1809, reigned for nineteen years. He was a nephew of his predecessor, who had been exiled to Waalo. His free-born subjects recognized him as Damel and Teeny. He put down the Marabout revolt in Kayor and defeated the Almami of Fouta, 'Abdul-Qadir (1790).

The twenty-fifth king, Birayma Faatma-Tyub (Geedy), 1809–32, was his predecessor's nephew. He reigned twenty-three years as Damel and was also Teeny of Baol.

The twenty-sixth king was Ma-Isa Tenda Dyor (Geedy), 1832–55. He was his predecessor's nephew and reigned for twenty-three years. On the advice of his slaves (the *Dyaam-Geedy* or Geedy slaves) he married his mother's sister; their two daughters, Ngone-Latir and Debo-Suko, both became *linger* (a title reserved for the close uterine kin of Wolof kings). He reigned over Baol as well as Kayor. His sister and his nephew were exiled to Waalo. He conquered the Trarza Moors. In 1849 he received a gift of a hundred and fifty guinea pieces in order to encourage the ground-nut trade. In 1853 he was looting wrecked ships.

The twenty-seventh king was Birahima Fal or Biram Ngone-Latir (Geedy), 1855–59, a daughter's son of his predecessor. He fought against Baol. In 1856 there was a rebellion led by his principal councillor, the Dyawdin Mbul, chief of the 'free men' (*dyaambur*) (see p. 265). In 1859 the province of Dyambur, inhabited mainly by Muslims, rose against the king. The Damel Birahima died of 'excessive intemperance'. During his reign Faidherbe stopped the 'custom' (a monetary tribute to the Damels) and replaced it by a duty on all exports from Kayor, collected by the Damel's agent. Birahima agreed to the installation of the telegraph.

The twenty-eighth king was Ma-Kodu Kudu Dyuf (Gelwar), 1859–61; he was his predecessor's father and son of the twenty-third Damel, Birahima Faatin-Penda, and a Gelwar woman from Salum, Koda-Kumba. An ill-natured drunkard, he was deposed by the French army for attempting to oppose the telegraph. He was replaced by Ma-Dyodyo Fal, a daughter's son of the twenty-fourth Damel, Amari Ngone.

The twenty-ninth Damel, Ma-Dyodyo Degen Fal (Dorobe), 1861 and 1863–64, was appointed by the French. He tried to prevent the looting of his soldiers (*tyeddo*). In 1862 Lat-Dyor Ngone-Latir (Geedy through his mother, but Dyop through his father) was chosen by malcontents to replace Ma-Dyodyo. He was the first Damel not to have Fal as his patronymic. Ma-Dyodyo was reinstalled as Damel in December 1863.

The thirtieth king was Lat-Dyor-Ngone-Latir Dyop (Geedy), 1862–82. He reigned intermittently between two rebellions. He made his submission in November 1868. He was Damel again between 1871 and 1882. He was killed in battle at Dyaqle on 26 October 1886.

The thirty-first king was Amari Ngone Fal (Dorobe), January–August 1883. His real name was Samba-Yaya Fal. He was a drunkard and kept company with griots and women. He fled before the forces of Lat-Dyor, and was exiled to Saint-Louis, where he threw himself into the river on 18 October 1891.

The thirty-second king, Samba Laobe Fal (Geedy), 1883–86, was the maternal nephew of Lat-Dyor. He was killed on 6 October 1886 at Tiwawan. After his death Kayor was annexed to the Colony of Senegal.[6]

Kayor Social Structure

Social classes in Kayor were ranked pyramidally. At the top were the nobles (*garmi*), followed by the Dyaambur, the free-born (*geer*) marabouts and commoner subjects. After these came members of the special caste groups (*nyenoo*), and at the bottom of the pyramid were the slaves (*dyaam*), who despised the *nyenoo*. The origins of the seven great royal matrilineages are complicated by constant intermarriage. Geedy women, for example, were several times married and divorced to kings of neighbouring states: the Emir of the Trarza, the king of the Mandinka, Saltigi Koli, Buur Siin, Buur-ba Dyolof, Teeny Baol, etc.

Linger were mothers, maternal aunts, or uterine sisters of the Damels. The title is also given to a Damel's daughter whose mother is a daughter of a Damel. The *linger* had her own villages and people whom she plundered at will. This provided a constant source of conflict with the Damel. *Linger* were highly respected, since it was through them that the royal blood was transmitted. They were at one time extremely powerful, and some of them achieved fame as warriors. About 1888 the queen mother of Salum, Kumba Daga, preferred death rather than serve a griot.

The king's court was composed of *dag* (courtiers), who resided at the capital. Dignitaries (*kangam*) were given territorial commands: they were known as *ndombo-y tank* after the anklets they wore as symbols of their office. There were seven principal officials: two governors or *dyawrin*, called Mbul and Dyinyen; the provincial chief of Guet (*Bör-Get*); the *Gankal*; the chief (*Dyaraf*) of the province of Ndyambur; the *Bördyak*; and the *Fara-Kaba*, an all-powerful officer who was chief of the throne slaves and was himself a slave. The *kangam* were famed for their courage: flight they considered a cardinal sin. The *kangam* present a difficult problem: their position is still unclear. It is not known how they were appointed, or what part they played in the election of the Damel, but they apparently retained a degree of independence and were not royals.

The Dyaambur were free-born commoners. One is tempted to look for the origin of their name in the two words *dyaam* (meaning slave) and *buur* meaning king. They were not, however, throne slaves (*dyaam-u Buur-i*). Nowadays the word *dyaambur* (with a short final vowel) has come to mean a sober member of the middle classes; and the derived word *dyaambure* is used to describe the quality of responsibility associated with a *dyaambur*. The explanation may be contained in this saying, associated with the Damels: *Kadyor yop, sama dyaam lenyu*—'all the people of Kayor are my slaves'. Mollien (1820: 95) mentions the fact that all Kayor subjects called one another 'slaves of the Damel'.

The majority of the Dyaambur were, of course, peasant farmers. Another name—*baadolo*—appeared in 1826, in J. Dard's *Grammaire wolofe*, as *badolo*. In 1685 it was given in the *Premier Voyage du Sieur de la Courbe* in the gallicized form of *basses doles*—'people of little cloth' (Cultru, 1913: 116). Henri Gaden (1914: 215) believes that the word was borrowed from the Fulani *baaydoola* (pl. *waasndoolBe*): a simple citizen, someone entirely at one's beck and call. The word itself is derived from the verb *waas/de* meaning 'to be without, to be poor'.

Wolof *baadolo* have the preoccupations of peasants the world over. Three things are necessary to subsistence according to them: seed (*dyi*), harvest (*goob*), and food (*lek*). Thus, three further things are vital to man: crops (*sakhle*), the grain-store (*sakkha*), and good chewing (*sakhami*). The same idea is expressed a little less crudely thus: 'The three good things of life are a healthy body, friendly neighbours and popularity.' A proverb celebrates the three qualities of a fortunate man: 'to have (*am*), to be able (*man*), and to know (*kham*).' Baadolo as well as Dyaambur had strong age-sets (*maas*), whose importance has recently been stressed by A. Sadji (1964: 52–56).

Kayor, like Waalo, Dyolof, Baol, Sine, and Salum—the other Senegalese kingdoms—had its marabouts. They were doctors, amulet-makers, and ran Koranic schools. They often acted as arbitrators in private and village disputes. In Kayor, as elsewhere, the pagan Damel favoured them from motives of prestige and charisma. They were also indispensable as scribes, being the only literates in the kingdom. This gave them a two-fold value in the eyes of the people. It was they who encouraged rebellions in Kayor. By 1862 they were so feared—even in Saint-Louis—that it was impossible to bring them to justice. 'No native will bear witness against a marabout' (Rapport Flize 14 November 1862: Papiers Ballot, No. 15). The *Seriny*—marabouts, farmers, soldiers, magicians, diviners, warriors, and scribes—occupied a prominent position in the social organization of Kayor.

The social groups so far considered consisted of free-born subjects who were not members of occupational 'caste' groups. The *nyenoo*, on the other hand, were endogamous 'castes', membership of which was based on birth, with which professional qualifications were associated. Among the Wolof there were jeweller and blacksmith castes (*tög*)—members of which were both despised and feared; woodcutters and carvers (*laobe*); and leatherworkers (*uude*) and weavers (*raba*). These distinctions may correspond to a former division of labour according to the material worked—metal, wood, leather, or cotton. A caste member may usually be identified by his patronymic (*sant*), indicative of his specialization. In Senegal the Thiam (*tyam*) are jewellers.

The caste of griots represent a special category. The Wolof call them *gewel*, the Fulbe *gaulo*, the Soninke *gesere*. In Kayor each Damel had his own kin group of griots. They were masters in the art of playing on names (*kheet* and *sant*): they referred obliquely to the object of their mockeries or praises without naming him. Only an expert would identify their subject and understand the implications. In former times the griot also filled a less peaceable function. In Kayor they bore the royal standard to war and could in no circumstances turn back. The story is told of a griot who, at the height of a battle, promised his Damel to capture the king of Baol. He arrived and, finding the king on his mat, said, 'The Damel wants you,' only to be felled to the ground and overcome by blows. At Guilé on 6 June 1886 the Kayor nobles advanced on horseback, preceded by their griots loudly shouting their families' praises. When Muse Buri Degen Dyeng, the Damel's lieutenant and friend, fell under fire his griot was killed ten paces ahead of him (Duguay-Clédor, 1931: 30–31).

Kayor society was sustained by a slave class (*dyaam*). Until recently *dyaam* were categorized according to their status. Slaves bought in the market worked for their masters from six in the morning until two in the afternoon, when they were free to work their own farms. Mondays and Fridays were free. If a slave of this category was 'maltreated by his master and wished to leave him and take refuge with another, he would make a cut in the ear of this person's child, or better still his horse. He then belonged to this man legally.'[7] Most slaves, however, were slave-born (*dyaam dyudyu*) and constituted the bulk of the domestic slaves. Their numbers are not known for Kayor, but Saint-Louis and Gorée in 1825 had 12,300 slaves out of a population of 16,000 (Archives Sénégal, Série 1 G 9). In a letter to the governor, dated 21 August 1865, the Marabout of Ndiagne (Seriny Ndyany) in Kayor stated: 'Whenever a slave market is established here I refuse to allow any to be sold until I am certain—through questioning them myself—that they are really slave-born. Each one must state "I am a slave and my mother was a slave" (*anaa*, '*abd*, *ummi jaariya*)' (Archives du Sénégal, I D 7).

The domestic slaves were 'treated as their master's children. . . . They might even buy slaves themselves.'[8] On 29 January 1836 Director Guillet wrote: 'It is not infrequent in Senegal to find slaves who are richer than their masters and who eat and drink at his table' (Archives, K 7). A Senegalese student, Mbaye Gueye, has reached the same conclusion (1962: 124): 'Domestic slaves lived as members of the family of their master, who was not their selfish oppresser but acted as their guardian and father.' Two-thirds of the day they worked for their owner. 'When work was done and the harvest brought in, these slaves travelled the country as weavers', to return in June for the rainy season (Carrère et Holle, 1855: 53–55). The Decree of 27 April 1848 suppressed domestic slavery in all the French colonies. However, it was not effective in the interior; the Governor had to ask the people of Kayor, Waalo, and Fouta to 'come and remove those slaves they had provided as securities in Saint-Louis and Gorée' (ibid: 151).

War captives constituted a third category of slaves. They were women for the most part, and usually became concubines (*taara*) as authorized in the Koran.

In Galam slaves were exchanged for iron bars—at least in the eighteenth century. A letter from Lat-Dyor in 1880 mentions that a horse was valued at two slaves (Archives, 13 G 260). On 23 April 1880 Ibra Faatim Sar, one of the Damel's ministers, wrote to the Governor: 'In our country slaves take the place of money' (Archives, 13 G 260). Traditions collected by the griot Marokhaya (1963: 3) for the period before Kayor's independence from Dyolof show that neither money nor gold (*khaalis amul*, *wurus amul*) were then in circulation. In Dyolof tribute in kind (*galak*) was levied on vassal provinces: fine sand from Kayor, salt from Gandiole, fish from Waalo, cotton from Sine, *buy* or monkey-bread (fruit of the baobab) from Salum. Gold was introduced only with the development of European trade.

Last but not least were those born in servitude, who belonged to the state—the throne slaves (*dyaam-u Buur-i*). We must be careful here not to let our modern anti-slavery prejudices distort our judgement of this capital and original institution.[9] Mahmoud Kati, author of the famous *Ta'rikh al-Fattaash*, writing of West Africa in the seventeenth century, said that the Negro states of Kanyaga, Mali, and Songhay all owed their supremacy to a bloc of twenty-four servile tribes which belonged successively to each empire.[10] In Kayor we have sixteen villages organized into the same number of patrilineages and matrilineages composed of throne slaves. They were slaves of the Geedy matrilineage. They made and unmade kings, won and lost their battles, and closely supervised their exercise of power. Among these Dyaam-Geedy we should single out the four sons of Dyor Mbay Ndendé (or Ndeede), herself the daughter of the chief of the throne slaves in Baol. Of her sons the most famous was Demba-Waar Dyor Sal, the *Fara-Kaba* of the Damel Lat-Dyor.

These state slaves were the only stable element in society, and this was the basis of their power. This is particularly true of Kayor. They were the only section of the population on whom the Damel could absolutely depend: they were his property and were not rebellious. The dispute between Lat-Dyor and his slave chief, Demba-Waar, was one of the reasons for his downfall. 'The greatest offices in the kingdom were usually confided to the throne slaves' (Papiers Ballot, No. 35, 1884). On 28 August 1883 the treaty instituting the French Protectorate was signed by the Damel of Kayor, Samba Laobé, and ratified by six throne slaves (Archives, 1 D 48). None the less, even these officers were expected to place irons above their bed to remind them of their servile condition (Mollien, 1820: 501).

It was from the *Dyaam-u Buur-i* that the Damel recruited his soldiers (*tyeddo*). *Tyeddo* is a word which in Wolof has now taken on the impious connotation of 'fetichist'. The Fulbe use it to refer to the 'blacks' (*tyeDDo*, pl. *seBBe*), as opposed to themselves and the Moors. The *tyeddo* earned a reputation as wild drunkards and incorrigible looters. So addicted were they to gin (*sangara*) that they would even go so far as to pawn their rifles to get hold of some (Archives, I D 24). In 1869 the Teeny of Baol sent horsemen to smash the demijohns of gin, to keep his soldiers sober by preventing its arrival in Baol (Archives, 13 G 264). Looting was their lesser vice. In 1864 their depredations in Kayor (condoned by the *linger*) brought a strong reaction from the Governor. In January 1865 the Ngigis post reported the plundering of the marabout villages in Kayor. The marabouts were put to ransom by the *tyeddo* of the Damel (Ma-Dyodyo) and 'the women were stripped naked' (Archives, I D 27). The exactions of the *tyeddo* caused the historic revolts of Kayor Muslims against their Damel. This was certainly the case for the 'Marabout War', which occurred towards the end of the seventeenth century.

In external appearances the *tyeddo* contrasted strongly with the rustic *baadolo* and the *seriny* (marabout) with his shaven skull and dignified mien. 'They wore long tresses, ear-rings and silver bracelets' (Ba, 1957: 584). The Abbé Boilat made a sketch of one, complete with his bottle of gin, in the *Esquisses sénégalaises*. In the sixteenth century Kayor's war of independence against Dyolof was fought with staves and cattle tendons. Damel Lat-Sukaabe bought his country's first guns from André Brüe in 1701. In 1818 (Mollien) soldiers were still fighting with bows and arrows. Bullets (made 'from bits of legs of metal pots') were used in the Guilé war of 1886 (Duguay-Clédor, 1931: 23, 29). European traders exchanged gunpowder for gold. We have no exact information on the size of the Kayor army, although at Guilé in 1886 it was 3,500 strong.

The *tyeddo* were intrepid combatants. Mollien recounts an incident during a battle between Kayor and Baol when each soldier 'to make flight impossible, filled his bulky breeches with sand, and overcome by the weight of the load, fell to his knees and prepared to shoot'. An official view published in 1876 is worth quoting at this point.

'The only army in Kayor was a guard composed of tiédos, lawless and faithless warriors, hostile to work of any kind, drinkers of absinthe and the adulterated *sangara*; on the other hand they were brave beyond compare. Without any exaggeration they may be likened to our brave medieval knights. Tiédos were called throne slaves and constituted a veritable army, irregular but redoubtable . . . . It goes without saying that their agricultural role was nugatory' (Notice sur le Sénégal, unsigned, dated 1876, Papiers Ballot, No. 26).

Lat-Dyor's grandson, Amadou Bamba Diop, told me that the *tyeddo* slaves preferred their servile condition. They had more influence than the free-born—certainly more than the unfortunate *baadolo*. They had power of life and death over the Damel; and even married his daughters. It is true to say of the *tyeddo* that 'although they belonged to the Damel, the Damel also belonged to them'. This fact is brought home by the history of Lat-Dyor, thirteenth Damel (1862–82)—the most typical and best known king of the nineteenth century.

The Life and Legend of Lat-Dyor

Lat-Dyor was born about 1842 in a pagan environment, for, contrary to general belief, he was not born a Muslim. He attended a Koran school run by the marabout Babakar Mbay—which goes to show only that princes took good care to 'recognize' Islam in order to gain the goodwill of the marabouts. He then moved to Ngigis, home of his maternal grandfather Ma-Isa Tende Dyor, then Damel of Kayor and Teeny of Baol (1832—55). From time to time he went back to stay with his father at Sagata. At the age of thirteen Lat-Dyor was appointed *Bör-Get* and *Dyogomay* by his eldest uterine brother, the Damel Borayma Ngone-Latir (1855–59). On the latter's death in 1859, the Geedy throne slaves (*Dyaam-Geedy-i*), Lat-Dyor's supporters, came into open conflict with the *dyaambur* (freemen) of Kayor, who backed the new Damel Ma-Kodu, the father of his predecessor. Ma-Kodu defeated Lat-Dyor's supporters, but in 1861 he got into trouble with the French and was replaced by Ma-Dyodyo. The malcontents (the Dyaam-Geedy-i) then turned to the youthful Lat-Dyor.

Lat-Dyor, nineteen years old, wanted to undergo the initiation rite of circumcision, which alone could make him socially adult. He went to his adviser, Demba Waar (born about 1837), who was chief of the throne slaves and said: 'Demba!' 'Dyop!' replied the other, calling him by his patronymic (*sant*). 'I wish to become adult!' (*dama bög nyu magal-ma*). The ceremony was held in Guet, at Tyilmakha, before a great crowd of people—much to the chagrin of Damel Ma-Dyodyo. When Lat-Dyor's father and his followers grew nervous of intervention the newly circumcised man's seclusion shed (*mbaar-du ndyuli*) was transferred to land belonging to the powerful Seriny Koki, Samba Aminata, whose mother, Aminata Dyop, was the daughter of the *Bör-Get*, Saa Khewer Faatma, paternal great-grandfather of Lat-Dyor. As always, everything hinged on marriage alliances and slaves. In 1862 the

Geedy pretender, Lat-Dyor Ngone-Latir Dyop, supported by Demba Waar, defeated the Damel Ma-Dyodyo. Lat-Dyor, his circumcision complete (*börlool*), was installed in his place as Damel. Following disputes with the French, he was obliged to spend four years in exile (1864–68). He tried unsuccessfully to win the kings of Sine and Salum over to his cause. Tradition tells that the former made a joke about Lat-Dyor's small stature and received the reply: 'A king does not carry his country around with him on his head!' (*kenna du-yenu reew-um tyi sa bop*). His only alternative was to sell his soul to Ma-Baa Dyakhou, which he did in 1864. Ma-Baa, the Tucolor marabout, was by then absolute ruler in Salum. He welcomed Lat-Dyor warmly as the son of the *Linger* Ngone-Latir, who had once given him a gun to help pay a fine following a court conviction. The year 1864 has always been remembered as one of locusts and famine (*at-um khiif-ba*). In 1865 Lat-Dyor was made Ma-Baa's assistant commander-in-chief. But, after invading and ravaging Dyolof, Ma-Baa was defeated at Nioro on 29 November and, two years later, on 18 July 1867, after a long campaign against the Serer of Sine, he was killed at Somb. 'Lat-Dyor, feeling that defeat was inevitable, abandoned the fight' (Baa, 1957: 585). In November 1868 he returned to Kayor to make his submission: with Ma-Baa he had lost his greatest ally and supporter; his Wolof followers refused to continue being exploited by Rip marabouts; and his mother was suffering from the climate of Salum. It was not until 12 February 1871 that he signed the treaty recognizing him as Damel of Kayor.

For ten years he ruled Kayor. During this time his main ambition was to bring Baol under his sway, as other Damel-Teeny had done in the past. He finally succeeded in 1874, when he defeated the Teeny of Baol, and ruthlessly put down his attempts to regain the throne. In 1875 Lat-Dyor and the French were allied against Amadou Sheikou, the Tucolor marabout who had rebelled in 1870. He was beaten at the battle of Boumdou on 11 February. But Lat-Dyor's opposition to the railway from Dakar to Saint-Louis then led to his flight to Baol, and Samba-Yaya Fal, a maternal nephew of Lat-Dyor, was installed as Damel by the Governor in January 1883. On 28 August 1883 a French Protectorate was proclaimed over Kayor and Samba Laobé became Damel. He reigned only three years. His jealousy of the Buur-ba Dyolof, Al-Buri Ndyay, led to the battle of the 'Guilé tamarind'

(*Dakhaar-u Güle*), where he was defeated (6 June 1886). The twenty-four-year-old Damel, a colossus of a man, was fined by the Governor and later accused of molesting the Tiwawan traders. He was killed on 6 October 1886 by Lieutenant Chauvey— in legitimate self-defence according to the official version. The *Réveil du Sénégal* of 10 October calls it 'execution' (Archives, 1 D 48).

Lat-Dyor, always at loggerheads with Baol, had possibly conceived a grand plan of action. In 1864 Colonel Pinet-Laprade had written to the Governor: 'Lat-Dyor is preparing a coalition of Wolof states against us, including Cayor, Baol, Sine, and Saloum —as well as the Trarza Moors' (16 January, Archives, 1 D 26). Only Waalo and Dyolof were left out. At all events it was clear to the French that Lat-Dyor was ambitious—Kayor had never been enough for him. And it was true that the kingdom he had inherited in 1871 had been deprived of the districts of Saint-Louis and Dakar, as well as the province of Dyander. He protested and tried to prevent it—but the Governor was adamant.

The all-important role of the throne slaves (*dyaam-u Buur-i*) had already been referred to. Under their chief, the *Fara-Kaba*, Demba-Waar Dyor Sal (1837–1902), they had supported Lat-Dyor as pretender and Damel. However, from 1879 tension began to mount between the two men. Lat-Dyor wrote to the Governor: 'I have given them territorial commands. But they are too greedy. They have treacherously tried to kill me and set traps for me.' And he asked the Governor for 'an officer to make my slaves obey their king!' On 28 November he wrote: 'They are trying to depose me in favour of my nephew Samba Laobé, a thing I shall never permit. They are my slaves, sons of my slaves. They shall all be disgraced and reduced to nothing. After I have finished with them they will be no more than the ashes left by a dry log which has been thrown into the flame' (Archives, 13 G 260). In the same year (1879) Lat-Dyor dismissed Ibra Faatim Sar and the *Fara-Kaba*, Demba-Waar Sal, once the 'veritable ruler of Kayor'.

The Damel cruelly missed the support of Demba-Waar when he found himself in conflict with the governor over the proposed railway. On 16 January 1877 Brière de l'Isle announced to Lat-Dyor his intention of building a line from Saint-Louis to Dakar through Kayor, with halts for the collection of groundnuts—now one of Senegal's principal exports, already totalling two and a half thousand tons in 1850. From 1873, according to a Gorée communication (Archives, 13 G 307/3), Lat-Dyor did all he could to stop the cultivation of groundnuts. 'He tells his followers that once there are no more nuts the White Man will go away and he will be absolute master of the country. . . . These views are not entirely without sense.' On 10 September 1879, however, Lat-Dyor had agreed to the railway, signing a treaty which he kept secret.

In June 1882 the Société des Batignolles was given the concession to carry out the construction. For two years (1881–82) Lat-Dyor made continual protests, taking advantage of most of his subjects' general hostility. The Governor's report (No. 750/DAP, 8 September 1882, 13 G 261) contained a letter from the Damel's councillor, Ibra Faatim Sar, which reveals their constant anxiety. He commented on the rumours which had been spread by Samba Fal, the Dakar interpreter:

'He told us that the proposed railway track was higher than a very tall man and that people from the western side would not be able to communicate with those from the east except when the gates were open —i.e. twice a day, in the morning and the evening.' Samba Fal also told Lat-Dyor: 'The Governor is only building this railway to trap you and kidnap you. He told us the railway would be faster than lightning. This is why Lat-Dyor grew frightened and opposed the new railway.'

Lat-Dyor felt the railway would bring the end of the Damels and ring a death knell for Kayor independence. He jibbed, argued, but finally gave way. His struggle had become anachronistic. He had really been beaten in 1859 by the installation of the Saint-Louis–Gorée telegraph through Kayor. He had been beaten by French artillery, the railway line, and the growing importance of groundnuts in the external economy. He had arrived on the scene too late—the ancient structure was cracking under the combined blows of French colonialism and egalitarian Islam. It was still too soon for African emancipation. Lat-Dyor had relied too much on the old proverb: *gan du-tabakh*, 'the stranger never builds': they were passers-by who had come to trade a little. But once they begin to build permanent posts, railway stations, and the like, they are here to stay.

In oral tradition the Damel is tenacious, proud, and bold—a

fearless and irreproachable knight, accompanied by his six favourite horses. Islam plays no part in popular legends and the herioc sagas of the griots. Lat-Dyor's death at Dyaqlé is recounted in a frankly pagan fashion. According to Marokhaya 'Samb', the griot, the Damel was killed by a bullet melted in gold (*bal-u wurus*) which an uncircumcised boy (*aat, pakhe*) had buried beneath a lavatory (*sawukay*) for a week. 'Samb' adds (1963: 56): 'This practice, being absolutely unknown to the white man, must be attributed to their *Black* followers. It is they who were immediately responsible for Lat-Dyor's death.' Another version is told by the griots of the family of Sal, chief of the throne slaves. At the battle of Dyaqlé Demba-Waar called out to his former master to take off the amulet he wore around his neck to keep him invulnerable (*tul*). Whatever happened, a defeated Damel could never return to face his subjects. He must die with his soldiers. Lat-Dyor removed the talisman and was killed by a bullet fired by Demba-Waar. His body was hidden in the Seriny Ndattu mosque, and later buried at the village of Ndukuman-u Dyere in Kör Garang Ma-Dyigen (Marokhaya, 1963: 55). Questioned on this point by a Senegalese audience after my lecture on 27 March 1963, Amadou-Bamba Diop replied simply: 'The whereabouts of a Damel's grave is never divulged. It is our tradition. Perhaps it is a pity, since our young people all want to make the pilgrimage, but that is how it is. Lat-Dyor's own son, my father Mbakhan, told me one day that he had seen it—in 1937.' The Lat-Dyor legend remains bathed in a haze of memories and native taboos. Yet Lat-Dyor himself had been converted to Islam, and his example led to the mass conversion of the Wolof of Kayor.

The Islamization of Kayor

When Lat-Dyor sought refuge in Salum in 1864 he stayed with the powerful marabout Ma-Baa Diakhou (Dyakhu), in the Rip. Ma-Baa was a descendant of the illustrious Denyanke who ruled over Fouta Toro until the era of the Almaami Tucolor (the end of the eighteenth century). At this time Ma-Baa had followers as far away as Saint-Louis, where Tucolor marabouts had been imprisoned for supporting his cause during the anti-*tyeddo* revolt (Rapport de Flize, 14 November 1862, Papiers Ballot, No. 15). On 24 June 1864 G. d'Arcy, Governor of British Gambia,

T

advised a concerted Anglo-French action against Ma-Baa, the 'Mahommedan Priest and warrior . . . perpetrator of atrocities under the cover of religion, fanatical destroyer of villages, who slays the men and takes the women and children as slaves' (Archives, 13 G 304). Between July and October 1864 reports from local posts call Ma-Baa a prudent and skilful man with a 'prophet-like gift for ubiquity'. He was said to be 'absolute ruler of Saloum (in August) with his sights fixed on Sine, then Baol and finally Kayor'. His army was estimated at four to five thousand men, all Muslim, with a majority of Tucolor. They were mostly armed with staves (Archives, 13 G 304 and 271).

On 17 April 1864 Lat-Dyor was in Sine. Between November and December of that year the French signed a treaty with Ma-Baa recognizing his authority in Salum. The Kaolakh commandant invoked this treaty when he asked Ma-Baa to drive out Lat-Dyor. Ma-Baa refused; instead he made the Damel his assistant commander-in-chief. In 1866 he agreed to invade Sine, but he died at Somb on 18 July 1867. He had 'firmly established the Moslem religion over a great part of Senegal; and is praised by griots and blind men alike. Ma-Baa's death was felt very strongly by the Moslems and his grave became the centre of pilgrimage into the very heart of pagan Sine' (Baa, 1957).

How did the converted Lat-Dyor behave after his submission in 1868 and his return to Kayor a year later? According to local officers' reports, Lat-Dyor let it be known that he would not agree to become Damel again unless 'everybody became marabout'. He announced his decision to abide by the 'advice of true marabouts'. In June 'many of the people are shaving their skulls and loudly announcing their intention to rally behind Lat-Dyor' (Archives, 13 G 264). Later, when he had been reinstalled as Damel, a petition from Rufisque traders accused him of being the 'marabout leader' whose religious fanaticism led him to attack Baol. On 9 February 1874 a letter from the Damel at Gorée began with the phrase 'Lat-Dyor, defender of the Moslem faith in Kayor'. On 19 February 1874 he wrote 'From the Sultan of Believers, Lat-Dyor Dyop. . . . My whole preoccupation is with the hereafter. . . . I can only pray for god's help and strength. . . . I am the Sultan of Believers in the country of the blacks' (Archives, 13 G 307/3). Moreover, this attitude, at least in the beginning, was far from being eyed with disapproval by the French authorities, mainly for reasons of trade and security. In 1876: 'The conversion of Lat-Dyor and all his tiédos to Islam may be a sign of the end of this plundering.' The people might be able 'to bring abundant supplies of groundnuts to our trading posts' (Notice sur le Sénégal, unsigned, 1876, Papiers Ballot, No. 26).

In those days converts were given the name of *silmakha*, meaning both blind-man and beggar. This had been the case with Lat-Dyor's great-grandfather Saa-Khewer Faatma Dyop. In the same way Lat-Dyor, on his return to Kayor in 1869, went begging for food for his soldiers as a sign of humility. When one village chief sent him away empty-handed he left without taking reprisals (Amadou-Bamba Diop, 1963). At all events, the Damel is called 'Silmakha' or 'Silmakha Dyop' in several letters from Kayor nobles (Samba Laobé, for example; 24 January 1880, 13 G 260). His behaviour bears witness to his conversion, although shades of traditional custom persist. He had nineteen wives ('for his amusement') and thirty-nine children (Marokhaya, 1963: 57); yet the Koran permitted him only four. Still it was the custom of the time, and it is followed by certain marabouts, even today: one of them has thirty-six wives.

The Archives of Senegal contain approximately 200 letters from Lat-Dyor: 95 cover the period from 1876 to 1877 (13 G 259); 40 from 1878 to 1880 (13 G 206); 40 from 1881 to 1882 (13 G 261); and a few for 1874 (13 G 307/3). The letters, in Arabic, were dictated in Wolof to his marabout scribes. These scribes were usually *cadis*: Momar Anta-Sali in 1868–69, Mori Kumba in 1877, Ma-Dyakhaté Kala in 1886. Lat-Dyor himself was illiterate, and his signature never appears on his letters, which, however, bear his seal in French and Arabic (6 February 1880, Archives, 13 G 260).

How was the process of Islamization achieved in Kayor, and what were its consequences? Arnaud (p. 9) wrote with rare insight in 1912:

'In Wolof country, at one time, the intrusion of Islam constituted a real social revolution. It was in fact a class struggle, a clash between the labouring classes and the aristocracy. The farmers detested the soldiers who exploited them. Thanks to Islam they were able to form a bloc against the pagan aristocrats. For a long time the marabouts were the natural leaders of the people against the oppressors. The soldiers never hid their contempt for the marabouts.'

The cause of this was clear. In the Wolof states, and especially in Kayor, the king was chosen from the princes of the blood by a body of electors who deposed him if he proved not to their liking. He received his only permanent and solid support from his 'legions'. His warriors, *tyeddo*, however, gave their backing only if he allowed them free rein to plunder the countryside undisturbed. Tensions consequently mounted between the plunderers and the plundered (the *baadolo*, peasants). The downtrodden *baadolo* were helped by the immigrant marabouts, who did their best to shelter them in their villages. The pagan *tyeddo* and the marabouts soon came into open conflict.

On the other hand, by the second half of the nineteenth century the kings represented a vanishing order (one of 'established disorder') and a dangerous despotism. These were the men who were confronted by a foreign colonial power. The French found the Damels unruly and intractable. 'The government, not content with setting the marabouts against the tiédos (while supporting the former), set tiédo against tiédo and Damel against Damel' (Notice sur le Sénégal, unsigned, 1876, Papiers Ballot, No. 26). The policy of the colonial government was expressed in the 'General Political Programme for the Colony of Senegal' presented in 1864 by Governor Faidherbe.

'We are not concerned with either the subjugation or the administration of these peoples (of the interior) . . . (nevertheless) we must never hesitate to establish posts on important lines of communication if the interests and protection of our commercial ventures demand it. . . . We shall eventually find that the chiefs of all the states will become our loyal allies, and be firmly clasped in our warm embrace.'[11]

When the Damel Lat Dyor was deposed or exiled he was only able to reassert his position through external intervention. Ma-Baa, the fighting marabout and ruler of Salum, was the only possible choice. The Damel sought him out as Al-Buri Ndyay, the Buur-ba Dyolof, had done before. The Almaami agreed to help on certain conditions: the pretender and his *tyeddo* were to accept Islam and join him in his 'Holy War'; and on his return to Kayor the Damel was to convert his people. This he set about doing. In 1869 he was back in Kayor and, according to Amadou-Bamba Diop, he suppressed looting (*moyal*) and rapine and converted his villages to Islam 'by persuasion'. He even conceived an idea for a 'profound social reform' based on Islamic tenets: theocratic and egalitarian. Unfortunately he was unable to overcome the basic obstacle standing in his way: neither his 'nobles' nor the colonial government would tolerate an 'oriental monarch'. Lat-Dyor succumbed because he opposed the groundnut trade and the railway. His new policy now led him into a final conflict with the throne slaves and their chief, Demba-Waar Sal. The Damel had to go; but Kayor remained. His Wolof subjects, having been shown the way, became Muslim to a man.

NOTES

1. A more detailed version of this essay, under the title of 'Lat Dior, Damel du Kayor, et l'islamisation des Wolofs', was published in *Archives de Sociologie des Religions*, Paris, No. 16, Juillet–Décembre, 1963, pp. 77–104.

2. *Chronique du Wâlo sénégalais* (1186?–1855), *Bull. de l'I.F.A.N.*, *T. XXVI*, Sér. B, Nos. 3–4, 1964, pp. 440–98.

3. Wolof is written phonetically: *e* and *o* are closed vowels; long vowels are doubled (*aa, ee, ii, oo, uu*); *kh* is a velar, close to the hard German *ch* and the Spanish *jota*. The liquid consonants (palatals) are followed by *y* (*ty, dy, ny*).

4. The information on Kayor economy is thin. Though the Wolof never had the same reputation for long-distance trading as the Serahuli or the Jula branch of the Mandinka, they formerly played an important part in the salt trade with the interior (Gamble, 1957: 36). According to Diagne (cited in Ames, 1962: 32), the mines of Gandiole were controlled by Kayor and the salt traded as far south as Fouta Jallon. Carrère and Holle (1855) state that men of Kayor bought Saint-Louis guns, powder, swords, iron bars, tobacco, printed cloths, and glass beads. Kayor furnished Senegal with grain, cattle, sheep, fowls, hide, soap, beans, fruit, palm wine, gourds, melon seeds, cassava, yams, groundnuts, and salt (cited in Ames, 1962: 34). *Ed.*

5. Gamble (1957: 56), citing Sabatié, gives as the electors in Kayor a council of seven: three representing the free-born, two the marabouts, one the warriors and one the royal slaves. *Ed.*

6. As noted by Gamble (1957: 50), the history of the Damels in the nineteenth century indicates certain characteristic features of succession: rivalry between son and sister's son, and marriages with close relatives across generations to secure the succession for own children. *Ed.*

7. Explanation: the guilty man is sent back to the owner of the horse

in 'compensation'. The same custom is reported for the Rgeibat and in Hoggar, in the Aïr.

8. 'Report on the Slaves,' by Hamet Fall, interpreter at Saint-Louis, 16 February 1884, Papiers Ballot, No. 35.

9. In the history of Islam a similar role was played by the 'white slaves' of Baghdad, Cordova, and Cairo.

10. French translation 1913, p. 107.

11. Papiers Ballot, No. 17. Faidherbe's text, a hundred years in advance, makes this curiously prophetic statement: 'I shall make no mention . . . of so-called Portuguese Guinea which exists only in the imagination of the Lisbon Government.'

REFERENCES

1862–86 Archives du Gouvernement du Sénégal, Dakar. Boxes 13 G (35, 259, 260, 261, 263, 265, 271, 304, 307/3); I D (22, 24, 26, 27, 32, 40, 48); O 33.

1862– Papiers du Gouverneur Victor Ballot (1853–1939), microfilmed in 1961 by the Archives Nationales, Paris, No. 185 M 1 (four reels).See the detailed list in 'Papiers d'Afrique', by Mlle G. Ganier, Bull. IFAN, Vol. XXV, 1–2, 1963, pp. 145–70.

Ames, D. 1962 'The Rural Wolof of the Gambia', in Markets in Africa, ed. by Bohannan, P. and Dalton, George, Northwestern University Press.

Arnaud, Robert 1912 'L'Islam et la politique musulmane française', Paris, Rens, col. de l'Afr. fr., January, pp. 3–29, 115–27, and 142–54.

Azan, Capitaine H. 1863–64 'Notice sur le Oualo', Paris, Revue marit. et col., Vols. IX and X, pp. 492–5.

Baa, Tamsir, Ousmane 1957 'Essai historique sur le Rip (Sénégal)', Bull. IFAN, Vol. XIX, B, 3–4, pp. 564–91.

Barthélémy, E. 1848 Notice historique sur les établissements français des Côtes françaises d'Afrique. Paris.

Boilat, Abbé P. D. 1853 Esquisses sénégalaises. Paris. XVI + 496 pp.

Brigaud, Félix 1962 'Histoire traditionnelle du Sénégal', Etudes sénégalaises, No. 9, 335 pp.

Carrère, F. &   1855   *De la Sénégambie française.* Paris, 396 pp.
Holle, Paul

Cultru, P.   1913   *Premier voyage du Sieur de la Courbe fait à la coste d'Afrique en 1685.*

Duguay-Clédor,   1931   'La bataille de Guilé', 143 pp. Contains
Amadou   'L'histoire des Damels du Kayor', from the *Moniteur du Sénégal*, J.O. 1864, and *Le Sénégal*, by Sabatié, undated (1925), pp. 109–32.

Faidherbe, Gl.   1883   'Notice historique sur le Cayor', *Bull. Soc. geog. de Paris*, Vol. IV, pp. 527–64.

   1889   *Le Sénégal.* Paris. 501 pp.

Gaden, H.   1914   *Lexique Poular-français.* Paris.

Gamble, D. P.   1957   *The Wolof of Senegambia*, together with Notes on the Lebu and the Serer, London (*Ethnog. Survey, W. Afr.*, XIV).

Marokhaya,   1963   *Essai sur l'histoire du Cayor*, translated
El-Hadj Assane   from the Wolof by Samba Fall Samb. Dakar. 63 pp.

Mbaye Guèye   1962   *La traite des Noirs au Sénégal, do la fin du XVIIIe siècle au milieu du XIXe siècle.* Dakar, D.E.S. (Fac. des Lettres). 173 pp. (TS).

Mollien, G.   1820   *Voyage dans l'intérieur de l'Afrique, aux sources du Sénégal et de la Gambie, fait en 1818.* Paris. 2 vols. Vol. I, 339 pp.

Monteil, Vincent   1962   'Une confrérie musulmane, les Mourides du Sénégal', *Arch. Socio. Relig.*, No. 14, pp. 77–102.

   1963   'Lat Dior, Damel du Kayor, et l'islamisation des Wolofs', *Arch. Socio. Relig.*, No. 16, Juillet–Décembre, pp. 77–104.

Rousseau, R.   1933   'Le Sénégal d'autrefois, Étude sur le Cayor, Cahiers de Yoro Dyâo', *Bull. CEHSAOF*, Vol. XVI, 2, Avril–Juin.

Sadji, Abdoulaye   1964   *Education africaine et civilisation.* Dakar. 92 pp.

INDEX

ABIODUN, Alafin of Oyo, 40–41

Abomey, *see* Dahomey

administrative systems: Ashanti, 221–3; Benin, 8–12; Dahomey, 75–78; Gonja, 188–92; Kom, 142, 143–6; Maradi, 100–4; Mende, 250–8; Mossi, 160–6; Oyo, 40, 48–50, 63, 64

adultery, 62, 89, 108, 116, 141, 146

Agadja, Dahomey king, 72, 73, 74

age grades, sets, 9, 67–68, note 10, 119, 126

Agyei, career of, 219, 220

Akinjogbin, Dr. I. A., 66, note 1

Alafin, *see* kings

Allada, kingdom, 37, 39, 70, 72, 75, 85

Amazons, 80, 84, 86, 87–88

ancestors, 9, 25, 26, 32, 48, 53, 56, 76, 78, 80, 84, 85, 90, 134, 146, 174

Ardra, kingdom, 39, 70

army: Ashanti, 210, 219, 226; Benin, 5, 7; Dahomey, 80, 86–89; Gonja, 198–200; Kayor, 269–71; Maradi, 118–19; Mossi, 171–2; Oyo, 57; *see also* Amazons; military organization, war

Asantehene, *see* kings

Ashanti, 87, 90, 159, 171, 181, 182, 183, 198–9, 206–36; — government, 206–36; accumulation of power, 223–8; applications of power, 228–32; apogee of power, 232–4; area, 212; chiefdoms (*amantoɔ*) 207–11, 228–32; emergent bureaucracy,

221–34; finance, 214–18; history, 207–8, 211–18; Kwadwoan revolution in government, 211–18; political service, 218–21; provincial administration, 221–3

associations, 6, 19–20, 127, 140–2, 158, 257–8; *see also* age grades, sets; societies

Atiba, Alafin of Oyo, 36, 44, 45–48, 49, 50, 55, 61, 65

authority, 9, 13–15, 28–29, 121, 143–4

Bafut, 123, 127, 132, 133, 144, 147

Bali, 123

Bamileke, 123, 127

Bamum, 123, 125, 127, 147

Bariba, 39, 44

Benin, kingdom of, 1–35, 39; boundaries, 3, 5; capital, 12–13; decline, 6–8; dynastic myth, 1–3; extent, 5–6; historical and territorial background, 1–12; the Oba, 28–34; palace organization, 18–24; political institutions, 12–34; territorial administration, 8–12

Bini, *see* Edo

Bowdich, R., 209, 211, 212–13, 215, 218, 219, 220, 221, 223, 226, 230

bride price, -wealth, 114, 134, 139, 242

British, 1, 7, 66, 199, 227, 228, 229, 233

Bum, 127, 128, 129, 133

bureaucracy, Ashanti, 214–23, 225

Set by Richard Clay (The Chaucer Press) Ltd
Bungay, Suffolk
and reprinted lithographically by
Fletcher & Son Ltd, Norwich